SHAKESPEARE'S DRAMATIC ART

SHAKESPEARE'S DRAMATIC ART

Collected Essays

WOLFGANG CLEMEN

LONDON
METHUEN & CO LTD

First published 1972
by Methuen & Co Ltd
11 New Fetter Lane, London EC4
© *1972 Wolfgang Clemen*
Printed in Great Britain by
Cox & Wyman Ltd
Fakenham, Norfolk

SBN 416 66930 1

Distributed in the U.S.A.
by Barnes & Noble Inc.

For Stanley Wells
and Inga-Stina Ewbank

CONTENTS

BIBLIOGRAPHICAL NOTE

Apart from Chapter 1, all the chapters in this book have been published previously as separate papers. Original publication is as follows:

2 *Wandlung des Botenberichts bei Shakespeare.* Sitzungsberichte der Bayerischen Akademie der Wissenschaften, Philosophisch-historische Klasse 1952, 4.

3 *Past and Future in Shakespeare's Drama.* Annual Shakespeare Lecture of the British Academy 1966. From the *Proceedings of the British Academy*, vol. lii, Oxford University Press.

4 *Shakespeare's Soliloquies.* The Presidential Address of the Modern Humanities Research Association, 1964, Cambridge University Press.

5 *Schein und Sein bei Shakespeare.* Festrede in der öffentlichen Sitzung der Bayerischen Akademie der Wissenschaften München 1959.

6 'Shakespeare and the Modern World' in *Shakespeare Survey* 16, 1963, Cambridge University Press.

7 'Das Drama Shakespeares'. Lecture given on the occasion of Shakespeare's 400th birthday to the German Shakespeare Society (West) 1964, published in *Shakespeare Jahrbuch (West)* 1965.

8 'Wie sollen wir ein Drama von Shakespeare lesen?' Introduction to a German edition of Shakespeare's works in 4 volumes by Winkler Verlag, München 1967.

The German versions of 2, 5, 7, 8 have also been reprinted in *Das Drama Shakespeares* 1969. In preparing the English versions of the German articles various alterations have been made.

Preface

Four of these eight essays go back to earlier articles which were included in a volume *Das Drama Shakespeares*, published by Vandenhoeck & Ruprecht in 1969. The opening one, however, on Shakespeare's art of preparation was written in 1970 and no German version has been published as yet. Of my English publications, the Annual Shakespeare Lecture of the British Academy 1966, the Presidential Address of the Modern Humanities Research Association of 1964, and a lecture given at the Tenth International Shakespeare Conference at Stratford in 1961, have been included. For permission to reprint them here acknowledgement is made to the British Academy, the Modern Humanities Research Association and the editors of *Shakespeare Survey*. References to the original places of publication are given in a bibliographical note opposite.

For advice and criticism I wish to thank Ernest Schanzer, Ina Schabert, Anne Barton, Muriel Bradbrook, and John Northam, and in particular Inga-Stina Ewbank and Stanley Wells, to whom the book is dedicated and who some years ago encouraged me to pursue my plans further, even if the originally intended full-length study of Shakespeare's dramatic art could not be completed for the time being.

Thanks are also due to my colleagues L. C. Knights and Henry Gifford who invited me to Bristol University in 1964, under the sponsorship of the Churchill Foundation, to give a series of lectures, in which several subjects treated in this volume were first discussed in lecture form.

For remarks and suggestions bearing on Shakespeare's technique of preparation I am indebted to unpublished theses by Friedrich Kastropp and Heinz Sprogies which will be referred to in the notes.

I feel particularly grateful to Charity Meier-Ewert and Gemma Geoghegan for their help in preparing the English version of the essays, to Ingeborg Boltz for compiling the index, and to Gisela Oswald for typing the manuscript and checking the quotations which as well as the line-numberings are based on the text of Peter Alexander (Collins-Shakespeare, London, 1951).

Wolfgang Clemen

I

Shakespeare's Art of Preparation.
A Preliminary Sketch

INTRODUCTION

Preparation is one of the most important elements of drama, but at the same time it is the most difficult to isolate and to define. This applies to Shakespeare even more than to other dramatists. In his plays preparation is a wide and complex phenomenon, which is manifested in many different ways and which presents itself to us in diverse contexts. Up to the present no attempt has been made to describe Shakespeare's art of preparation,[1] and the most probable explanation of this lies in the difficulty of delimiting and categorizing so varied and complex a process. For preparation may mean the announcement of a new character about to enter for the first time, but it may also mean the gradual working towards a catastrophe or a climax, extending over several acts; it may include the insertion of omens, portents, dreams and supernatural appearances, and may extend to the use of dramatic irony, of prophetic hints concealed in the imagery, and premonitions of the characters themselves.

Preparation can appear in one recurrent obvious device, but it may also operate through the structure of a whole scene, an act, or an

---

[1] The most coherent discussion still is Arthur Colby Sprague's chapter on 'Preparation and Surprise' in *Shakespeare and the Audience*, Camb., Mass., 1935. For scattered remarks on the subject see the books by William Archer, Brander Matthews, Sir John Squire, B. Evans, H. S. Wilson, V. K. Whitaker, N. Coghill, W. Rosen, J. R. Brown, J. L. Styan quoted on the following pages. Of earlier critics S. T. Coleridge gave a good deal of attention to preparation in Shakespeare (cf. J. R. de Jackson 'Coleridge on Shakespeare's Preparation' *Review of English Literature* 7 (1966)). Of twentieth-century critics it is H. Granville-Barker who in his *Prefaces* shows much awareness of the aspect of dramatic preparation. In Germany Otto Ludwig in his *Shakespearestudien* Leipzig, 1872 made some pertinent remarks on Shakespeare's dramatic preparation. A subtle and detailed analysis of the preparatory function of first scenes in Shakespeare is to be found in E. Th. Sehrt, *Der dramatische Auftakt in der elisabethanischen Tragödie*, 1960.

extended dialogue, in which case it is much more difficult to demonstrate. Finally, what we call preparation is very closely linked with other aspects of dramatic art, with the technique of exposition, with the creation of dramatic tension, suspense and expectation, and even of dramatic contrast. How then are we to make the necessary distinctions and divisions?

In view of these difficulties it may at first seem advisable to examine individual aspects of Shakespeare's art of preparation separately. One could for instance trace recurrent conspicuous devices, such as the use of omens and portents, or examine the part played by premonitions, or study the preparation for the first appearance of main characters – one could treat them as we treat clearly defined aspects like the aside. But in this way we cannot grasp the complexity of the subject; we do not see how Shakespeare usually, in aiming at a particular effect, works on several, different levels and with 'infinite variety', nor can we show how closely the different aspects of dramatic art are interwoven and conditioned by one another. In order to recognize and demonstrate the interdependence and co-operation of the individual means of preparation, it is advisable to abandon systematic treatment of this sort and make a new start proceeding in a selective way. One will have to omit some points of importance and refrain from going into questions related to the art of preparation yet mainly connected with other aspects of dramatic technique. An exhaustive discussion of dramatic preparation would in any case necessitate a whole book, probably a long one. The present study, concentrating on only eight plays (of which the selection will be justified on p. 11) cannot therefore hope to be more than a preliminary sketch of a complex subject which calls for more detailed and full treatment in the future.

A brief study of the subject will have to limit itself to those forms of preparation which can be demonstrated by quotations. For as with other elements in drama there are some aspects of preparation which can be illustrated from the text and others which are much more difficult to demonstrate because they are less tangible and less evident in individual passages, affecting rather the whole 'lay-out' of an episode. Such forms of preparation would need a detailed interpretation of a whole scene or act in order to become manifest. We therefore give preference to forms of preparation which are articulated at particular points in the play.

Why is preparation in drama particularly important, and a distinctive characteristic of this genre? For one thing the dramatist works within limitations which do not apply to the story teller. The novelist may describe at length the setting in which his story is to take place, he may tell us something about the whereabouts of his characters, about their background, their ideas, their previous history. In the course of his narrative he can pause whenever he likes to record the changing conditions which are to influence the conduct of his characters, and he can analyse those factors which are to motivate and explain future actions. The dramatist cannot avail himself of this freedom. He must put all these elements, background, description, motivation, psychological analysis into dialogue. Gesture, setting and spectacle may help him in conveying these elements to the audience, but the spoken words of the characters will always remain his chief resource. Moreover, the need to limit length is a constant pressure on the dramatist. He must be economic, concise, selective. Condensation must be his aim and hence he must try to do several things at once. While informing the audience, he must carry on the conversation on the stage and make the characters reveal themselves; while painting the background and atmosphere he must move the action forward. He cannot pause to comment, describe, prepare and explain, unless this is done under another pretext by the characters themselves. This means that much of what belongs to the substance of preparation must be 'smuggled in' as an unobtrusive and convincing part of their utterance. A criterion for good drama is therefore the degree to which the matter which serves the purpose of information and preparation is turned into lively dialogue and action.

The less leisurely quality of drama as compared to the novel is connected, as was shown, with the fact that the dramatist has no opportunity for direct comment. This leads to a further distinction: not only is the progress of the action on the stage, during a scene, identical with the progress of the author's narration, but also with the progress in the minds of the audience. While in a novel we can pause or slow down the tempo of reading for moments of retrospection, reflection and interpretation, and, on the other hand, can take in an elaborate description, an analysis of a state of mind at one sweeping glance, as it were, the play is in constant motion, and in watching it we proceed from one moment to the next. We cannot look back to the top of the page, we cannot obtain a comprehensive contemplation of a whole passage; we have to go on at the same speed at which the action on the stage proceeds. Steady progress, or – as Thornton Wilder put it – 'forward movement',[1] is one of the basic laws of drama.

Another criterion for good drama is therefore the degree to which we are drawn into this process; and on the other hand an understanding of the nature of it may give us a key to the principles underlying the art of preparation. In a successful play the audience not only watches what is happening on the stage at the present moment, but is also constantly looking out for what is going to happen next. We want to see and know more of what we have just seen, our minds are stretching forward, our awakened interest asks for continuation and clarification. The building up of impressions which is going on all the time in the minds of the audience while the play is in progress also includes a building up of expectations.[2] While fixing our attention on the immediate presence of the spectacle, the dramatist also keeps our imagination busy with speculations about the further development. What we see at the present moment we judge on the basis of what we have learned so far about the characters and on the basis of what we have been expecting all the time (only at the very beginning of the play is this different). But this does not mean that our previous knowledge and our expectations must always be fulfilled by the course of the action. The clash between expectation and fulfilment constitutes an important source of dramatic effect. Shakespeare, in his handling of the art of preparation, made rich use of it.

The 'progress of time' of which we have spoken also means that the dramatist is under greater pressure of time in shaping his plays than the novelist. A whole life's tragedy may be compressed into a three hours' 'traffic of the stage'. More things happen as a rule, more conflicts and developments are presented to us, in a play than in a novel limited to three hours' reading. Without proper preparation the audience would be overwhelmed by the impact of these inner and outer events following closely one upon another. Preparation, used subtly and unobtrusively, is a means for the dramatist to stretch out time, to create the

[1] Thornton Wilder 'Some Thoughts on Playwriting' in *Playwrights on Playwriting*, ed. Toby Cole, New York, 1960.
[2] Cf. J. L. Styan, *The Elements of Drama*, Cambridge, 1960, Ch. 6, 'Building the Sequence of Impressions'.

illusion of 'double time', to convey to us the experience of the gradual ripening of a decisive action, of the seemingly slow approach of a catastrophe or crisis. We are ready to accept a radical change in a character's mind or a fatal reversal of inter-human relationships though they may take place within half an hour's time, because we have been led up to them little by little.

On the other hand, by informing us beforehand about the circumstances and conditions under which a climax, a catastrophe will take place, the dramatist may concentrate the audience's entire attention on the emotional impact of the event, excluding all informative detail. Preparation thus becomes a means of economy, of saving up the resources of stagecraft.

Another aspect of the art of preparation derives from the foreknowledge of the audience. Shakespeare, as a rule, takes the audience into his confidence at an early stage. The audience thus possesses knowledge which is superior to that shared by the main character or characters. This foreknowledge makes the spectator watch the development of the play, the delusions, hopes, discoveries, the 'false' and the 'right' actions of the characters on the stage with a mixture of pleasure, apprehension, and critical detachment. He feels at once remote, looking at the play with an almost god-like prescience from a superior vantage-point and he also feels involved,[1] for he will suffer for and with the characters, looking through their false hopes and illusions and foreseeing the fatal consequences of their doings. He may identify himself with their reactions and attitudes and may at the same time judge and reject them on account of his superior knowledge. In his comedies Shakespeare made ample use of this 'gap of awareness', which has a direct bearing on the peculiar technique of preparation characteristic of these plays.[2]

But although Shakespeare gives to his audience, as a rule, a good deal of foreknowledge, he does not tell them everything. There is also a certain amount of guess-work on the part of the audience. We must not know too well what is going to happen, or if we know, we must not know *how* it will happen. The art of preparation consists in establishing

[1] On the concepts of 'involvement' and 'detachment' see William Rosen, *Shakespeare and the Craft of Tragedy*, Oxford, 1960, p. 57; cf. V. Whitaker, *The Mirror up to Nature. The Technique of Shakespeare's Tragedies*, San Marino: California, 1965, p. 154.
[2] See B. Evans, *Shakespeare's Comedies*, Oxford, 1960.

a balance between certainty and uncertainty, between an assured fore-knowledge and a vague presentiment. The dramatist must alternately unveil and veil, promise and again withdraw his promise, he must proceed rather by 'hints and guesses' than by obvious and obtrusive indications. Straightforward and direct preparation will fit certain developments only, but it is not the best solution for most cases. At this point we see that the often-repeated maxim enounced by Alexandre Dumas Jr. 'The art of the theatre is the art of preparation' needs some modification, and it is worth quoting William Archer, who, in reply to Dumas, wrote: 'Yes, it is very largely the art of delicate and unobtru-sive preparation, of helping an audience to divine whither it is going, while leaving it to wonder how it is to get there.'[1] Thus the rousing of curiosity, of conjectures as to *how* things will develop, and as to how certain 'riddles' put to us at the play's beginning will be solved, form a strong element in Shakespeare's art of preparation. Dramatic art, as John Dover Wilson once defined it, is an art of 'progressive revela-tion'.[2] A play begins by showing us an unsolved situation, an issue not yet cleared up, a latent conflict of which we do not know the outcome. By and by we shall know more, for more things will be 'revealed' to us. Preparation is one of the means of setting this process in motion and of keeping it going. For every utterance which goes towards revealing an additional detail acts at the same time as preparation for other things which we may be expecting.

Preparation is often combined with the creation of tension and suspense. For an expectation of which the fulfilment is delayed acts as a stimulus to keep our interest alive and to put us into a state of keen alertness. We have been promised something and now we have to wait for it longer than we had expected; at the same time we may grow uncertain, wondering how it will take place or even whether it will take place at all. Tension depends a good deal on the amount of pre-paration the dramatist has put into operation. Delay and suspense, on the other hand, will increase the tension while deliberate preparation goes underground, having previously built up certain unforgettable expectations in the minds of the audience. We find many examples in Shakespeare of this use of delay through the insertion of episodes or

[1] William Archer, *Play-Making. A Manual of Craftmanship.* Re-issued ed. J. Gassner, New York, 1960, p. 132.
[2] J. Dover Wilson, *What Happens in Hamlet*, Cambridge, 1935, p. 231.

scenes which appear to interrupt, or branch off from, the main action, the audience having been previously prepared for certain issues.[1]

Dramatic preparation, not only in Shakespeare's plays, is usually judged and appreciated on the assumption that the play will be attended by an audience which has no previous knowledge of it. The ideal spectator is taken to be someone who not only sees the play for the first time in his life on the stage, but who has not even heard about it before. Surely most playwrights have this type of audience in mind when writing their plays, and this must have been true to a certain extent of Shakespeare too. But even Shakespeare, when composing plays like *Richard III*, *Julius Caesar* or *Antony and Cleopatra* (and a good many others), could count on his audience's knowledge of the story in its rough outline. And his audience, too, consisted of different groups of spectators with differing degrees of information about the contents of his plays. Some of these spectators would probably see the play for a second time. Much the same applies to a modern audience, although today a greater proportion will be familiar with a play by Shakespeare which they are going to see. However, previous information about a play does not invalidate the use of dramatic preparation, nor does it basically diminish the rousing of curiosity and interest which are so essential to the full enjoyment of a theatrical experience.[2] For although we have, at the back of our minds, knowledge of how the play will develop and end, we may nevertheless forget about it as we sit in the theatre and enter into the mood of someone watching the play for the first time. In identifying ourselves with these spectators and also with the characters on the stage we may experience the same tensions, qualms, uncertainties and hopes, no matter what we know of the happy or unhappy conclusion.

In fact, a spectator who has read the play beforehand will be in a better position to appreciate the subtlety of early preparatory devices or forebodings, not to mention the ironies which would escape a spectator seeing the play for the first time in any case. The playgoer who already knows the story will be able to switch his interest with more eager attention from the 'what' to the 'how' – and this is where dramatic art (and art in general) is revealed.

[1] Cf. Nevill Coghill, *Shakespeare's Professional Skills*, Cambridge, 1964.
[2] 'In the drama, our knowledge of the end of a play in no wise interferes with our enjoyment' Brander Matthews, *The Study of Drama*, London, 1910, p. 193.

The study of Shakespeare's technique of preparation will constantly cause one to ask what is happening in the minds of the audience. Analysing this process of accumulating impressions, expectations, and interests set in motion by the play as it is performed would shift the emphasis from mere textual explication towards another method of dramatic interpretation that has relatively seldom been tried out as yet.[1]

However, no principle can be laid down for this interplay between the audience and the stage, as too many different forms and degrees of preparation are involved. Even the requirement that preparation must not be too direct and straightforward but should provide for an element of uncertainty and guess-work (as was pointed out above) does not apply to all kinds of preparation. Indeed, any rigid categorization of dramatic devices and situations which lend themselves to the purpose of preparation would oversimplify the matter and would blur the distinction between the different degrees of expectation in the minds of the audience.

Even among the more indirect forms of preparation there are some to which the concept of 'expectation' does not appear to apply. For of the many dramatic or tragic ironies woven into the texture of the tragedies only very few theatre-goers will catch the premonitory meaning; quite a number of these ironies will in fact only disclose themselves as deliberate forebodings to someone who reads the play for a second or third time, with a thorough knowledge of what will be said and acted in the later parts of the play. These ironies may be deciphered – as it were – only if one goes through the play in the opposite direction; from the end backwards to the beginning.

Among these subtle and hidden forms of preparation we may also include the use of certain recurring key-words or the use of imagery. Again 'expectation' or 'curiosity' would not be the right term for describing what happens in the minds of the audience. For these words or images act on our subconscious; they may create a mood of apprehension or danger, they may put us into another frame of mind in which we may more readily accept what the next act will present to us. We are 'tuned in' and imperceptibly drawn into an altered imaginative mood. These delicate effects are most difficult for the critic to assess and will differ from one theatre-goer to another, according to the degree of his sensitivity and imaginative capability.

[1] John Northam, *Ibsen's Dramatic Method*, London, 1953.

Shakespeare has always been praised for the way in which he takes up, in the later scenes of his plays, suggestions, phrases, hints or even situations which occurred in the first acts. There are seldom 'loose threads' in his plays, especially in those of his maturity. Again and again, when watching or reading attentively a later act or scene, we are reminded of a phrase or an image or even of a situation in the earlier parts of the play. There are numerous echoes, correspondences, variations and repetitions in each of the tragedies which help to bind the parts of the play together and make it a living organism of which all parts are interrelated. These echoes and correspondences establish links between the scenes, and often build a bridge between parts which at first seem unrelated. In studying the various forms of preparation our attention will be directed to a considerable extent towards this important aspect of Shakespeare's dramatic art. But here, too, the question arises as to whether all these echoes, which revive our memory of earlier scenes, enable us to place these earlier passages under the heading of 'preparation'. To quote a famous example: Is Lady Macbeth's sleep-walking scene which contains many echoes from an earlier scene (ii, ii) therefore 'prepared' by this earlier scene? Surely, this 'preparation' (if we want to keep to this term at all in this connexion) is recognized only in retrospect.[1] The utterances made by Lady Macbeth in the earlier part of the play, soon after the murder of Duncan, may linger on in our memory because of their symbolic impact, but they do not rouse expectation of any kind in our minds. And this is true of a great many similar echoes and correspondences found in Shakespeare's later plays.

However, the consideration of this significant aspect may warn us that 'preparation' in Shakespeare's plays is not only evident in what the characters themselves say in the way of anticipation. Besides, fore-boding or explicit anticipation are for Shakespeare's characters only one way of anticipating the future. As has been set out in another connexion,[2] Shakespeare makes full and frequent use of those natural attitudes and feelings in man which point towards the future. Any observer who looks out for utterances which, by drawing the future into perspective, may serve the purpose of preparation, will be struck by the great number of phrases expressing hope and fear, or stating promises, vows, threats, and warnings or indulging in wishful thinking.

[1] See the paragraph on *Macbeth* p. 84.
[2] See the chapter on 'Past and Future in Shakespeare's Drama'.

A strong subjective element thus comes in. The relevance of these utterances in view of their preparatory function will differ greatly and they cannot be taken at their face value. For in as much as the anticipation expressed in these utterances may be misleading, it will clash with the superior foreknowledge of the audience or with the even more superior omniscience of the dramatist himself. It is by such clashing that the intense interest with which we watch a performance is reinforced.

But apart from such anticipatory feelings expressed by the characters themselves the dramatist has at his disposal other means of preparing the audience. Some of these means, such as the acceleration or the slowing-down of tempo, the change in versification, the transformation of the vocabulary, the building up and organization of a long passage of dialogue or of a speech, cannot be discussed here; other means, such as the use of delay and suspense, will be considered briefly. With all these aspects, however, we shall become aware of the boundary beyond which preparation is an intangible and altogether too diffuse and complex subject to be demonstrated in a study of this kind.

On the other hand it is just this intricacy and many-sidedness which make a study of this phenomenon 'preparation' especially fascinating and fruitful. Studying this single aspect we may learn more about the whole play. For we shall see how in each play the forms of preparation are determined by the overall principles of structure and style, and we shall find that the manner in which preparation is handled even reflects the play's theme and meaning. It is one of the aims of this study to enquire into the correspondence existing between the kind of preparation used and the other constituent elements of each play. Thus the study of preparation could open up a new approach for which this preliminary and fragmentary sketch is designed to give some suggestions.

The eight plays which will be treated individually on the following pages have been chosen because they illustrate the range of techniques of preparation as well as the range of meaning which the very concept of preparation – as suggested above – involves. All of these plays differ from one another considerably as to the technique of preparation used and as to its relationship with the nature of the play and its major characters. Some additional aspects of the art of preparation, which could not be examined in these eight sections, will be mentioned and briefly discussed in a concluding chapter.

SHAKESPEARE'S ART OF PREPARATION

Of Shakespeare's histories *Henry VI*, *Richard III* and *Richard II*
have been selected because, on the one hand, a remarkable development
can be traced in these plays, for they exemplify the advance from
'technique of preparation' towards 'art of preparation'. On the other
hand, these histories also display strong contrasts as far as the function
of preparation is concerned, which will be revealed in particular by a
comparison between *Richard III* and *Richard II*.

Of Shakespeare's tragedies *Romeo and Juliet*, *Julius Caesar*, *Hamlet*,
Othello, and *Macbeth* were chosen. In these five plays we find not only
a wide variety of different techniques and functions of preparation but
also, in each case, an illuminating connexion between the general
character of the drama and the specific art of preparation. The development of the art of preparation culminates in *Macbeth*, the concept of
preparation becoming at the same time so complex that its investigation
by the methods tried out so far becomes a problem. The romances and
comedies have not been included in this study. The comedies in particular would require an altogether different and detailed approach. For
the manifold intrigues, disguises, mistaken identities, discoveries and
deceptions are in each play tied up with a good deal of preparation and
most (although not all) of Shakespeare's comic effects depend on preparation rather than on surprise. In some comedies we even find scenes
of eavesdropping which have been beforehand carefully rehearsed. One
would have to go into great detail in order to disentangle the threads of
intrigue, leading up to the comic confrontations and confusions. Moreover, a study of preparation in the comedies would have to take into
account Shakespeare's art of building up several levels of awareness,
especially of a discrepancy of awareness[1] which acts as a powerful agent
in preparing the minds of the audience for the ensuing comic effects.
An examination of the comedies from the point of view of preparation
therefore constitutes a major task.

A FIRST SCENE AS AN EXAMPLE: A MIDSUMMER NIGHT'S
DREAM, I, i.

However lest the comedies be altogether omitted, we propose to start
by looking at the first scene of *A Midsummer Night's Dream*. For this
scene can well illustrate a number of points which were made about the

[1] Cf. Bertrand Evans, *Shakespeare's Comedies*, 1960.

features of preparation in our introduction. Combining exposition with preparation the scene not only gives us the information we need in order to understand the following events, introducing in a skilful manner the various strands of the action, but it also prepares us for the mood, atmosphere and theme of this comedy. We can see how the art of preparation consists in the playwright's ability to do several things at once, 'smuggling in' his bits of information in an unobtrusive manner. But we can also note the part played by imagery and by 'key-words' in attuning us to what is to come and we shall see how the time-element too has an important share in rousing expectations for the future.

Some of this can already be shown in the very first lines of the scene:

> *Theseus.* Now, fair Hippolyta, our nuptial hour
> Draws on apace; four happy days bring in
> Another moon; but, O, methinks, how slow
> This old moon wanes! She lingers my desires,
> Like to a step-dame or a dowager,
> Long withering out a young man's revenue.
>
> *Hippolyta.* Four days will quickly steep themselves in night;
> Four nights will quickly dream away the time;
> And then the moon, like to a silver bow
> New-bent in heaven, shall behold the night
> Of our solemnities.
>
> *Theseus.*   Go, Philostrate,
> Stir up the Athenian youth to merriments;
> Awake the pert and nimble spirit of mirth;
> Turn melancholy forth to funerals;
> The pale companion is not for our pomp.
> Hippolyta, I woo'd thee with my sword,
> And won thy love doing thee injuries;
> But I will wed thee in another key,
> With pomp, with triumph, and with revelling.
>
> (I, i, I)

It is not a matter of chance that Theseus is the first character to speak. For he and Hippolyta not only form what we may call the 'enveloping action' which binds together the various plots, and which will be taken up again in the fourth act when the world of dreams and errors is to merge into the world of reality; Theseus also acts as arbitrator in the love dispute between Hermia and Demetrius and it is on his wedding day that the final decision about Hermia's fate will be made.[1] This wedding day is mentioned here as the goal towards which the play is moving, and we are given the exact time and date. But the first conversation between Theseus and Hippolyta also conveys to us a twofold awareness of time which is important for the whole way in which we, the audience, are to experience the events of the following scenes and acts. This emerges when Hippolyta's 'Four days will quickly steep themselves in night; Four nights will quickly dream away the time' (6) is contrasted with Theseus' 'But, O, methinks, how slow this old moon wanes' (4). At the same time these lines introduce us to the atmosphere of the moonlit scenes that follow; we hear the keywords 'dream', 'night' and 'moon' in different contexts. In fact 'moon' and 'night' each occur five times, 'dream' three times in this scene alone. On the other hand, these first lines also suggest the aristocratic world of the court and we realize that the comparison of the moon with 'a stepdame or a dowager long withering out a young man's revenue' is very apt. Theseus' order to Philostrate 'Stir up the Athenian youth to merriments; . . .' not only introduces the subplot of the mechanics who are to rehearse a play for the occasion of the wedding day, but also evokes that 'pert and nimble spirit of mirth' which is to dominate the mood of the comedy, not forgetting, however, the darker undertones of melancholy and vexation which also constitute an ingredient of the play's atmosphere. Theseus' last lines, in which he reminds Hippolyta of his former manner of wooing her 'with my sword' 'doing thee injuries' and announces his intention to 'wed thee in another key', pose an antithesis which will be meaningful for other love-relationships in this play too. Finally, in the concluding line, the three formal and suggestive nouns 'pomp', 'triumph', 'revelling', besides pointing forward towards the wedding festivities with the dramatic entertainments, again set the key for the style and manner of courtly life which is one sphere of the action of the play.

But very soon we are again reminded of conflict and the darker issues of life. Egeus begins his complaint against Lysander with a telling phrase

[1] Cf. my edition of *A Midsummer Night's Dream*, The Signet Classic Shakespeare, New York, 1963.

> Full of vexation come I, with complaint
> Against my child. . . .
>
> (I, i, 22)

There will be dissension, anger and discord again and again in this comedy. For we shall hear of Oberon and Titania's quarrel, which is underlined by the tumult in nature described at length in II, i, 81 ff., and of other conflicts in the fairy world and even among the mechanics. Moreover, Egeus' dispute with his daughter and Lysander is only the first of several clashes and indignant, sometimes even raging encounters between the four Athenian lovers. The episode in which Egeus, Hermia, Lysander, and Demetrius appear before Theseus skilfully links the 'enveloping action' of Theseus and Hippolyta with the plot of the four lovers and leads up to the following confusion, for the verdict passed by Theseus on Hermia makes her flee with Lysander into the wood near Athens. Thus of the four plots which are combined in this play, three are introduced and linked up with each other in this first scene. But even more important as an introduction to the whole play are those passages which suggest and foreshadow its themes. Egeus accuses Lysander of having 'witched' his child. His lines

> Thou hast by moonlight at her window sung,
> With feigning voice, verses of feigning love,
> And stol'n the impression of her fantasy. . . .
>
> (I, i, 30)

are full of dramatic irony and so are the references to the 'judgment by eyes' which will play such an ambiguous role later on:

> *Hermia.*   I would my father looked but with my eyes.
> *Theseus.*   Rather your eyes must with his judgment look.
>
> (I, i, 56)

or Helena's later lines in this scene

> Love looks not with the eyes, but with the mind;
> And therefore is wing'd Cupid painted blind.
>
> (I, i, 234)

These lines are preceded by another ironical statement which foreshadows Titania's falling in love with Bottom turned into an ass[1]

---

[1] Cf. Stanley Wells in his edition of *A Midsummer Night's Dream* (New Penguin Shakespeare, London, 1967) p. 23.

Things base and vile, holding no quantity
Love can transpose to form and dignity.

(I, i, 232)

However, there is one passage which, more than any other, condenses into a suggestive image the whole movement and mood of this comedy as well as its central theme. It occurs at the end of Lysander's and Hermia's rather superficial repartee and strikes us by the sudden effusion of lovely poetry after so many shallow lines (which yet give expression, though in a very different manner, to the hazardous nature of love to be witnessed in the following scenes). To permit appreciation of this unique transition it will be necessary to quote the entire passage together with the preceding repartee:

Lysander.	Ay me! for aught that I could ever read,
	Could ever hear by tale or history,
	The course of true love never did run smooth;
	But either it was different in blood—
Hermia.	O cross! too high to be enthrall'd to low.
Lysander.	Or else misgraffed in respect of years—
Hermia.	O spite! too old to be engag'd to young.
Lysander.	Or else it stood upon the choice of friends—
Hermia.	O hell! to choose love by another's eyes.
Lysander.	Or, if there were a sympathy in choice,
	War, death, or sickness, did lay siege to it,
	Making it momentary as a sound,
	Swift as a shadow, short as any dream,
	Brief as the lightning in the collied night
	That, in a spleen, unfolds both heaven and earth,
	And ere a man hath power to say 'Behold!'
	The jaws of darkness do devour it up;
	So quick bright things come to confusion.

(I, i, 132)

This last speech not only expresses the play's central theme, the transitoriness and inconstancy of love, it also conveys to us the peculiar rhythm of quick movement and dreamlike wonder which is to take hold of us during the next few scenes. The central image of lightning in the night which comes and goes 'ere a man hath power to say "Behold"',

15

serves as a symbol for what will be enacted in this play, whereas the coming disorder is anticipated by the last line 'So quick bright things come to confusion'. Nor is it by chance that the two keywords 'shadow' and 'dream' occur in these lines.

Though this is the most suggestive and imaginative passage to prepare the audience for the kind of love which is to be enacted in the play, it is not the only one. Hermia's following answer adds more significant touches, enumerating what is 'due to love' and what goes under the heading of 'poor Fancy's followers'.

> If then true lovers have been ever cross'd,
> It stands as an edict in destiny.
> Then let us teach our trial patience,
> Because it is a customary cross,
> As due to love as thoughts and dreams and sighs,
> Wishes and tears, poor Fancy's followers.
>
> (I, I, 150)

But at the end of this scene it is Helena who, in the fashion of the early comedies, indulges in a series of definitions of love which in this comedy become more than a mere display of wit and ingenuity. For they point in each case towards those qualities of love which will prove conducive to the ensuing confusions and mishaps. The lines about love's ability to transform 'things base and vile' and the following lines on the 'blindness of love' have already been quoted, but the rest of the passage is equally revealing:

> Nor hath love's mind of any judgment taste;
> Wings and no eyes figure unheedy haste;
> And therefore is love said to be a child,
> Because in choice he is so oft beguil'd.
> As waggish boys in game themselves forswear,
> So the boy Love is perjur'd everywhere;
>
> (I, i, 236)

Against this background of love 'perjur'd everywhere' Hermia's swearing 'By all the vows that ever men have broke' (175) and Helena's account of Demetrius' first hailing down oaths which were soon forgotten ('showers of oaths did melt' 245) are an ironical anticipation.

No supernatural element has as yet been introduced in this first scene. Nevertheless we begin to feel that this is going to be a world in which irrational and incredible things may happen. A case in point is Theseus' inhuman verdict pronounced against Hermia, should she persist in refusing to marry Demetrius. For twice (65 and 86) she is told by Theseus

> Either to die the death, or to abjure
> For ever the society of men.
>
> (I, i, 65)

Thus the date of 'the next new moon' (83) on which we expect the wedding festivities for Theseus and Hippolyta to take place, could also – according to this decree – be the day on which Hermia will be sentenced to death, this double expectation attuning us to a twofold course and perspective of events. But menacing a disobedient daughter with a death-sentence is in itself a motif which removes this world of Theseus, Egeus, Hermia, Demetrius and the other Athenians into a fairy-tale sphere of strange and incredible happenings. Even an Elizabethan audience, accustomed to the punishment by death for minor offences, would have wondered at the monstrosity of such a notion and would have felt that this belongs to the unreal world of comedy in which we frequently find laws of similar incredible severity (cf. for instance *Comedy of Errors*, I, i, 147).

Looking at the very beginning of this scene we observed the way in which Shakespeare makes Theseus unobtrusively and skilfully prepare us for the moonlit scenes which are to follow. But even in Theseus' stern speech of which we have just quoted the beginning ('Either to die the death') the moon comes in, though this time in quite a different connexion. For as an alternative to death (in case of persistent disobedience) the unhappy life of a nun 'in shady cloister mewed' is offered to Hermia

> To live a barren sister all your life,
> Chanting faint hymns to the cold fruitless moon.
>
> (I, i, 72)

When, however, later in the scene, Lysander and Hermia actually plan their 'lovers' flight' into the woods near Athens, the nocturnal scenery of this meeting can be anticipated with more fullness, though in the stylized poetical manner ('Phoebe' replaces the moon) of which we shall have more in the following scenes:

> To-morrow night, when Phoebe doth behold
> Her silver visage in the wat'ry glass,
> Decking with liquid pearl the bladed grass, ...
>
> (I, i, 209)

Thus this first scene reveals preparation on several levels, it bears out Coleridge's observations 'Shakespeare showed great judgment in his first scenes . . .' and 'that in all his plays he takes the opportunity of sowing germs, the full development of which appears at a future time'.[1]

HENRY VI

Turning to the three parts of *Henry VI* we already find a rich use of preparation, although it is still of a fairly obvious, direct and often even primitive kind. These three plays are crowded with characters, episodes, events and intrigues which follow one another in rapid succession. The multiplicity of detail often obscures the overall development, so that a reader (as well as a spectator) of these plays may find it hard to follow up the various threads of the action and recognize their relevance and connexion. Whereas in his later histories, for instance in *Richard II*, Shakespeare tends to select only a limited number of events and figures from the great mass of material the chronicles offered him, in *Henry VI* he still tries to dramatize as many events as possible in order to cope with the fullness of the historical record. Consequently in *Henry VI* he is compelled to give more space to explanation, factual information and documentation than in the later histories. The technique of preparation occurring most frequently in *Henry VI* serves this purpose. For a great many passages and lines which we could single out as pointing towards the future are of this expository, informative kind. The emphasis in these three plays is on outward rather than inward action – on battles, feuds, dissensions, plots and political intrigues. Plans tend to be carried out speedily; the performance of an action usually follows shortly on its announcement. Thus the most frequent form of preparation in *Henry VI* is the straight-

[1] S. T. Coleridge, *Shakespearean Criticism*, ed. T. M. Raysor, London, 1960, vol. II, pp. 230, 232.

forward announcement of future purpose, the bragging proclamation or threatening prediction of impending events. The appropriate place for such boastful and self-assertive predictions is the soliloquy. Thus, at the end of *2 Henry VI*, III, i York proclaims his aim:

> I will stir up in England some black storm
> Shall blow ten thousand souls to heaven or hell;
> And this fell tempest shall not cease to rage
> Until the golden circuit on my head,
> Like to the glorious sun's transparent beams,
> Do calm the fury of this mad-bred flaw.
>
> (III, i, 349)

Such lines may recall the grandiloquent braggings of Marlowe's tragic heroes. However, it should be observed that, contrary to the wishful thinking of Marlowe's characters couched in extravagant and hyperbolic terms, the language of Shakespeare's characters keeps more within the confines of reality. For most of the announcements made by Shakespeare's characters come true later on, whereas the predictions of Marlowe's heroes only partly fulfil themselves. For either they move in an imaginary world of impossibilities, or the audience is left wondering which of these bragging announcements will materialize and which not.

When Shakespeare's characters, in these plays, declare their intentions, they state the issue in a clear-cut and definite manner, as if determination already meant achievement. Especially the statements made at the end of a scene have this apodictic turn which the rhyme sometimes helps to underline. Thus Winchester concludes the first scene of *1 Henry VI* with his announcement:

> The King from Eltham I intend to steal,
> And sit at chiefest stern of public weal.
>
> (I, i, 176)

In a similar vein Plantagenet reveals his purpose at the end of the Second Act:

> And therefore haste I to the Parliament,
> Either to be restored to my blood,
> Or make my ill th' advantage of my good.
>
> (II, v, 127)

In *2 Henry VI* it is York who, in this straightforward manner, announces a whole programme of action in a few lines, again at the end of the scene:[1]

> Then will I raise aloft the milk-white rose,
> With whose sweet smell the air shall be perfum'd,
> And in my standard bear the arms of York,
> To grapple with the house of Lancaster;
> And force perforce I'll make him yield the crown,
> Whose bookish rule hath pull'd fair England down.
>
> (I, i, 249)

In *3 Henry VI* the character of Warwick has come into the foreground and now we hear from him a similar proud affirmation of future action, condensed into a concise formula:

> I was the chief that rais'd him to the crown,
> And I'll be chief to bring him down again;
> Not that I pity Henry's misery,
> But seek revenge on Edward's mockery.
>
> (III, iii, 262)

The plans announced to us in this way always appear to be final; they imply prompt execution. The sense of expectation on the part of the audience is diminished by the fact that there does not seem to be any interim 'between the acting of a dreadful thing/And the first motion' (*Julius Caesar*, II, i, 63), any hesitation or uncertainty, any qualm or genuine apprehensiveness. Moreover, we do not watch the 'hatching' of such a plan, for it is put forward as a ready-made design. We are not allowed a glimpse of what is passing in the speaker's mind, we are given the final result and not what leads up to it.[2]

The only exception seems to occur in Richard Gloucester's great soliloquy in *3 Henry VI*, III, ii, 124. Gloucester's desire for the crown and his planning for the future command far more interest and attention on the part of the audience, for his passionate wish finds expression in appropriate images which may suggest to us the speaker's

---

[1] Cf. too, III, i, 380 f.
[2] For remarks on this aspect and related issues the author is indebted to an unpublished thesis by Heinz Sprogies, *Die Kunst der Vorbereitung in Shakespeares Historien*, Munich, 1964.

strong personality ('like one that stands upon a promontory' 135; 'like one lost in a thorny wood' 174). We also watch a mind at work 'toiling desperately to find it out'. And we hear a question at the end of this soliloquy preceding the final resolve:

> Can I do this, and cannot get a crown?
> Tut, were it farther off, I'll pluck it down.
>
> (III, ii, 194)

To appreciate the new elements in this soliloquy we should look back to York's soliloquy at the end of the first scene of *2 Henry VI* and compare the manner in which he expresses his desire for the crown and his future intentions:

> And therefore I will take the Nevils' parts,
> And make a show of love to proud Duke Humphrey,
> And when I spy advantage, claim the crown,
> For that's the golden mark I seek to hit.
>
> (I, i, 235)

The use of such explicit formulas by which future plans are candidly disclosed also goes to strengthen the didactic tendency of these early histories. Shakespeare's characters in these early plays become their own prophets and commentators to a much greater extent than in later plays, but there too we may find this feature every now and then. They not only define the role they are going to play (as e.g. the Duchess in *2 Henry VI*, I, ii, 12), they also announce their imminent death as if they were their own Presenters. Thus in *1 Henry VI* we are warned that Talbot is going to die soon not only by characters like the General and Sir William Lucy (IV, ii, 37; IV, iii, 38; IV, iv, 38) but also by Talbot himself in three consecutive scenes (IV, v–vii).[1] The detached manner in which a character may comment on his own future plans or fate, stepping aside as it were, and looking at himself as an outward observer, is typical of many passages. That a character on such an occasion should sometimes speak of himself in the third person is a revealing detail (e.g. 'A day will come when York shall claim his own' *2 Henry VI*, I, i, 234).

But it is not only their own plans and intentions that the characters disclose. They also predict the ominous course of events in general and prophesy the grim consequences which 'civil dissension' will lead to.

---

[1] Cf., too, the scene with dying Mortimer (*1 Henry VI*, II, v).

All three parts of *Henry VI* are interspersed with prophetic utterances such as Warwick's at the end of the Temple Garden scene:

> And here I prophesy; this brawl to-day,
> Grown to this faction in the Temple Garden,
> Shall send between the Red Rose and the White
> A thousand souls to death and deadly night.
>
> (*1 Henry VI*, II, iv, 124)

or Exeter's comment again at the end of a scene:

> But howsoe'er, no simple man that sees
> This jarring discord of nobility,
> This shouldering of each other in the court,
> This factious bandying of their favourites,
> But that it doth presage some ill event.
>
> (*1 Henry VI*, IV, i, 187)

In passages like these the characters serve as a mouthpiece for the playwright to point the moral of his chronicle plays. The passages are 'preparatory' not so much in a specific sense as in the wider and more general pattern suggested in my chapter on 'Past and Future' (see p. 127). For in Shakespeare's early histories there is – running parallel and sometimes even contrary to the characters' personal intentions – a sequence of superpersonal prophecies, predictions and anticipations which are to bring to light the inevitable course of history. Shakespeare, in making dramatic use of omens, portents, dreams, prophecies and curses, could draw on his own chronicle-sources as well as on traditional beliefs and folklore. However, as I have shown elsewhere, he extended this traditional stock of premonitory devices by developing new means of expressing premonition and anticipation.[1] The impersonal choric comment which has no relation to the speaker's character and role may thus become a personal utterance. When a character's prophetic utterance is charged with his own emotions, his own fears and hopes, his passionate desire or his intense hatred, a process of dramatic integration and identification may take place on which the success of preparation in drama depends to a considerable degree. Only in *Richard III*, however, did this become completely true.

[1] 'Anticipation and Foreboding in Shakespeare's Early Histories', *Shakespeare Survey*, 6 (1953).

As to the foreshadowing of the generally dire course which history will take, those scenes should be noted in which verbal prophecy is underlined by symbolism on the stage. The very beginning of *1 Henry VI* with the black-draped stage signifying a dark future,[1] but also the plucking of the red and the white roses in the Temple Garden, (II, iv) may exemplify this. There are also certain recurring stock situations which in themselves are premonitory. When in *2 Henry VI* we watch the final leave-taking between Suffolk and the Queen we cannot but realize its ominous impact:

Suffolk. Even as a splitted bark, so sunder we:
      This way I fall to death.
Queen. This way for me.

          (III, ii, 411)

Comparing this, however, with anticipation in scenes of leave-taking in *Richard III* and *Richard II*[2] we may note the finer and richer use Shakespeare later made of such potentialities.

A special aspect of Shakespeare's technique of preparation is the way in which he prepares us for the first entry of his major characters. The convention of self-introduction and self-presentation was handed over to Shakespeare from the Moralities and Mysteries ('Deus sum') and he made good use of it in plays like *Richard III*, though in a far more skilful and refined form. In *Henry VI*, however, there still are examples of the clumsy and primitive manner in which characters introduce themselves, describing their position and announcing their intentions (cf. *1 Henry VI*, II, ii, 72; II, iv, 6; II, v, 1; etc.). The audience in these cases is not previously prepared, but receives all the information from the characters themselves. The brief informative remarks which immediately precede the entry of a new character ('But who comes here? It is the Lord . . .') can scarcely be described as 'preparation', for they have no other purpose than to identify him or her, although this information may sometimes also include some hints as to the physical appearance, the dress and the background of this new character.[3] But

---

[1] See the comments by E.Th. Sehrt, *Der dramatische Auftakt in der elisabethanischen Tragödie*, 1960, p. 106 ff. and H. T. Price, *Construction in Shakespeare*. The Univ. of Michigan Contributions in Modern Philology 17 (1951), p. 26.

[2] Cf. *Richard III*, II, iv; III, iii; IV, i; *Richard II*, II, ii; v, i.

[3] Cf. *Richard II*, II, iii, 57.

as 'preparation' should involve the building up of some kind of 'expectation', we may dismiss these short-term informative announcements as not particularly revealing for Shakespeare's art of preparation. It is more rewarding to follow up the development of the technique by which Shakespeare, usually in a preceding scene, gives us a portrait of a new character or prepares us for him by some account or some pertinent remarks. In *Henry VI* we may watch the very beginnings of this device. For already in the first scene we are given a messenger's report about Talbot (who does not appear on stage before the fourth scene) telling us 'of a dismal fight/ Betwixt the stout Lord Talbot and the French' (I, 1, 105) and praising him, who 'above human thought,/ Enacted wonders with his sword and lance'. The epic-descriptive manner in which this account is given here *en bloc*, as well as the bragging glorification of the play's hero, are typical of the style of these early Histories.

A good deal more lively and more colourful is the report about Jack Cade which we are given by York in *2 Henry VI*, and which not only prepares us for the role Jack Cade will play, but also fills us with some curiosity about this odd character. In fact, through York's account we receive just the right amount of necessary background-information to enable us to appreciate the comic side of the later scene where Jack Cade, together with Dick Butcher, Smith the Weaver and others, will appear for the first time on the stage.[1] But apart from these instances there is not much in *Henry VI* to show us how Shakespeare prepares his audience for a first appearance of an important character.

Let us sum up to what extent the technique of preparation in the three parts of *Henry VI* also characterizes the general style and manner of these plays. The obviousness and explicitness of the 'preparatory links' (announcements, plans, warnings) is a feature to be traced on other levels of dramatic representation too. Nothing is held back or merely hinted at, full information is as a rule supplied. The 'short-term' preparation which we have observed is an outcome of the structure of these plays in which one short episode follows another. That preparation (for the appearance of a major character, for sieges, battles, etc.) is very often made *en bloc* and is not, as in Shakespeare's later plays, scattered in small pieces over a whole scene, is in keeping with the epic, descrip-

[1] Cf. A. C. Sprague, *Shakespeare and the Audience*, London, 1935/1966, p. 141.

tive mode of these chronicle plays. The impersonal quasi-choric manner of many premonitory utterances bearing no relationship to the speaker's character is typical of the 'documentary'[1] style in these chronicle plays. Furthermore, events take place just as they have been previously announced and prepared for, i.e. the preparation is straight-forward and direct – in contrast to later plays there is hardly any disparity between preparation and fulfilment. As the emphasis in these plays is on outward events rather than on what happens in the minds of the characters, preparation, too, tends to remain on the surface and pertains to factual details rather than to inward changes. And there is, lastly, little preparation of atmosphere or mood.

RICHARD III

With *Richard III*, preparation becomes a much more deliberate and differentiated instrument in the hands of the dramatic craftsman. Not only do we find preparation on several levels simultaneously, but we can also discern a close connexion between the play's meaning, the role of its chief character, and the methods of preparation used in the drama.[2]

Richard III is Shakespeare's first major achievement in the art of plot-construction. Any careful study of this play would reveal its close-knit structure, the consistency and logic of its action, the skill with which several minor actions are linked together within an 'Enveloping Action' (Moulton). We do not lose sight of the main issue, as we do in *Henry VI*; the maze of many characters appearing in the course of the play, of many intrigues and many incidents has been made clear for the spectator. On the level of outward events Shakespeare keeps us well informed and as a rule prepares us well for every new character, for every change of place and every new episode. It is therefore not

[1] A. P. Rossiter, 'The Structure of *Richard the Third*', *Durham Univ. Journal* 1938 (following a distinction made by C. Leech in *Durham Univ. Journal*, 1937).
[2] In my *Commentary on 'Richard III'* (London, 1968) the various techniques of preparation are given some attention and examined in connexion with the relevant passages occurring within this scene-by-scene interpretation. The present discussion therefore refrains from quoting these passages again and limits itself to stating the principles guiding the use of preparation.

surprising that we find, dotted all over the play, many links and references which build a bridge from one scene to another and provide us with the necessary information but also with some expectation of what is to come.[1]

However, the key to the play's elaborate construction is its main character. For each minor action is built round the central figure of Richard Gloucester himself. Even when he is absent from the stage, his presence is felt because of the references to him, so that each scene without him prepares us in fact for the next scene with him. One might even say that the well-organized structure of the play derives in some way from the specific conception of his role. For this well-planned structure has its equivalent in Richard Gloucester's deliberate scheming and cunning plotting. The action is determined to a large extent by his own planning and his capacity to utilize every new turn and event, and even every unexpected move of his future victims, for his own secret purpose. Richard Gloucester, the arch-schemer, holds most of the threads of the action in his own hands and secretly directs the action of the play and the movements of the minor characters. He even acts as his own producer, rehearsing a counterfeit scene which he and Buckingham are going to stage in presence of the Mayor a few moments later (III, v). This is a new means of preparation, drawing its grim actuality from the practice of the theatre.[2] Richard's soliloquies, his asides, his detailed orders to subordinates, his threats and warnings to his foes are rich in announcements of future acts and plans. But we feel that the wealth of preparation contained in his utterances is legitimate, for indeed this master-plotter's chief intellectual activity consists in hatching out plans, preparing intrigues and paving the way for his various undertakings.

Thus we shall find it quite natural that he takes us into his confidence from the very beginning, his first soliloquy combining in a masterly manner exposition, character-self-portrayal, preparation for some major issues and announcement of the first intrigue. The tension with which we watch the play results to a certain degree from the large amount of foreknowledge not only given to the audience at the

[1] Thus for example the imminent execution of Rivers, Gray and Vaughan is referred to six times in the preceding scene III, ii. In IV, ii we are prepared by many informative hints for the new events of Act V. For more examples see the *Commentary*.

[2] For more instances of this relationship, see Anne Righter, *Shakespeare and the Idea of the Play*, London, 1962.

beginning but supplemented and extended in practically every scene. We have been told about Richard's aims by Richard himself. Now we wonder how he will achieve them and we watch his victims' blindness, false security, weakness and helplessness, but also their true forebodings, and their futile efforts to resist or to escape. All this implies an intricate network of preparations which again and again link promise and fulfilment, planning and execution, apprehension and grim accomplishment.

But this is only one level on which preparation operates. For as early as the third scene another chain of 'pointers towards the future' is established. Margaret's curses, prophecies, and warnings build up a new system of promises and predictions waiting for fulfilment. Through Margaret, who stands somewhat outside the action, the superpersonal powers of Destiny and Nemesis are brought into the play. Margaret's curses and prophecies (later on, in IV, iv, reinforced by the curses of the Duchess of York and Queen Elizabeth) act as a forceful means of preparation, but they awaken a different kind of expectation, counteracting – as it were – the expectation roused by Richard Gloucester's dire predictions and sly announcements. For they not only prepare us for the failure and the defeat of Richard's many victims, but also for his own fall and destruction. From this moment we shall watch Richard's preparations as well as the reactions of his enemies and allies with a divided awareness. For the prescience given us by Richard himself is superseded by foreknowledge of another kind which makes the audience recognize that in the net Richard is weaving for his victims he will eventually be caught himself.

Curses, prophecies and warnings had also been used as a device of preparation in the three parts of *Henry VI*; they belong, together with portents, omens and ghosts, to the traditional elements of foreboding which Shakespeare found in Senecan drama and in his own sources, the chronicles of Holinshed and Hall. However, these devices are now used as deliberate structural links and brought into a rigorous system. Moreover, in the person of Margaret the curses and prophecies have found a convincing voice, for Margaret embodies the power of prophecy, recalling Ate and Nemesis in classical tragedy. It is furthermore significant that all the curses will be remembered when they are fulfilled, thus binding together earlier and later passages of the play. Contrary to the more general and vague contents and use of curses in pre-Shakespearian drama, here the reference is to concrete circumstances. Moreover, they act as preparation for other imprecations, for those cursed by Margaret will themselves call down evil upon others when their hour of death predicted by Margaret arrives (e.g. Vaughan III, iii, 7; Hastings III, iv, 109). In some cases these curses and imprecations are even used ironically, for the characters unwittingly curse themselves (I, ii, 26; II, i, 32). Thus the curses, warnings and prophecies in *Richard III*, embracing almost all the characters figuring in this play, assign, as it were, a place to everybody within a pattern of guilt and expiation, of crime and punishment. All characters take part in this 'cycle' of which we observe the beginnings in the play's first scenes and which is rounded off, character by character, in the last two acts. The 'Nemesis pattern' of the plot is built up in such a way that each minor 'Nemesis action' prepares us for the next one, whereas they all together point towards the 'major Nemesis action' involving Richard himself and ending with his downfall. The 'chain of destruction' which is suggested by this systematic sequence of corresponding actions,[1] demands a particular use of the technique of preparation. For the inevitability and inexorability of the destined events rather than their 'possible' fulfilment must be emphasized. The ironical utterance made by Richard in his encounter with Queen Elizabeth 'All unavoided is the doom of destiny' (IV, iv, 217) gives expression to this feeling of a predetermined fate which in fact is aroused in the audience early in the play, being enhanced by almost every scene with that cumulative and repetitive method so characteristic of this drama.

On the other hand, the forcefulness of this cyclical operation of curses, prophecies and nemesis actions gives the play an additional dimension which was still lacking in *Henry VI*. As Kitto has observed, the action of this play refers 'to the whole framework of our universe', not only to certain individuals. Richard stands for more than for a single wicked tyrant, so that the final disaster 'is not merely bad luck, but is a typical recoil on man of his own inhumanity'.[2]

The superpersonal and supernatural element which is thus suggested is also manifest in a few other devices of preparation, namely the appearance of ghosts, the mention of omens and the ominous function

[1] R. G. Moulton, *Shakespeare as a Dramatic Artist*, Oxford, 1885/1929, p. 110.
[2] H. D. F. Kitto, 'A Classical Scholar Looks at Shakespeare', *More Talking of Shakespeare*, ed. J. Garrett, London, 1959.

of dreams. Again, these devices are used more systematically and deliberately than in *Henry VI*. The long procession of eleven ghosts (v, iii) all pronouncing and predicting death and defeat for Richard, but victory and success for Richmond, once more reflects Shakespeare's tendency to accumulate effects, to repeat the same device and to make the ultimate issue overwhelmingly clear.

Even the use of irony, by its very nature a subtle instrument of preparation, contributes through its frequency and obviousness to this cumulative effect. It is made convincing by the ironical and cynical temperament of Richard, who through his ironies displays his intellectual superiority. But at the same time he is not aware of those tragic ironies which will be directed against himself and in fact forecast his own destruction. Thus the many ironical and ambiguous utterances, scattered all through the play, also help to establish that two-fold expectancy which we referred to above.

However, apart from these various types of intellectual and rational preparation establishing a tight and logical connexion between expectation and fulfilment, we also find other forms of foreboding of a more imaginative and subjective kind. The most outstanding example is Clarence's dream (I, iv), which by means of suggestive symbolism and evocative imagery foreshadows not only Clarence's own death but the impending disaster in general.[1] The rich poetic language of this dream-narrative acts on the imagination of the audience quite differently from the clear-cut and definite speech used in most of the other scenes; it builds up a presentiment of awe and vague fear which will be confirmed in a more specific way by the following events. The same method of evoking an atmosphere of dark forebodings, which are as yet indeterminate but which will subsequently be borne out by the events, is manifest in the choric scene with the three citizens (II, iii). It is the first time that Shakespeare, for the purpose of preparation, employs this type of 'mirror scene'[2] the main function of which is to create an atmosphere of ominous foreboding, fear and alarm. *Fear*, one of the key-words in the play's vocabulary,[3] also occurs in some utterances of

[1] For a detailed interpretation of this dream-narrative see my *Commentary on Shakespeare's Richard III*, p. 67 ff.

[2] Cf. H. T. Price, 'Mirror Scenes in Shakespeare', *Joseph Quincy Adams Memorial Studies*, ed. J. G. McManaway, New York, 1948.

[3] Other key-words which could also be taken as a means of preparation are: woe, sorrow, grave, death, hell, blood.

individual characters expressing this kind of subjective and indefinite presentiment[1] that is so effective in influencing the audience's expectations.

While these different forebodings spread the feeling of *uncertainty* among those characters who are conscious of the dangers threatening them through Richard's actions, Shakespeare presents us Hastings, cocksure, confident and ignorant of what will shortly be coming to him.[2] Thus, by an ironical reversal, Shakespeare uses the security of Hastings as a preparation for his own downfall and for the destruction of several others.

Discussing the indirect methods by which Shakespeare prepares his audience we must not forget the way in which Richard's growing insecurity is depicted in the last talk with Buckingham, how he loses his self-control, 'gnaws his lips' (IV, ii, 27), staggers at the mention of an earlier prophecy (IV, ii, 92), issues conflicting orders to Ratcliffe and Catesby (IV, iv) and betrays a gradual loss of confidence. In the famous scene on Bosworth Field Shakespeare shows us a Richard Gloucester who has lost his balance of mind and betrays to us by his reactions[3] and his abrupt and changed language that now he, too, is aware of his coming defeat. These scenes thus reveal to us a new mode of expressing anticipation and foreboding not by explicit statement but by skilful dramaturgy based on an interplay between gesture and movement, language and behaviour. This is the direction towards which Shakespeare's art of preparation will develop in his later, mature plays.

However, looking at the play as a whole we receive the opposite impression. For preparation consists too much in explicit verbal statement, in repetition and obvious demonstration. The play appears to be permeated by a network of interlinking preparatory and anticipatory devices. The characteristic feature of Shakespeare's early style (outlined above p. 24) – that everything is made obvious and clear – still holds true of this play, although there is greater variety and a more systematic

---

[1] Cf. Queen Elizabeth I, iii, 40–1; Prince Edward III, i, 148. And cf. too the occurrence of this word in Richard's own speech v, iii, 214.
[2] Cf. the warning given to the audience by III, i, 193 and III, ii, 11 and Hastings' own utterances in III, ii.
[3] His helmet seems to him 'easier than it was' (v, iii, 50) he 'will not sup to-night' (48). For further instances and the transformation of language and verse-structure see my *Commentary*, p. 208 ff.

organization of the various means of preparation. But on the whole, too much is announced beforehand and this ample preparation may sometimes seem obtrusive to us. The final outcome of this tragic history is brought home to us in an almost overwhelming manner. It seems that a great dramatist must strike a balance between our foreknowledge and our ignorance, between our positive expectation and our doubt. In *Richard III*, however, we are in no doubt as to how the play's action is to develop.

RICHARD II

Richard II displays several new aspects of Shakespeare's manner of preparing the audience. It is true that this play also begins with a speech (though a very short one) spoken by the King himself, but it leaves us guessing as to what kind of person he will turn out to be. It is his manner rather than his actual purpose that we become acquainted with. Coleridge, in fact, commenting on this first scene, quoted it as an example of 'the judgment with which Shakespeare always in his first scenes prepares, and yet how naturally and with what concealment of art, for the catastrophe. How he presents the germ of all the after-events in Richard's insincerity, partiality, arbitrariness, favouritism and in the proud tempestuous temperament of his barons'.[1] But it is doubtful whether Richard's bearing in this first scene, although proud, ceremonious, conceited and somewhat biased, does in any explicit way prepare us for his impending defeat and downfall. The varying glimpses we are given of his character tend rather to arouse a divided response on the part of the audience. We may feel that his actions (rather than his bearing) – his whimsical departure from legality – prepare us for his downfall in the sense that we see him devaluing the very foundations of his own position, but on the other hand we shall have to admit that the King is still in command of the situation. Nor do Bolingbroke's utterances and his banishment at the end of the third scene make us foresee his early return, his rise to power and his eventual accession to the throne. It is in fact not before the fourth scene that the king, in his account of Bolingbroke's 'familiar courtesy' with the common people, ironically foreshadowing future events, calls up the vision[2]

[1] Coleridge, *Shakespearean Criticism*, ed. T. M. Raysor, 1960, vol. I, p. 138.
[2] Compare, too, the King's doubts expressed in I, i, 20 ff.

As were our England in reversion his,
And he our subjects' next degree in hope.

(I, iv, 35)

It has been argued[1] that the audience was familiar with *Woodstock*, so that Shakespeare's depiction of the two major characters would have been appreciated against this background. But (and this holds true for all history plays by Shakespeare) even if the audience knew the general drift of the story, their curiosity would still be directed towards the way in which Shakespeare set out to dramatize it and characterize both Richard and Bolingbroke.

To look once again at the first three scenes: it is typical of the oblique use of preparation in this play that the deadly combat between Bolingbroke and Mowbray which we have been expecting throughout these scenes never takes place, but is cancelled at the last minute by the king. Moreover, the actual issue between Mowbray and Bolingbroke, Mowbray's so-called treason, his share in Gloucester's murder and Bolingbroke's alleged former guilt, is never fully resolved. Our attention in these first three scenes is directed towards issues which do not play an important part in later events and which furthermore seem to have little bearing on the central action of the play, which is the great conflict between the declining king and the ascending Bolingbroke. Direct preparation for this conflict is held back, instead there are warnings, fears and apprehensions of a more general kind,[2] so that even before we can grasp any actual signs of the approaching catastrophe a vague feeling of foreboding is aroused in us. This feeling is enhanced in the following scenes when certain characters express subjective sentiments of anticipation, for which they cannot yet give any rational explanation.[3] A new feature of Shakespeare's art of preparation is thus revealed which differs from the deliberate and direct forecast evident in *Richard III*. At the beginning of II, ii we find the Queen strangely stirred by some inexplicable sorrow:

[1] By A. P. Rossiter. Preface to his edition of *Woodstock*, London, 1946.
[2] See for example the valedictory speech of the Duchess at the end of I, ii, 'I take my leave before I have begun, / For sorrow ends not when it seemeth done' or Mowbray's 'And all too soon, I fear, the King shall rue' (I, iii, 205). See also York's warning in II, i, 212.
[3] For the following paragraphs cf. my article in *Shakespeare Survey* 6 (1953).

> yet I know no cause
> Why I should welcome such a guest as grief,
> Save bidding farewell to so sweet a guest
> As my sweet Richard. Yet again methinks
> Some unborn sorrow, ripe in fortune's womb,
> Is coming towards me, and my inward soul
> With nothing trembles.

(ii, ii, 6)

This is presentiment as yet unfounded in concrete knowledge. The audience, however, at the end of the previous scene, has already learnt of some of the facts which give substance to the Queen's apprehensions. For there Northumberland, Willoughby and Ross, who up to that point have been loyal to the king, decided to abandon him; Northumberland, moreover, revealed to his companions the news of Bolingbroke's imminent return to England. The audience has also heard lines like:

Willoughby.   The King's grown bankrupt like a broken man.
Northumberland.   Reproach and dissolution hangeth over him.

(ii, i, 257)

In addition the audience would remember Gaunt's famous prophecy at the beginning of that scene and York's warnings. Thus we could say that these events, unknown to the Queen, have been transformed, as it were, into an inward feeling of foreboding to which she gives expression. Nor have we long to wait for the action to respond to these forebodings, for a few minutes later Green brings the news of Bolingbroke's arrival and of Worcester's flight. The Queen receives this news as a confirmation of her 'unborn sorrows', her metaphorical language establishing the same connexion between foreboding and event as between conception and birth:

> So, Green, thou art the midwife to my woe,
> And Bolingbroke my sorrow's dismal heir.
> Now hath my soul brought forth her prodigy;
> And I, a gasping new-deliver'd mother,
> Have woe to woe, sorrow to sorrow join'd.

(ii, ii, 61)

33

But the scene does not end here. York's sorrowful figure and his ominous announcement 'Now comes the sick hour that his surfeit made . . .' add to the grief already expressed. When, a few moments later, the news of the death of the duchess is brought, the promise of York's presageful entrance seems to have come true. At the end of the scene Shakespeare again makes use of the foreboding potentialities of leave-taking. Comparing the passage with the parting of Margaret and Suffolk (*2 Henry VI*, III, ii)[1] we find that this time more expression is given to the feeling of dark foreboding experienced by the characters at this moment:

> *Bagot.*　Farewell: if heart's presages be not vain,
> We three here part that ne'er shall meet again. . . .
>
> (II, ii, 141)

The audience cannot fail to see the parallelism between the ending of this and of the preceding scene. This technique of parallel structure is yet another means of preparation which Shakespeare constantly used and refined and of which there will be more examples in *Henry IV*, and even more in the tragedies. As regards *Richard II*, one further instance may be mentioned. The beginning of the play shows us the king in his capacity as judge, pronouncing judgment on the two conflicting lords. We are reminded of this situation in IV, i, when Bolingbroke acts as a judge over Aumerle and Fitzwater. By an ironical reversal the judged has now become judge. But this later scene, too, had to a certain degree been prepared for by III, i, where Bolingbroke, also acting as judge, sentences Bushy and Green to death.

The play as a whole is less crowded with incident, intrigues and minor episodes than *Henry VI* and *Richard III*. More space is given to reflection, to the expression of sentiment, to the poetic elaboration of thought and feeling. Preparation in this play is therefore less concerned with outward events, with the linking of details of the outward action. The emphasis is rather on anticipation through feeling, inner vision and imaginative foreboding. It is not a matter of chance that whole scenes and situations are built into the structure of this play with a primarily anticipatory function. Thus the scene between Salisbury and the Welsh Captain obviously serves this purpose. The scene ends with Salisbury's vision of Richard's impending fall:

[1] See the Section on *Henry VI*, p. 23.

Ah, Richard, with the eyes of heavy mind,
I see thy glory like a shooting star
Fall to the base earth from the firmament!
The sun sets weeping in the lowly west,
Witnessing storms to come, woe, and unrest;
Thy friends are fled, to wait upon thy foes;
And crossly to thy good all fortune goes.

(II, iv, 18)

This is a more complex and imaginative use of preparation than is to be found in the early histories. It conveys the inner vision through nature-imagery yet at the same time supplies factual evidence. Anticipation is expressed simultaneously on different levels. An examination of the scene (II, i) in which the dying Gaunt voices his prophecy (reiterated by York and later on by Carlisle: IV, i, 114 ff.), but also an analysis of the Garden-scene (III, iv), would show that Shakespeare in *Richard II* took special care to place foreboding passages within a dramatically convincing framework and to link them closely with the appropriate situation and character.[1]

However, the most notable example of Shakespeare's manner of establishing a correspondence between a specific mode of preparation and a character's cast of mind is to be found in the speeches of the king himself. For it is fair to say that Richard by his very nature anticipates his abdication even before the political need for it has arisen. He enters into his role of martyr before he has actually been made a martyr. His early thoughts of death and woe, of worldly loss and decay cast a dark colour over many of the speeches which we hear from him after the middle of the play (from III, ii onwards). He indulges in these gloomy thoughts and ominous visions, elaborating them through telling imagery and rhetorical devices. His manner of anticipation, which prepares us for his own end, is an outcome of his deep-rooted escapism.

The great scene in which Richard (after his disappearance from the play for no less than four scenes) greets the English soil near the coast of Wales (III, ii) gives us an ironical reversal of his anticipations. For

[1] For further examples see my article in *Shakespeare Survey* 6 (1953). A comparison with Shakespeare's source (Holinshed) would show to what extent Shakespeare extended the role of foreboding, prophecies and warnings, developing those characters who like Gaunt are important in this connexion and creating specific scenes and situations which are to serve this purpose.

by this second speech, in which he still relies on the invulnerability of the anointed king, we are prepared in an ambiguous way for his encounter with Bolingbroke in the next scene:

> So when this thief, this traitor, Bolingbroke,
> Who all this while hath revell'd in the night,
> Whilst we were wand'ring with the Antipodes,
> Shall see us rising in our throne, the east,
> His treasons will sit blushing in his face, . . .
>
> (III, ii, 47)

These lines are certainly not ironical in the way that Richard Gloucester's predictions are ironical – for Gloucester virtually turns truth upside down. What Richard utters here is a profound truth which will be kept alive even in *Henry IV*, although he himself is soon to be disposed of. In the course of this scene, however, Richard's confidence changes into fear of the worst. For even before Scroop, the bearer of bad news, has unfolded 'his tiding of calamity', the king salutes him with these lines:

> Mine ear is open and my heart prepar'd.
> The worst is worldly loss thou canst unfold.
> Say, is my kingdom lost?
>
> (III, ii, 93)

Not waiting for Scroop's disclosures he ends this speech with the ominous imprecation:

> Cry woe, destruction, ruin, and decay—
> The worst is death, and death will have his day.
>
> (III, ii, 102)

Death, in fact, is the subject of the long speech which follows a little later on (144). As if preparing for his own role Richard condenses the ensuing tragedy into a single formula:

> A King, woe's slave, shall kingly woe obey.
>
> (III, ii, 210)

After this we are not surprised at the conclusion of the scene; for the dismissal of his retinue is in itself an anticipation of his dethronement:

> Discharge my followers; let them hence away,
> From Richard's night to Bolingbroke's fair day.
>
> (III, ii, 217)

It is not merely by chance that most of the lines in this play which have a preparatory or foreboding meaning are spoken by the king himself. For his is a mind particularly prone to imaginative anticipation which he exploits and even relishes just as much as his theatrical role and his lyrical effusion.

Thus, in *Richard II*, the art of preparation has become altogether more subtle and indirect, being more than in the previous histories linked up with imaginative vision, subjective foreboding and poetic anticipation.

TITUS ANDRONICUS

Before discussing five major tragedies at some length, let us look briefly, by way of contrast and as it were 'negative proof', at *Titus Andronicus*, the first tragedy attributed to Shakespeare – though he may have had only a share in it. For here we do not find much in the way of dramatic preparation. There is in this play, in keeping with the tradition of the tragedy of blood, an accumulation of atrocities, horrors and murders, mostly performed on the open stage. But in spite of the glaring presentation on stage of these deeds of violence we are not greatly moved. If we ask 'why?', one answer will be that these atrocities are insufficiently prepared for; they are too numerous, too abrupt, too unmotivated. They fail in their effect because of the absence of convincingly drawn and motivated characters; which prevents us from being sufficiently attuned to an acceptance of these violent happenings. Admittedly there is preparation on the level of plot and the play is not unskilfully constructed.[1] In fact, some of the deeds are announced before they take place. But this does not suffice to prepare us adequately for what we see on the stage. In *Richard III*, composed not long after *Titus Andronicus* and therefore offering itself for comparison on this issue, fewer atrocities take place on stage, for the greater part of Richard's bloody murders are made known to us through reports. But those deeds of which we are eye-witnesses are better prepared for, and

[1] Cf. H. T. Price, 'The Authorship of *Titus Andronicus*', *J.E.G.P.* XLII (1943).

even for off-stage murders we receive some preparation. What we find in *Titus Andronicus* thus appears to bear out the truth noted by Coleridge in his *Summary of the Characteristics of Shakespeare*:[1] 'Expectation in preference to surprise. God said, "let there be *light*, and there was *light*" not there *was* light. As the feeling with which we startle at a shooting star, compared with that of watching the sunrise at the pre-established moment, such and so low is surprise compared with expectation.'

ROMEO AND JULIET

Turning to *Romeo and Juliet*, Shakespeare's first major tragedy, we may again observe the appropriateness of the various forms of preparation to the play's particular mood and theme. Applying to the many preparatory lines in this tragedy the criterion of 'necessary preparation', one might well say that Shakespeare could have done with much less. The audience would have been sufficiently prepared for the great turns in the play, for the various developments and for the final catastrophe if only half of these anticipations and predictions had been inserted. However, anticipation of the impending tragedy as well as foreshadowing of the inevitable course of fortune is at the very heart of *Romeo and Juliet*. The high degree of self-awareness with which the two 'star-crossed' lovers give expression to this feeling of 'some consequence yet hanging in the stars' from the very beginning, may seem improbable from a psychological point of view, yet it conveys to us that distinctive mood of an inescapable dark fate moving towards them. But although the prologue to the play clearly announces 'the fearful passage of their deathmarked love' we are left guessing as to what particular form this dark fate will take, and there are up to the last act moments at which a better course would seem likely.[2] The two lovers often express a dark presentiment of impending doom, but they do not know how and when it will come. This hovering between knowing and not-knowing contributes greatly to the tragedy's dramatic impact. On the other hand, the prescience given to the audience at the outset of the

[1] S. T. Coleridge, *Shakespearean Criticism*, ed. T. M. Raysor, 1960 (Everyman), Vol. I, p. 199.
[2] See e.g. Friar Lawrence's exposition of Romeo's 'fortunate situation' in III, iii, 135 ff.

play makes them appreciate many of the utterances spoken by the two lovers as examples of tragic irony. Tragic irony, in this play, is a particularly powerful and at the same time subtle form of anticipation.[1] But whereas in other plays the characters are in fact mostly unconscious of the truths which they disclose in their ironical statements, in this tragedy we sometimes wonder to what extent Romeo and Juliet – be it consciously or subconsciously – actually foresee what is ahead of them. If Juliet, for instance, as early as the fifth scene of the first act, refers to her grave, we may wonder how far this is 'tragic irony' and how far presentiment:

> Go ask his name. – If he be married,
> My grave is like to be my wedding bed.

> (I, v, 132)

Many of the premonitory passages in *Romeo and Juliet* express the notion that events are controlled by the stars, by fortune, and sometimes by what could be called 'Providence'. As has been pointed out by V. K. Whitaker, 'it is nowhere clear whether the stars symbolize blind fate or chance or . . . the operation of natural forces which may be resisted or modified by human will'.[2] But no matter how one might define the metaphysics of this tragedy, Shakespeare has established a kind of interplay between these superpersonal forces and the inward qualities of the two lovers, although this relationship is not conclusive and absolute, as has been shown by T. J. B. Spencer.[3] Fate and chance can act like this because the two lovers meet them half-way, because their passion, their determination, their weakness and their strength are of just the kind the stars and 'chance' can make use of. A closer examination of the numerous passages bearing on anticipation would reveal this interplay between inborn character and fortune acting from outside. It would even be possible to discern a difference between the manner in which both lovers express their presentiments. Out of Romeo's first full utterance of foreboding at the end of the fourth

---

[1] 'The method of *Romeo and Juliet* is that of anticipatory irony', H. S. Wilson, *On the Design of Shakespearean Tragedy*, Toronto, 1957, p. 49.

[2] e.g. IV, v, 94; v, iii, 292; see V. K. Whitaker, *The Mirror up to Nature, The Technique of Shakespeare's Tragedies*, 1965, p. 111 f.

[3] T. J. B. Spencer, Introduction to *Romeo and Juliet*, New Penguin Shakespeare, London, 1967, p. 18 ff.

scene rings bitter pathos and stern determination even at this early moment:

> for my mind misgives
> Some consequence, yet hanging in the stars,
> Shall bitterly begin his fearful date
> With this night's revels and expire the term
> Of a despised life clos'd in my breast,
> By some vile forfeit of untimely death.
>
> (I, iv, 106)

whereas the first premonitory lines coming from Juliet's lips reflect a rather different attitude, more cautious and reflective, hesitant in the face of Romeo's repeated solemn assertions that he would swear:

> Well, do not swear. Although I joy in thee,
> I have no joy of this contract to-night:
> It is too rash, too unadvis'd, too sudden;
> Too like the lightning, which doth cease to be
> Ere one can say 'It lightens'.
>
> (II, ii, 116)

Even at a relatively early stage both lovers think of their death, their grave, their dark end, but again in a slightly different manner. Thus even before the beginning of the fateful third act with Mercutio's and Tybalt's death, Romeo, after he has just been married to Juliet by Friar Lawrence, defies 'love-devouring death';

> Do thou but close our hands with holy words,
> Then love-devouring death do what he dare;
> It is enough I may but call her mine.
>
> (II, vi, 6)

The lines spoken by Juliet in I, v, 138 have already been quoted as an instance of irony. But very soon she becomes more explicit when, at the end of III, ii, after having heard about Romeo's banishment, she exclaims:

> Come, cords; come, nurse; I'll to my wedding-bed;
> And death, not Romeo, take my maidenhead!
>
> (III, ii, 136)

Three scenes later, before the parting with Romeo, the sight of him in the dim garden below melts for her into an ominous vision:

> O God, I have an ill-divining soul!
> Methinks I see thee, now thou art below,
> As one dead in the bottom of a tomb;
> Either my eyesight fails or thou look'st pale.
>
> (III, v, 54)

This is a fine example of the way in which Shakespeare makes use of the scenic situation (Romeo below in the garden at dawn) to evoke a suggestive vision of the future.[1] Its dramatic effect at this moment is all the more poignant as Romeo has just expressed his confidence in the future:

> ... all these woes shall serve
> For sweet discourses in our time to come.
>
> (III, v, 52)

But earlier in the scene he, too, had his ominous misgivings. Before the nurse interrupts the leave-taking of the lovers, he rounds off their dialogue with

> More light and light – more dark and dark our woes!
>
> (III, v, 36)

The contrast between light and dark, day and night, constantly brought out by the play's imagery (as was first demonstrated by Caroline Spurgeon), is also frequently made use of for the purpose of anticipation and foreboding.[2]

Some of the minor characters also add to the network of warnings and anticipations displayed throughout the play. The form and style of their warnings, too, appear well adjusted to their role. This is particularly true of Friar Lawrence who – in keeping with his calling – likes to utter wise maxims and sayings. In the scene in which we first see him with his basket (II, iii), he concludes his soliloquy (which in fact prepares us already for the poisonous potion of Act IV) with the line 'Full soon the canker death eats up that plant' and this line is given

---

[1] e.g. III, i, 126.
[2] Cf. the two other references by Juliet to death in the same scene, both instances of irony, the first reinforced by the syntax: 95, 203. And compare, too, Lady Capulet's outcry: 'I would the fool were married to her grave!' (140).

ironical meaning by Romeo's entrance following immediately. At the end of this scene Romeo is warned by the Friar: 'Wisely and slow: they stumble that run fast'. This warning, anticipating Romeo's fatal rashness in the last act, contains a significant reference to speed and time.

Contrary to his source, Brooke's poem which makes this love story last several months, Shakespeare condensed the action into four or five days, thus giving us the impression of fatal precipitation. The time-element therefore plays an important role in the art of preparation. Again and again we are reminded of the rush of time, of the brief hours allowed to the lovers, of the too short space of time left at the disposal of those who want to avert the final catastrophe. An analysis of this use of time in *Romeo and Juliet* would show how even small details like the fixing of the marriage day for Paris on Thursday (instead of on Wednesday as originally planned) are devised to arouse tension and eager expectation as to what may happen next. Friar Lawrence himself comes back to his warning about the danger of running too fast. For his famous prediction pronounced to Romeo at his cell begins with the line

> These violent delights have violent ends,
> And in their triumph die;
>
> (ii, vi, 9)

and ends:

> Too swift arrives as tardy as too slow.
>
> (ii, vi, 15)

In the scene (iii, iii) in which Friar Lawrence informs Romeo of 'the prince's doom' his warnings become more explicit. The impetuous haste with which Romeo draws his sword to end his own life ('that I may sack the hateful mansion') prompts the Friar to a long admonitory speech which in fact points forward to what will happen in the last act:

> Wilt thou slay thyself?
> And slay thy lady that in thy life lives,
> By doing damned hate upon thyself?
> . . .
> Take heed, take heed, for such die miserable.
>
> (iii, iii, 116)

We have already noted the manner in which Shakespeare in this tragedy not only prepares us in an indirect way for the final event but sometimes even anticipates the scene in which the event will take place by divinatory vision and imaginative description. A case in point was Juliet's early vision of Romeo 'dead in the bottom of a tomb' (see p. 41). In the same act she refers to the scene of her own end when she defies her mother with

> Delay this marriage for a month, a week;
> Or, if you do not, make the bridal bed
> In that dim monument where Tybalt lies.

(III, V, 200)

However, the 'dim monument' grows fully alive in her imagination in all its repulsive and grim horror when we find Juliet (at the end of IV, iii) alone, preparing to drink the potion prescribed for her by Friar Lawrence. She visualizes the tomb in which she will be laid, together with all the terrors that belong to it:

> Shall I not then be stifled in the vault,
> To whose foul mouth no healthsome air breathes in,
> And there die strangled ere my Romeo comes?
> . . .
> Where bloody Tybalt, yet but green in earth,
> Lies fest'ring in his shroud; where, as they say,
> At some hours in the night spirits resort—
> Alack, alack, is it not like that I,
> So early waking – what with loathsome smells,
> And shrieks like mandrakes' torn out of the earth,
> That living mortals, hearing them, run mad—
> O, if I wake, shall I not be distraught,
> Environed with all these hideous fears,
> And madly play with my forefathers' joints,
> And pluck the mangled Tybalt from his shroud,
> . . .
> O, look! methinks I see my cousin's ghost
> Seeking out Romeo, that did spit his body
> Upon a rapier's point. Stay, Tybalt, stay.
> Romeo, I come. This do I drink to thee.

(IV, iii, 33)

The passage from which these lines are quoted is one of the longest descriptive passages in the whole tragedy and its function is primarily one of preparation. Juliet voices here a mixture of imaginary fears and frenzied visions centring in a suggestive account of the gloomy monument which we shall see five scenes later. Although Juliet's brain-sick phantasies here are not yet founded in reality, they will nevertheless be fulfilled, for she as well as Romeo will die in that gruesome place. The description, abounding in concrete and graphic details, conveys to us a whole range of emotions which all point towards the future. Her premonition does not hit upon the exact and irrevocably fatal course events will take, but it tells her truly enough that something terrible may happen. Again this blending of mistaken fears, vague guesses and clear presentiment is more powerful and suggestive than a straightforward anticipation precisely corresponding to the later event could ever be.

Shakespeare does in fact sometimes make use of presentiments which deceive those who experience them. The contrast between the audience's awareness of this delusion and the confidence felt by the characters on the stage is a device which will be further developed in later tragedies, particularly in *Julius Caesar* and in *Macbeth*. In *Romeo and Juliet* it is Romeo rather than Juliet who is momentarily taken in by such deceptive forebodings. We have already quoted Romeo's hopeful lines spoken just before Juliet's vision of him lying in a tomb (see page 41). But there is a more striking example at the beginning of the fifth act when we see Romeo soliloquizing in a street of Mantua:

> If I may trust the flattering truth of sleep,
> My dreams presage some joyful news at hand.
> My bosom's lord sits lightly in his throne,
> And all this day an unaccustom'd spirit
> Lifts me above the ground with cheerful thoughts.
> I dreamt my lady came and found me dead—
> Strange dream, that gives a dead man leave to think!—
> And breath'd such life with kisses in my lips
> That I reviv'd, and was an emperor.
>
> (v, i, 1)

Promising though this dream is, as taken by Romeo, it contains a line which speaks the truth: 'I dreamt my lady came and found me dead'.

A moment later Balthasar enters and brings the news of Juliet's (apparent) death. The dream had been an ironical preparation for an anticlimax.

There are in this play more examples of this art of achieving dramatic effects of a peculiar kind by creating a mood or a situation which is immediately followed by its reversal. Granville-Barker points to the first scene of the second act in which, after the chorus, we see Romeo alone but disappearing again behind the wall. Benvolio and Mercutio's bawdy talk serves as a foil, as a contrast not only for what is to come but also for the 'unseen' presence of Romeo who during this short interval had to listen to Mercutio's ribaldry: 'The discord thus struck is perfect preparation for the harmony to come'.[1] There is a similar effect with the transition from the scene in Capulet's house, when the date for Juliet's marriage to Paris has just been agreed upon (III, iv), to the balcony scene (III, v) beginning with Juliet's 'Wilt thou be gone?'.[2]

Sometimes a few lines spoken by a minor character before leaving may give an edge and an ironical foreboding to what will be enacted immediately afterwards by the chief characters. Thus the warning pronounced by Tybalt before he leaves the stage

> I will withdraw; but this intrusion shall,
> Now seeming sweet, convert to bitt'rest gall.
>
> (I, v, 89)

will linger on in our ears when we watch the first encounter between the lovers. Tybalt does not speak of the vengeance he himself would be likely to take on Romeo. He states his threat in the form of an impersonal prediction. Spoken at this very moment it will impress itself on the audience which has already been let into the secret.

Preparation, however, is not a rule to be followed by Shakespeare throughout this tragedy. Some things happen which we did not expect and which take us by surprise; it is the shock-effect itself which completely changes the mood of the play. Mercutio's death occurs unexpectedly, for the warning uttered by Benvolio at the very beginning of the scene

[1] Cf. H. Granville-Barker, *Prefaces to Shakespeare*, Second Series, 1930, 1946, p. 10/11. See also J. L. Styan, *The Elements of Drama*, 1960, pp. 71, 129.
[2] Granville-Barker, *op. cit.*, p. 22.

And if we meet we shall not scape a brawl;
For now, these hot days, is the mad blood stirring.

(III, i, 3)

would scarcely have been taken by the audience as a premonition of the death of Mercutio, who moreover did not – as Romeo and Juliet did – feel a dark fate moving towards him. And yet he was destined to die first and his death in fact leads the way to major changes in Romeo's character and in the course of the whole action.

Shakespeare's deliberate art of preparation in *Romeo and Juliet* becomes even more evident when a comparison with the source, Brooke's poem, is made.[1] Most of the premonitory passages which have been quoted on the preceding pages have in fact no counterpart in Brooke. But whatever, in Brooke's account, could be made use of for this purpose was taken over by Shakespeare and transformed or elaborated so as to give relief and imaginative depth to these moments of warning and anticipation. From several examples a few lines from Brooke's poem may be quoted by which this process of transformation may be illustrated. After having been told by her mother that she is to marry Paris Juliet protests:

First, weary of my paineful life, my cares shall kill my heart,
Els will I perce my breast, with sharpe and bloody knife;
And you my mother shall become the murdress of my life.

(194 ff)

Shakespeare, however, at this point makes Juliet (with her corresponding lines) already anticipate the exact situation of act v:

Delay this marriage for a month, a week;
Or, if you do not, make the bridal bed
In that dim monument where Tybalt lies.

(III, v, 200 ff)

Even more illuminating is the way in which Shakespeare changed details of Brooke's story in order to endow the action with more motivation, and more coherence, in other words, in order to prepare

[1] For the following remarks I am indebted to F. Kastropp's unpublished thesis, *Die Rolle der Vorahnungen und Voraussagen in Shakespeares Tragödien*, Tübingen, 1952.

his audience better for the course of his tragedy. Only a few changes may be mentioned in this connexion. Contrary to Brooke, who refers to the 'ancient grudge' between the two families only in passing, Shakespeare makes this family-feud the very starting-point of his tragedy from which all further complications derive and it serves, moreover, as a dividing line and a frame of reference for almost all characters in the play. The servants, exchanging in their skirmish jests and puns, hint at the 'ancient grudge' in a more casual though subtle, allusive manner and we might believe at first that we were watching the beginning of a comedy, had not the prologue prepared us for a 'fearful passage' of tragic events. It is only after this witty prose-encounter between the servants has been going on for some time that members of the two families arrive who take up this quarrel in a slightly comic way, which may shed some light on the perspective under which this family feud is to be seen. Shortly afterwards Prince Escalus appears to put an end to this brawl of his 'rebellious subjects' 'on pain of torture' (I, i, 85). After he and his train together with the Capulets have left the stage, Romeo's name is mentioned for the first time. This masterly introduction, leading us step by step towards Romeo's first entry, does more than merely inform us about the situation. For in the swift meeting of all these figures, in their quick coming and going and in the suddenness with which the trivial 'ancient quarrel' is raised and again subdued, with swift transitions from jesting to heated strife, the scene prepares us for the mood of the play, in which so much depends on trifling causes, on chance and on inconsiderate haste.[1] The atmosphere of the Italian town with its narrow streets, its excitable inhabitants, and its readiness to swing over from comedy to tragedy, is conveyed to us throughout these first hundred lines and by a number of subtle touches and veiled allusions we are prepared for some of the tragedy's central themes.[2]

The preparation for Romeo's first appearance is equally remarkable. The question put by Lady Montague to Benvolio 'O, where is Romeo? saw you him to-day?' gives rise to Benvolio's melodious and beautiful lines painting the scenery in which the shy Romeo tries to hide himself.

---

[1] Cf. the chapter 'They stumble that run fast' in Brents Stirling, *Unity in Shakespearian Tragedy*, Columbia, 1956.
[2] See E.Th. Sehrt's excellent analysis of this exposition (*Der dramatische Auftakt in der elisabethanischen Tragödie* 1960, p. 148 ff).

But Montague's ensuing account of Romeo's love-sick behaviour, conveys to us only one side of him, the sentimental and romantic lover 'posing to himself..., more in love with love than with Rosaline, posing to his family and friends.'[1] This Romeo, however, who instantly appears will be superseded by the 'actual Romeo' who will soon turn into a tragic hero. This preparatory scene is of course not in Brooke, nor does Brooke present the exchange of Rosaline for Juliet and Romeo's 'transformation' in the same light as Shakespeare. But Shakespeare nevertheless made use of many minor details of his painting of the background.[2]

Another important change concerns the role of Tybalt and the way in which Shakespeare leads up to his death. Whereas in Brooke he comes in only at the fatal clash with Romeo and his friends, Shakespeare makes him appear at the very beginning, even before Romeo, embodying, as it were, the hatred between the two houses. He appears again at the feast at Capulet's house, threatening death for Romeo and predicting 'bitterest gall' for the future (I, v, 94). That he sent a challenge to Romeo, as we hear in II, iv, from Benvolio, is another 'preparatory' detail which we find only in Shakespeare, just as his killing of Mercutio augments his guilt and prompts Romeo to revenge his friend. Romeo's initial reluctance to answer Tybalt's impudent challenge, his subtle allusion (well understood by the audience but not by Tybalt) to 'the reason of my love' which he bears towards the 'good Capulet' Tybalt, and his effort to prevent the fight between Mercutio and Tybalt – all this goes towards building up more tension, more suspense. In fact it gives more meaning to Tybalt's death, which together with Mercutio's death (not to be found in Brooke) forms a turning-point in the tragedy, preparing the way for the final catastrophe: 'This day's black fate on moe days doth depend' (III, i, 116). – Romeo's foreknowledge expressed immediately after Mercutio's death will be shared by the audience and will assume even more poignancy through Tybalt's death following directly afterwards.

Thus a comparison with Shakespeare's sources – here and elsewhere – can throw much light on an aspect of Shakespeare's art of preparation

---

[1] H. Granville-Barker, *op. cit.*, p. 53; Cf. J. L. Styan, *The Elements of Drama*, 1960, p. 129.
[2] See G. Bullough, *Narrative and Dramatic Sources of Shakespeare*, London, 1957, vol. I, p. 276 ff.

which without such a comparison would be hard to grasp. For Shakespeare, in transforming a story, a chronicle-account or an episode into a dramatic plot, must always have kept an eye on the needs of dramatic motivation and preparation. How to lead up to a crisis or to a catastrophe, how to incorporate suspense and delay, how to develop the seeds sown in the play's beginning, how to take up, intertwine and disentangle the threads of the plot, how to insert expository scenes, all this has a bearing on the art of preparation and reveals Shakespeare's deliberate manner of re-shaping his material in order to turn it into good drama. To demonstrate this, however, would demand a thorough examination of the construction of Shakespeare's plays.[1]

At the end of this section, however, we should like to ask which aspects of the art of preparation are particularly characteristic of this tragedy. To begin with the way in which the two lovers express their presentiments reflects the interplay between character and the operation of fortune, whereas the use of tragic irony and of 'false forebodings' sheds light on the deceptiveness of Romeo in particular. The use of the time-element for the purpose of preparation is an important factor in the play's peculiar rhythm. Lastly the descriptive and metaphorical character of many passages of anticipation helps the audience to visualize the impending disaster and to build up that imaginative vision which is part of the playgoer's essential experience in *Romeo and Juliet*.

JULIUS CAESAR

In *Julius Caesar* as in most of the other tragedies Shakespeare prepares us beforehand for the first appearance of his hero. But compared with *Romeo and Juliet* the procedure has become more complicated. For no portrait of Caesar is given before his first appearance, scarcely even an indication of his character. Our attention is simply drawn to the dangers which threaten him, or rather to the dangers apparent in his ascent. Yet the first scene has a significant expository and preparatory function. For it is, as John Dover Wilson said, 'a brilliant overture introducing the fundamental fact of the situation: the fickle populace, with its love

[1] Marco Mincoff's article 'The Structural Pattern of Shakespeare's Tragedies', *Shakespeare Survey* 3 (1950); his earlier study *Plot Construction in Shakespeare*, Sofia, 1941; and H. T. Price's essay 'Construction in Shakespeare', *The Univ. of Michigan Contrib. in Modern Philology* 17 (1951) are important examples of this kind of approach.

of a strong man, be he Pompey or Caesar'.[1] Against this 'strong man' a resistance is announced, a secret threat. We hear the last lines of this scene immediately before Caesar enters the stage 'in solemn procession', and in this way we are warned even before we see Caesar:

> These growing feathers pluck'd from Caesar's wing
> Will make him fly an ordinary pitch,
> Who else would soar above the view of men,
> And keep us all in servile fearfulness.

(1, i, 73)

But with this the preparation for Caesar is by no means complete. For Shakespeare continues to prepare us for him throughout the next two scenes. Caesar appears twice in the second scene, but each time very briefly. Yet in both cases the fleeting impression given to us by these appearances is modified immediately after Caesar leaves the stage and supplemented by the conversations between Cassius and Brutus, joined later by Casca. Through this continuing characterization of Caesar, which both looks back to previous episodes (e.g. 1, ii, 100) and reports and reflects on what is happening offstage on the Capitol, our own view changes, so that when Caesar next appears we see him differently – our judgment of him becoming uncertain.

This manipulation of our sympathies, which continues during the following scenes, gives rise to that 'divided response' with which we regard not only the figure of Caesar but also that of Brutus.[2] The repeated, or rather continued, characterization of Caesar, which Shakespeare proceeds with in the third scene, too, not only has the function of enriching and complementing the impression which his short appearances on stage have made on us; it also adds a contrapuntal element by showing us how Caesar's figure is reflected in the consciousness of others, and we may be influenced by their viewpoint. At the same time Shakespeare succeeds in making his hero occupy our minds (and those of his friends and enemies) continuously, although he only appears on stage for a comparatively short time. This is a subtle and not immediately apparent aspect of Shakespeare's art of preparing us for the successive entrances of his major character.

[1] *Julius Caesar*, ed. J. Dover Wilson, The New Shakespeare, Cambridge, 1949, p. xvii.
[2] Cf. Ernest Schanzer, *The Problem Plays of Shakespeare*, London, 1963.

But if one thinks of *Julius Caesar* in connexion with the art of pre-paration the many omens, portents, prophecies, warning dreams and premonitions which Shakespeare uses in this play immediately spring to mind. Most of them Shakespeare found in Plutarch, but a comparison with the source shows us how deliberately Shakespeare shapes this material, supplements it and even alters it in part, so that the prepara-tory and dramatic function of these omens may be intensified and brought to bear directly on the characters; sometimes the omens even seem to mark the point at which the different reactions and spiritual conflicts of the individual characters harden and take shape. Thus the portents which precede the murder of Caesar, and which Casca first reports to Cicero in I, iii, occur in Plutarch too, but in order to increase the effect Shakespeare makes additions of his own invention: the escaped lion and the panic-stricken women. Even more important is the way in which these portents are integrated dramatically: the stormy night shaken by thunder and lightning, the 'strife in heaven' hanging ominously over Casca and Cicero's meeting in the street, create a natural background for Casca's report of the several 'strange and won-derful signs'. In this way the portents are related to the immediate natural events which the audience also experiences. In the following scenes[1] the audience is reminded several times of these natural events, and recalls at the same time the foreboding significance they had at these earlier moments.

Particularly revealing are the different attitudes which Cicero, Casca and Cassius display towards the omens in the third scene.[2] In the his-tories omens and portents were still presented, as a rule, as objective facts; their prophetic function was accepted without question. But here the characters react to them in quite different ways. Casca insists on their evil significance and even anticipates the objection of the sceptics:

> let not men say
> 'These are their reasons – they are natural'
> For I believe they are portentous things
> Unto the climate that they point upon.
>
> (I, iii, 29)

---

[1] Cf. II, i, 44, 103, 199, 265; II, ii, 1.
[2] Cf. T. S. Dorsch's introduction to his edition of *Julius Caesar* (New Arden Edition, London, 1955).

Cicero is the one who formulates this sceptical attitude clearly in his answer, while Cassius – insisting with elevated rhetoric on the search for the 'true cause' and enumerating once more the prophetic phenomena – uses the portents for his own purposes, even if he scornfully makes nothing of the night's disturbances and does not react to them with fear and trembling as Casca does. Yet Cassius too, like Cicero, does not believe in portents. Only towards the end of the play does he alter his opinion,[1] so that when we hear him then we may think of this third scene and take it doubly seriously, if so sane a man is now also to become a prey to sinister premonitions. Cassius, who initiates the conspiracy, sees in the nocturnal storm and in the omens an incitement to Caesar's murder, a sign of the indignation of Nature at Caesar's actions. As if born of the dark and sinister disturbances of the night, Caesar's figure is recalled at the end of Cassius's speech, a brilliant example of the gradual emergence of the central character, round whom the entire action of the first part of the tragedy revolves:

> Now could I, Casca, name to thee a man
> Most like this dreadful night
> That thunders, lightens, opens graves, and roars
> As doth the lion in the Capitol . . .
>
> (I, iii, 72)

In the scene between Calpurnia and Caesar, too, the relationship between the nocturnal storm and the omens is established, and these are described here once more by Calpurnia (supplemented by new suggestive details not found in Plutarch). So emphatic a repetition – for Plutarch has Calpurnia describe her dream but not the portents – creates a link, a parallel to the third scene of the first act, and gives the portents another different function, that of a warning to Caesar, and this is reflected in Calpurnia's fear and premonitions. These premonitions are felt by the audience too; they are also suggested by the frequent references to 'fear', 'danger', 'threat' etc. in this scene and by Caesar's apparent lack of concern in the face of these, and earlier, warnings. Caesar's feeling of his own security and invulnerability,

---

[1] You know that I held Epicurus strong,
And his opinion; now I change my mind,
And partly credit things that do presage.

(v, i, 76)

strengthens the anticipation and expectation of the audience who knows him to be a man doomed to death.

Calpurnia's dream (II, ii) is another effective instance of the double interpretation of a prophecy, or rather of the different reactions to it. Plutarch, too, describes a dream of Calpurnia's,[1] which Shakespeare transformed into a most suggestive dream vision providing a specific preparation for the following scene on the Capitol. This direct and concrete significance is even suggested to the audience by Caesar in an unconsciously ironic way, when he says of Calpurnia

> And these does she apply for warnings and portents
> And evils imminent,
>
> (II, ii, 80)

But because of the positive interpretation which Decius gives to Calpurnia's dream Caesar relinquishes his original intention to stay at home on this day and not go to the Capitol, and this again makes the audience realize that an unmistakable warning has been pronounced, which Caesar first took seriously but then pushed aside after all. For Caesar confesses the first effect of the dream in the subsequent conversation with Decius.

While he wishes to inform the Senate that the reason for his absence lies in his free will ('The cause is in my will: I will not come'), he admits to Decius 'for your private satisfaction' what the real reason was, and tells now for the first time of Calpurnia's dream – a most effective stroke of dramatic art through which we may guess at what must have been taking place in Caesar's mind. Because now we see that the warning brought to Caesar a little earlier from the augurs by a servant (in the victim there was no heart) must have made a deeper impression on him than appeared from the self-assured words of dismissal with which he acknowledged the news. At this point the remark made by Cassius in the previous scene, 'For he is superstitious grown of late', and Caesar's belief in the 'holy chase' of the Lupercalia celebrations (I, ii, 7) may spring to mind. Shakespeare deliberately altered Plutarch's

[1] In Plutarch (SK. 98) she dreams that a decorative pinnacle on the house, conferred as an honour upon Caesar, has broken down. Shortly before this we read: 'She dreamed that Caesar was slain, and that she had him in her arms'. For further observations on Shakespeare's use of his source with regard to anticipation and foreboding, the author is indebted to Friedrich Kastropp's unpublished thesis (see p. 46).

version of the episode with the victim, and inserted it at this point as a further rung in the ladder of preparation.

The discrepancy which exists between the growing feeling of pre-sentiment in the audience and Caesar's denial of the significance of the portents is considerably strengthened, in this scene as in others, by dramatic ironies, of which we quote here only one example.[1] When Caesar pushes aside the predictions which Calpurnia anxiously reveals to him with the words

> for these predictions
> Are to the world in general as to Caesar.
>
> (II, ii, 28)

These lines may be understood in two different ways: in a 'reassuring sense' – 'not only to Caesar but to the whole world these warnings apply', or 'not only for the world in general but also for Caesar these predictions are valid'. But Caesar thinks only of the first meaning, so that at this point, as at certain others, Caesar's self-deception in spite of the unwilling admission of truth is made evident. The expectation with which the audience looks forward to future developments and is prepared for them time and again is given an additional stimulus. In fact these and some other remarks of Caesar's sound almost as if he knew what was in store for him, and what was being hatched out against him. The audience asks, 'Does Caesar see so clearly, or not at all?'[2] Torn between two alternatives by this irony, the audience may look ahead with increased curiosity.

When speaking of the warnings which are brought to Caesar's attention, one naturally thinks first of the words of the soothsayer, at the beginning of the tragedy: 'Beware the Ides of March'. Shakespeare has made revealing changes to the warning as it occurs in Plutarch. To begin with he has brought forward the warning, which occurs in Plutarch later on a different occasion, and he has formulated it less precisely, which led A. W. Verity to the appropriate comment: 'here the vague sense of undefined peril inspires greater awe'.[3] From the

[1] For further examples and a detailed discussion of verbal irony in Shakespeare's tragedies cf. Beate von Loeben, *Shakespeares sprachliche Ironie und die Entwicklung seiner Dramatik*, Diss. Munich, 1965.

[2] Cf. von Loeben, *op. cit.*, p. 56.

[3] *Julius Caesar*, ed. A. W. Verity, The Pitt Press Shakespeare, Cambridge, 1924 (1st ed. 1895).

beginning Caesar's future is overshadowed by this early warning, but we are still uncertain as to how it will develop in detail. In order that this 'Beware the Ides of March' may impress itself upon us, Shakespeare has the warning repeated three times in the first scene and he has the soothsayer meet Portia in the street – in what might be called a preparatory scene – shortly before the central scene on the Capitol. Portia's anxiety about Brutus is added to the soothsayer's anxiety about Caesar, and therefore our apprehensions are drawn in two directions at once. When Shakespeare begins the following murder scene with Caesar's own self-assured words, 'The Ides of March are come', to which the soothsayer replies 'Ay Caesar; but not gone', the circle is complete and the audience receives an indication of the future from the reminder of the past.

Directly after this confrontation between the soothsayer and Caesar follows Artemidorus' final attempt to warn Caesar in time. Shakespeare has prepared us for this carefully, too, by letting Artemidorus appear on his own in II, iii; the apostrophe to the absent Caesar, with which his speech closes, rouses a last hope, only to predict, in the second line, the disaster:

> If thou read this, O Caesar, thou mayest live;
> If not, the fates with traitors do contrive.
>
> (II, iii, 12)

Thus here, as in most of Shakespeare's tragedies, a moment is contrived shortly before the catastrophe at which 'everything might have turned out all right after all'.

The passages listed here present only a few selected aspects of a complex structure. For the first two acts are in their entirety and in many details of action, characterization and thematic exposition a preparation for the death of Caesar.

The skill with which Shakespeare grafts the first part of the tragedy, leading up to Caesar's murder, to the second part which ends with the death of Brutus, has often been emphasized by the critics. If we take a close look we find that the art of preparation plays an important part in this. Shakespeare succeeded in making Caesar's murder, which ends the first thread of the action, the starting-point of a new sequence of events, but he also established numerous correspondences, echoes and links between the first and second parts,[1] so that some of the things which were implied or prepared for in the first part are fulfilled or extended in the second part. To demonstrate this it would be necessary to examine above all the development of the main characters, Brutus, Antony and Cassius, and the further development of the conspiracy. Only a few selected examples, drawn from single passages of the text, may be cited here: Calpurnia's prophetic dream, 'many lusty Romans/ Came smiling and did bathe their hands in it' (i.e. Caesar's blood) is fulfilled after Caesar's death when Brutus calls to the conspirators 'Stoop, Romans, stoop/And let us bathe our hands in Caesar's blood' (III, i, 106). Or to cite another example: before the great scene of Caesar's murder is ended, that is to say, before the counter-movement has begun, we hear from Antony's lips a prophetic curse:

> Domestic fury and fierce civil strife
> Shall cumber all the parts of Italy; ...
>
> (III, i, 264)

As early as II, iii we see the fulfilment, and again it is Antony who, with his famous speech over Caesar's body (in iii, 2), begins a new line of action and then foresees the now unalterable course of events:

> Now let it work. Mischief, thou art afoot,
> Take thou what course thou wilt.
>
> (III, ii, 261)

So in this instance, too, we may see how what is enacted in later scenes is prepared for beforehand by thoughts and visions.

Apart from the figure of Brutus, it is probably the two appearances of Caesar's ghost which impress the connexion between the first and second parts of the tragedy most forcibly on the audience. Here, as in *Hamlet* and *Macbeth*, Shakespeare introduces the supernatural as a significant prophetic element not only in descriptive passages (including omens and portents) but also as a visible reality. In Antony's prophetic curse at the end of the great scene of Caesar's murder there was a vision of Caesar's ghost ('and Caesar's spirit, ranging for revenge' III, i, 270). But when now – in the fourth act – the ghost of Caesar

---

[1] 'there is scarcely a line in this play which does not create echoes in the mind of something past or arouse anticipations of something, which is yet to come'; John Palmer, *Political Characters of Shakespeare*, London, 1945.

actually appears, this momentous apparition is carefully prepared for too. The music, sounding here at Brutus' command as an accompaniment to Lucius' song, has the function of attuning the audience to the appearance of the ghost, of forming an atmospheric preparation. The low-pitched prose to which Brutus changes, the kind, concerned words to the boy who has fallen asleep, his sitting down and turning over the leaves of the abandoned book – all this helps to slow down the tempo and create an atmosphere which by its very quietness and intimacy rouses the expectation of the audience. The intrusion of the ghost comes at a moment of heightened attention.

Plutarch has the appearance of the ghost, but not the short preparatory scene with Lucius. Shakespeare leaves the significance of the ghost open to doubt, and this increases the effect which it makes. And this effect consists for the audience for the most part in a feeling of premonition. For the audience will associate Brutus' decision to meet the enemy at Philippi (which he insisted on a short while before, against Cassius' advice) with the ghost's assurance 'thou shalt see me at Philippi', and this association will make them fear for Brutus' safety at Philippi from this time on. The fact that the ghost appears again 'in Philippi fields', as reported by Brutus in the last scene, sets the seal on what must by now be regarded as unavoidable. Again we have come full circle.

But many other words and events also prepare us for Brutus' death. As so often in Shakespeare, the self-awareness of the tragic hero is enhanced in the face of his approaching death, which he himself predicts.[1] As early as the first act we find Brutus indirectly preparing us for his own death, for it is only in retrospect that we can understand his words in this sense; for the lines

> For let the gods so speed me as I love
> The name of honour more than I fear death.

(I, ii, 88)

betray the ideal according to which Brutus will himself act later (v, i, 111). But at this point we have no notion of the turn events will take.

Not only with Brutus but also with the other characters the audience is repeatedly faced with the question: 'How will this character behave now? How should we judge him? What or who can he really be?' As

[1] Cf. the end of v, i, and v, iii, 96; v, v, 19.

Ernest Schanzer has shown,[1] *Julius Caesar* belongs to Shakespeare's problem plays inasmuch as the main characters demand from us 'a divided and complex response'. Shakespeare leaves the question open as to how a character should ultimately be judged, we are kept unsure of our bearings with regard to the central moral issue. It is therefore certainly not a matter of chance that this question, 'How will a character behave in the future, how should we judge him?' is frequently put by the characters in the play themselves; and it often has an important function in the dramatic conflict between them. The divided response to the principal characters applies not only to the audience but also – to a certain extent – to the relationship of the characters to one another. This has a certain relevance to the art of preparation. The second scene of the play is already rich in judgments and opinions which the characters form about one another. How will Caesar behave? Will it be possible to win Brutus for the conspiracy (I, ii, 312)? Caesar too, foresees who will be a danger to him (I, ii, 193), as his famous words about Cassius show. When at the end of the scene Casca takes his leave of Brutus and Cassius, he is assessed differently by each, whereby Cassius in his judgment of Casca is clearly thinking of future possibilities (I, ii, 299).

Most important for the later course of the action are the varying judgments passed on Antony in the great conspiracy scene. Cassius warns against him – he will become dangerous and should therefore fall with Caesar. But Brutus contradicts this in a lengthy speech, not only on moral grounds but also because his picture of Antony is quite different ('for he is given/To sports, to wildness and much company'). Trebonius ends this disagreement with two lines which predict the future with uncanny dramatic irony:

> There is no fear in him. Let him not die;
> For he will live, and laugh at this hereafter.
>
> (II, i, 190)

Cassius' warning against Antony is repeated after Caesar's death and receives added significance in what follows – while Brutus again lends his support to Antony, Cassius cannot suppress his fears:

Brutus.   I know that we shall have him well to friend.

[1] Ernest Schanzer, *The Problem Plays of Shakespeare*, 1963.

Cassius.   I wish we may. But yet have I a mind
              That fears him much; and my misgiving still
              Falls shrewdly to the purpose.

                          (III, i, 144)

Julius Caesar is a political play. Groups are formed and jeopardized, plans are considered and rejected, guesses about the future actions of partners and opponents are hazarded, mistrust and fear, trust and miscalculations alternate with one another and time and again direct the attention of the characters and of the audience to the future. In this way a new dimension of the art of preparation is opened up, a dimension of which there was little evidence in *Romeo and Juliet*. If we look closely we find further means and effects of the art of preparation which differ greatly from those employed in *Romeo and Juliet*. We are prepared for the future less by inner premonitions, as in *Romeo and Juliet*, than by omens, portents, supernatural appearances and prophecies as well as by surmises and calculations of the type we have just referred to. Although the individual characters, as we have seen, react differently to the portents and even, in part, doubt their validity, their effect on the audience will persist. The portents and the prophecies raise the murder of Caesar and also the decline of Brutus to the level of historical events of almost cosmic significance. The anticipatory passages too (such as the great prophecy of Antony) show the audience repeatedly that more is at stake than an individual destiny or the fate of a few people; it is a matter of a whole nation, a supreme political decision, a historic event.

Finally, the art of preparation is not restricted as it is in *Romeo and Juliet* to two lovers and their downfall, it covers more developments, characters and events. In the first two acts we have, beside the diverse preparations for the murder of Caesar, and the preparation for Caesar's various appearances, those for the inner conflict which is growing in Brutus's soul, and about which we even learn something *expressis verbis* on some occasions, as for instance in the famous monologue 'Between the acting of a dreadful thing . . .'. But this turn of Shakespeare's dramatic art, 'that he has moved his crucial action into the soul of Brutus' and that 'the crucial step from an external to an internal action was taken in *Julius Caesar*',[1] cannot be fully demonstrated from selected passages, it can only be indicated here and there.

[1] V. Whitaker, *The Mirror up to Nature*, 1965, p. 131 ff.

HAMLET

While in *Julius Caesar* it was possible to distinguish climaxes in the action, to which the technique of preparation gradually leads us, in *Hamlet* this has become much more difficult. In *Hamlet* there is no clear climax; instead of a direct line leading to a goal, we have a network of twisted and often broken lines. The action of *Hamlet* always takes place on several levels; to a much greater degree than in *Julius Caesar* there emerges, behind the external action in the foreground, a region of 'internal action'. We found it possible to penetrate to the core of *Julius Caesar* with the help of passages explicitly contributing to preparation, but we can scarcely do so with *Hamlet*. This does not mean that in *Hamlet* Shakespeare neglected the technique of preparation. But only now and then can it be illustrated from 'explicit passages'; for the most part it has gone beneath the surface of verbal statement, and is implicit in the construction of whole scenes and dialogues and in the intricate sequence of events.

But this same difficulty that we have in demonstrating Shakespeare's art of preparation from single passages in *Hamlet* may help us to understand the peculiar quality of the play. We gain an insight into the complexity, the elusiveness, and the ambiguity of expression characteristic of this tragedy if we look at the different utterances of anticipation or foreboding appearing in a single scene or spoken by one character. This is true above all of the speeches in which Hamlet himself announces, foresees or predicts future events or issues. There are even a few passages in which *Hamlet* informs us directly about his future plans and aims, as for instance with his intention 'To put an antic disposition on' (I, v, 172) or with the disclosure of what he wants to achieve with the performance of 'The Mousetrap':[1]

> I'll have these players
> Play something like the murder of my father
> Before mine uncle. I'll observe his looks;
> I'll tent him to the quick. If 'a do blench,
> I know my course. The spirit that I have seen
> May be a devil; and the devil hath power
> T' assume a pleasing shape; yea, and perhaps

[1] Cf. also III, ii, 73–85.

> Out of my weakness and my melancholy,
> As he is very potent with such spirits,
> Abuses me to damn me. I'll have grounds
> More relative than this. The play's the thing
> Wherein I'll catch the conscience of the King.
>
> (II, ii, 590 ff.)

Similarly what Hamlet says to his mother at the end of the closet scene (III, iv, 202) about his forthcoming journey to England is an exact preparation for the events of the following scenes. Hamlet clearly sees through the intrigues which are being woven against him, he anticipates the plans of his opponents and will frustrate them. After a long scene of passionate conflict with his mother his lines bring us back to the progressing action, take up the earlier threads (III, iii, 2 ff.) and establish a link with what follows. Together with the plans devised by the king, which aim at Hamlet's destruction through this journey to England, Hamlet's utterances establish a fresh network of external preparations which arouse corresponding expectations in the audience.

These speeches of Hamlet's, each of which fulfils a preparatory function, testify to his sense of reality and the astuteness of his plans. On a different plane are the pronouncements at the beginning of the play in which he divines future evil but does not yet know what form it will take ('foul deeds will rise . . .' I, ii, 256; cf. also I, ii, 158).

The same rather general 'pointing towards the future' may be seen in some of Hamlet's most famous utterances, as for instance his lines at the end of the first act

> The time is out of joint. O cursed spite,
> That ever I was born to set it right!
>
> (I, v, 189)

or his words after the killing of Polonius

> I do repent; but Heaven hath pleas'd it so,
> To punish me with this, and this with me,
> That I must be their scourge and minister.
> I will bestow him, and will answer well
> The death I gave him. So, again, good night.
> I must be cruel only to be kind;
> Thus bad begins and worse remains behind.
>
> (III, iv, 173)

However, these and similar 'key-passages'[1] may give us a clue as to the play's general meaning or rather to Hamlet's self-interpretation, but they cannot be taken as 'dramatic preparation' in its proper sense.

Of Hamlet's references to the future, some stand in ironic contrast to their fulfilment. His appeal to the ghost

> Haste me to know't, that I, with wings as swift
> As meditation or the thoughts of love,
> May sweep to my revenge.
>
> (I, v, 29)

and his assurance in the soliloquy a little later

> And thy commandment all alone shall live
> Within the book and volume of my brain,
>
> (I, v, 102)

and even his firm words at the end of the last great soliloquy which we hear from his lips:

> O, from this time forth,
> My thoughts be bloody, or be nothing worth!
>
> (IV, iv, 65)

only sound like anticipation; in reality they serve to reveal Hamlet's inner dilemma to us.

Finally we find a series of veiled comments which Hamlet makes under the protection of the 'antic disposition', compelled not to betray himself, but at the same time driven to let something be known of his knowledge, which is often 'foreknowledge'. His threat that 'those that are married already, all but one, shall live' (III, i, 151), directed to the king who is listening in the background, is an example of this, as is the conversation with the king shortly before the departure for England:

Hamlet.   For England
King.   Ay, Hamlet.
Hamlet.   Good!
King.   So is it, if thou knew'st our purposes.
Hamlet.   I see a cherub that sees them.

(IV, iii, 46)

[1] As e.g. Horatio's response 'Heaven will direct it' to Marcellus's 'Something is rotten in the state of Denmark' (I, iv, 90).

We also find a whole series of veiled ironical comments in which Hamlet uses quite common sayings in obscure form, in such a way that an attentive Elizabethan audience could hear the warning or 'prognosis' hidden in them.[1] Sketchy as it may be, this cursory examination of those comments of Hamlet's which may be placed in the category of anticipation or preparation shows how complex this phenomenon has now become, and how difficult it is to draw conclusions about the technique of preparation from such passages.

It is more rewarding to examine the way in which individual scenes are prepared for. *Hamlet* is a play of suspense, of retarding episodes, of digressions. Over and over again the action apparently fails to move forward, it seems to be held up, its movement reflecting the delaying disposition, the hesitation which we see in Hamlet himself. With a structure of this sort it is particularly important that the audience should be carefully prepared for important scenes and that our interest should be drawn from one episode to the next. Thus we have several examples of deliberate and careful preparation for individual scenes and entries. The most famous example of this is the preparation for the revealing conversation between Hamlet and the ghost, which is preceded by the preparation for the ghost's first appearance. Various critics have commented on the artistry with which we are gradually prepared for the eventual revelations of the ghost during five scenes,[2] and it is therefore not necessary to go into this matter at greater length.

The most distinctive feature of this preparation lies in the variety of ways in which Shakespeare here creates presentiments, anticipation and tension. Atmosphere, historical reminiscences and references to other phenomena of foreboding, questions and uncertainties, graphic details, suspicions and speculations all contribute to the extreme tension which accompanies the appearances of the ghost and fills the audience with new questions all the time. Already in the course of the first scene 'this

---

[1] Illuminating examples of this are given by H. Weinstock in his chapter 'Hamlets prognostischer Spür- und Tiefsinn' in *Die Funktion elisabethanischer Sprichwörter und Pseudosprichwörter bei Shakespeare*, Heidelberg, 1966. Cf. also Beate von Loeben, *Shakespeares sprachliche Ironie und die Entwicklung seiner Dramatik*, Diss. Munich, 1965.

[2] Cf. Marco Mincoff in *Shakespeare Survey* 3 (1950) p. 58 ff; H. Granville-Barker, *Prefaces/Hamlet*, London, 1944³; 'A First Movement', Otto Ludwig, *Shakespeare Studien*, 1901, p. 103; K. Burke, 'Psychology and Form' in *Perspectives on Drama*, edited by J. L. Calderwood and K. E. Toliver, New York, 1968.

thing' (the first reference to the ghost, made by Horatio (21)) has become 'this portentous figure' (109); and so the announcement at the end of the scene of a future meeting between Hamlet and the ghost is already linked with a quite distinctive form of expectation. But we know, too, how Shakespeare delays the final realization of this meeting several times, interrupts the main stream of the action, draws our attention in other directions, and yet continues to prepare us step by step for the great scene of confrontation. The art of preparation makes use of diversion and suspense, but also of a deliberate continuous accumulation of information, of descriptive details which influence our own idea of the appearance of the ghost, augment our curiosity and lead our expectations in a particular direction. The repetition of the ghost's appearance under similar circumstances is also used as a means of preparation. Our interest in the imminent appearance of the ghost has become so intense that it continues beneath the surface while we watch other things happening on the stage. Yet in spite of all the preparation, the moment at which the ghost appears before Hamlet and his friends in the fourth scene takes us by surprise. For although the audience has been waiting for the ghost all the time from the beginning of the scene, he appears at the one point in the conversation where the audience does not expect him. And then, before Hamlet is really given a clear picture of the circumstances of the murder, another hundred lines pass, so that we have a second phase of preparation and delay, in which uncertain ties, confirmed suspicions ('O my prophetic soul!' 41), new questions and new fragments of information combine with gestures and spectacle to heighten the tension and anticipation, until finally the dreadful truth is revealed. It was a particular stroke of genius on Shakespeare's part to make this great scene of revelation, for which we were being prepared during five scenes, now in its turn point towards further events, thus endowing it with an essentially preparatory function.

The subtle and complex preparations which precede the appearance of the ghost and his revelation contribute considerably to the especial weight which is given to the figure of the ghost in the play. The ghost overshadows the subsequent development and some critics have even wished to see in him the 'agent' of the play's action. The fact that the appearance of the ghost is prepared for in such detail, while Hamlet is scarcely introduced at all before his first appearance, has even led one critic to the conclusion that not Hamlet, but his father, is the main character in the play.[1]

Anyone who had only a casual acquaintance with *Hamlet* might feel that it was a loosely constructed play with a number of disconnected interludes and episodes, in which the main thread of the action tends to be lost. But in fact the individual scenes and appearances are deliberately linked to one another, and over and over again an attentive reader or spectator may discover indications, links in the chain, and preparatory references which draw his attention in good time to what is to come. Both the dramaturgy of the individual scenes and the interlocking links between the different scenes are carefully thought out, and follow an exact plan. Here preparations of a particular kind arise, and some of these may be mentioned.[2]

In the first scene of the second act Ophelia 'affrighted' tells her father of her most recent meeting with Hamlet, whose nature and behaviour she can no longer understand[3] (II, i, 75–97). We have been prepared for such a transformation by Hamlet's words in the preceding scene ('How strange or odd some'er I bear myself . . .' I, v, 170), but we do not know whether this is already the 'antic disposition' which Hamlet had announced, or still the result of the genuine horror which filled him after the meeting with the ghost, or sad despair at the parting with Ophelia which has now become necessary, or even something still unknown to us. We shall ask these questions again when we see Hamlet next (in the following scene). But Ophelia's account of Hamlet, full of telling and unforgettable impressions of his gestures, appearance and behaviour, prepares us also for the next scene between Hamlet and Ophelia (III, i). We have seen Hamlet as she sees him, now we compare this picture with the reality of his own appearance shown to us in the third act. New questions arise in the audience and this is an effective means of preparation which Shakespeare uses in *Hamlet* with particular mastery.[4]

In the scene between Laertes and Hamlet at Ophelia's grave we find a form of preparation which we have not as yet discussed. The action

[1] Richard Flatter, *Hamlet's Father*, London, 1949, p. 1 ff.
[2] Some further instances of this sort of preparation are given in the chapter on 'Shakespeare's Use of the Messenger's Report', p. 112.
[3] Cf. Granville-Barker, *Prefaces*. 3rd Series *Hamlet*, London, 1944, p. 64.
[4] On the significance of the question as a form of speech see Harry Levin, *The Question of Hamlet*, Oxford, 1959, I: Interrogation.

is designed in such a way that it may be taken as a symbol of what happens later. The struggle between Laertes and Hamlet appears as an overture to the fatal duel later on. Hamlet's jumping down into the grave[1] has the function of an omen, as has Laertes' wrestling with him in the grave – in which both of them will soon be lying. Certain comments of Hamlet's also foreshadow with tragic irony the disastrous end (e.g. v, i, 260).[2]

We mentioned above that the extent of the preparation devoted to the figure and entrance of the ghost impresses upon us his particular significance. The same may be said of the way in which Shakespeare prepares for the scene with the players, and then has Hamlet plan and prepare the 'Murder of Gonzago' play. Both are key scenes, which establish a level of illusion different from that of the other scenes and therefore offer many and varied possibilities for echoes and reflexions, both retrospective and prospective. But this is not to be examined here. As far as the preparation for the arrival of the players in the second act (II, ii) is concerned, it is significant that here too, Shakespeare makes use of the device of delay in order to draw the attention of the audience to this episode. At the first meeting between Hamlet and Rosencrantz and Guildenstern the players are only mentioned in passing (II, ii, 320), but this mention causes Hamlet to put a number of questions. For almost fifty lines the conversation revolves round the players, so that we await their appearance with increasing interest. A little later their arrival is announced by a fanfare off stage (*Guildenstern*: 'There are the players' 365). But still they do not appear. Instead we see Polonius, who comes to announce their arrival (398) after another delaying dialogue. Once more the conversation takes a different turn, drawing the attention of the audience not to the players, but instead to Ophelia. And only then, after another fifteen lines, do the players themselves appear. Thus the preparation for their appearance extends over more than a hundred lines, and as a result it is afforded great significance, although we do not yet know why.

This second scene of Act II is the longest in the whole play. In it

[1] Granville-Barker doubts the justification of this stage direction, but it has always been followed, and clearly dates from a stage practice in Shakespeare's time (*Prefaces, Hamlet*, 1944, p. 162).
[2] On the way in which Shakespeare prepares us for Laertes' death cf. H. D. F. Kitto, *Form and Meaning in Drama*, London, 1956, 'The Problem of Hamlet'.

there are no less than seven individual episodes of which five are prepared for or at least announced shortly beforehand,[1] and in this preparation the technique of delay is used several times. Thus a scene which is characterized by a certain stagnation in the external action is given movement, tension and variety. The stage business provided by Shakespeare's text counterbalances the 'inaction'. To mention only one example in addition to the preparation for the entrance of the players which we have already discussed: at line 39 Polonius appears in order to report the return of Voltemand and Cornelius. But before he leaves the stage to fetch the two ambassadors he begins to intimate to the king that he has found 'The very cause of Hamlet's lunacy' (49). The king urges him: 'O speak of that, that do I long to hear'. But Polonius puts off what he had to say: 'Give first admittance to th' ambassadors'. So the long report of the ambassadors intrudes before the conversation with Polonius is taken up again, and because of Polonius' circumstantial manner this conversation, too, needs time before it reaches the subject which the king and the queen, as well as the audience, are waiting for so eagerly. Polonius' bustling to and fro, and the kind of usher's function he is given, become, in this scene as in others, part of the technique of preparation.

The preparation of the Gonzago play which is to be performed in the next act also begins in this scene, shortly before the players leave the stage (541). Here the technique of dramatic preparation leading up to the central play scene[2] can be combined with the necessary preparatory arrangements for the production of the 'play within the play'. But Hamlet is not just preparing for some theatrical production or other, but also for the purpose it is designed to serve, the unmasking of the king. And the king's own words too, which with ironic ignorance, encourage and favour the ensuing performance, are part of this preparation.[3] So we are prepared on different levels for the 'Murder

[1] Apart from the entrance of Voltemand and Cornelius, the entrance of the players and Polonius' two entrances, one might list Hamlet's entrance and the second entrance of Rosencrantz and Guildenstern. We do not take into consideration the conventional fanfare which announces the entrance of the king and queen at the beginning of the scene.

[2] J. Dover Wilson calls it 'the climax and crisis of the whole drama' (*What Happens in Hamlet*, 1935, p. 138).

[3] Good gentlemen, give him a further edge,
And drive his purpose into these delights.
(III, i, 26)

of Gonzago' play. The dumb-show comes as the last rung in the ladder.

Thus the relationship between the technique of preparation used in *Hamlet* and the peculiar nature of this play is less obvious and more difficult to grasp than with other tragedies. On the one hand, there are those 'gnomic utterances' and dark prognostications which may give us a clue to the tragedy's general meaning or to the notions of its hero, but do not prepare us for specific events. On the other hand, some of the play's climactic scenes, the encounter of Hamlet and the Ghost, the arrival of the actors, the 'play within the play' are very elaborately prepared. Lastly, the technique of preparation throws some light on the interplay between delay, digression and short-term tension which is a peculiar feature of *Hamlet*.

OTHELLO

In *Othello* too we have preparation on different levels and of varying kinds. Nevertheless, as far as the technique of explicit verbal preparation is concerned, we can find more of it in the text of the play and we can grasp it more easily than in *Hamlet*. This derives largely from the fact that a good deal of the action results from Iago's scheming, is calculated, steered and utilized by him, and therefore also prepared for by him, sometimes down to the most minute details. With considerable frankness Iago lays his cards on the table right from the beginning, reveals not only his plans but also the methods he will use to accomplish them. He makes a diagnosis, takes the strength and weakness of his opponents into account, and devises a strategy which will rise to the occasion and lead to success. Much of this scheming and manipulation of the plot is reminiscent of *Richard III*, in which Richard also holds the threads of the action in his hands, and acquaints us with his plans for the future at each stage. Some of this can be traced back to the character role of the Vice, whose characteristics included cunning scheming and announcement of intended actions.[1] There can be no doubt that the free and open way in which Iago acquaints the audience with his aims for the future is evidence of the revival of a primitive stage convention. But if Shakespeare, in his later period, revives 'primitive stage conventions' this is not a relapse into imperfections long since over-

[1] Cf. B. Spivack, *Shakespeare and the Allegory of Evil*, Oxford, 1958.

come, but a skilful use of the effects and limitations of conventional devices. Not only does Iago's villainous role demand to be equipped with these features which traditionally belonged to it, but also his particular function in the play and the distinctive relationship between him and the audience make it suitable for these conventions to be employed.

In fact the high degree of awareness of the audience, which is acquainted with Iago's aims from the very beginning, is an essential aspect of the technique of preparation in the play. Not only does the audience learn at an early stage what Iago intends to do at every turn, they also see how Iago lays his snares, pre-arranges individual situations for his own purposes and even directs the movements and appearances of others so that his plans may be fulfilled. Against this background of awareness the audience then follows the sequence of events and episodes. Will things turn out as Iago has planned? And how will he utilize or overcome unforeseen opportunities or hindrances? The dramatic preparation thus evident in numerous speeches of Iago's creates a particular kind of tension in the audience's attitude to the stage action.

Iago has more soliloquies and asides than the other characters. In them most of the planning and preparation is accomplished. Not only do Iago's soliloquies set the action in motion time and again, they also provide an occasion for these plans to be hatched out.[1] The convention whereby future events are announced in a soliloquy receives an inner justification and becomes, in spite of all the unpsychological elements, psychologically credible. At the end of the first act Iago describes his coming campaign against Othello, which is based, as always, on a correct estimate of him; the soliloquy ends with the couplet:

> I ha't – it is engender'd. Hell and night
> Must bring this monstrous birth to the world's light.
>
> (I, iii, 397)

At the end of the next scene Iago has another soliloquy in which his plans are presented and described in a rather more concrete way. Similarly he ends:

[1] Cf. H. Granville-Barker, *Prefaces*, Second Series, London, 1946, *Cymbeline*, p. 241.

'Tis here, but yet confus'd:
Knavery's plain face is never seen till us'd.

(II, i, 305)

In the next scene but one, again at the end of a soliloquy, which discusses his further actions, Desdemona is drawn into his calculations:

So will I turn her virtue into pitch;
And out of her own goodness make the net
That shall enmesh them all.

(II, iii, 349)

In this way it would be possible to follow step by step the process of scheming and planning which stems from Iago. But the developments which he himself has instigated are also commented on by him. For like the Vice in the morality plays Iago observes the evil he causes, and himself notes his own success with approval. From the success reported to date, new prospects for the future can be deduced. In the great 'poisoning scene', in which Iago succeeds in finally corrupting Othello's mind, we have such a sequence of analysis and prophecy:

The Moor already changes with my poison.
Dangerous conceits are in their natures poisons
Which at the first are scarce found to distaste
But, with a little act upon the blood,
Burn like the mines of sulphur.
> *Re-enter Othello*
>   I did say so:
Look where he comes!
>   Not poppy, nor mandragora,
Nor all the drowsy syrups of the world,
Shall ever medicine thee to that sweet sleep
Which thou owed'st yesterday.

(III, iii, 329)

The ideas and imagery emerging from this passage (Iago as poisoner and physician), have of course been prepared for and developed over a long period[1] and belong, as Robert B. Heilman has shown,[2] to a pattern

---

[1] Cf. for instance I, i, 68.
[2] Robert B. Heilman, *Magic in the Web. Action and Language in Othello*, University of Kentucky, 1956. See especially pp. 91–8.

which enables Iago's role to be interpreted on several levels. The study of the different sequences of imagery, metaphors and themes, as carried out by Heilman, reveals many aspects of the technique of preparation.

But how is the audience affected by the fact that so much of the dramatic preparation in this play is provided by Iago himself? As is shown by the passages quoted above, Iago's diagnoses and the prognoses resulting from them are in many cases so accurate that the audience will accept the expectations and predictions expressed by Iago. They will have to acknowledge Iago to be an almost entirely reliable guide to the action, but they will admit it against their will, and it would be going too far to say that the audience see the course of the action just as Iago does. On the contrary, our animosity and antipathy towards Iago grow in the same measure as his predictions turn out to be correct and his machinations meet with success, and the hope grows too that his prophecies may in the end remain unfulfilled. From this paradoxical state of affairs, that the character who accurately judges and predicts so much is the one whom we watch with increasing revulsion, a conflicting mood arises in the audience. On the other hand, Iago's perspective is often so distorted that the audience is not prepared to accept it. Thus some of his statements contradict the opinions which the audience have formed of Desdemona and Othello to such an extent that they feel they must be on their guard against Iago. This applies for instance to the various passages in which Iago comments with base cynicism on the love between Othello and Desdemona, assuming that it will not last for long, and classing it as 'merely a lust of the blood'. To quote a few sentences from the remarks addressed to Roderigo:

It cannot be long that Desdemona should continue her love to the Moor – put money in thy purse – nor he his to her: it was a violent commencement in her, and thou shalt see an answerable sequestration – put but money in thy purse. These Moors are changeable in their wills – fill thy purse with money. The food that to him now is as luscious as locusts shall be to him shortly as acerbe as the coloquintida. She must change for youth; when she is sated with his body, she will find the error of her choice. Therefore put money in thy purse.

(i, iii, 342)

This is an example both of false judgment and of false prediction; and one may suspect that Iago is himself aware of this but nevertheless argues in this way deliberately with the intention of influencing Roderigo, his unintelligent and easily misled companion. But one of the fatal aspects of this tragedy is that warnings and predictions justified neither by morality nor by character are realized in the diabolical manœuvres arranged by Iago, and may have disastrous effects. This applies for instance to the famous warning given by Brabantio to Othello as he leaves (which Iago cunningly turns against Othello in III, iii, 206)

> Look to her, Moor, if thou hast eyes to see:
> She has deceiv'd her father, and may thee.
>
> (I, iii, 292)

If we enquire into the preparation for the first entrance of the main characters in the early scenes, we find again that it is Iago who prepares us for Othello's appearance and he does so in a distorted way. His remarks to Roderigo are primarily concerned with his own relationship to his lord, but they do not give us a 'portrait'. Nevertheless we receive an inaccurate and unfavourable impression of Othello, which he has to overcome when he appears for the first time a little later. So right from the beginning the audience have been warned and their sympathy will go out to Othello, who faces Iago's accusations with such unsuspecting innocence, and has no idea of what Iago has in store for him. But the tension with which the audience follow Othello's path grows in proportion to their feeling that Iago's predictions concerning his credibility and gullibility are correct, although they know that Iago cannot grasp the depth either of Othello's love for Desdemona or his noble humanity (in spite of his occasional admissions: 'The Moor is of a free and open nature' I, iii, 393; 'The Moor, howbeit that I endure him not,/Is of a constant, loving, noble nature' II, i, 282).

The relationship between the active intriguer Iago and his passive victim Othello helps to explain the fact that very little in the way of explicit dramatic preparation for future events is spoken by Othello. However, at the climax of Othello's joyful reunion with Desdemona in Cyprus, Shakespeare has him express, with his great happiness, the fear that it may not last:

> If it were now to die,
> 'Twere now to be most happy; for I fear
> My soul hath her content so absolute
> That not another comfort like to this
> Succeeds in unknown fate.
>
> (II, i, 187)

This premonition, to which Iago's aside following a little later gives the first response, has as yet no concrete foundation. There is a more ominous tone of foreboding in Othello's prophetic lines after Iago has succeeded for the first time in rousing his suspicions against Cassio, and after Desdemona has appeared in order to appeal for him:

> Excellent wretch! Perdition catch my soul
> But I do love thee; and when I love thee not
> Chaos is come again.
>
> (III, iii, 91)

This exclamation is in the first part of the scene. But after 350 lines the situation has developed in such a way that Othello, with his powerful call for vengeance, summons up an irrevocable future:

> Arise black vengeance, from the hollow hell.
>
> (III, iii, 451)

The apostrophe leads almost at once to the oath:

> my bloody thoughts, with violent pace,
> Shall ne'er look back, ne'er ebb to humble love,
> Till that a capable and wide revenge
> Swallow them up.
>
> (III, iii, 461)

With this declaration Othello expresses in his own words a fatal prophecy which must make the audience realize that from now on there will be no way back. At the end of the scene Othello for the first time gives an explicit announcement on the level of the external action:[1]

> I will withdraw
> To furnish me with some swift means of death
> For the fair devil.
>
> (III, iii, 480)

[1] Cf. the continuation in IV, i, 217, 'Get me some poison Iago, this night'.

and this is a significant indication of the inner reversal which has taken place in him. In fact everything here is preparation, leading to the diametrically opposed situation at the end of the scene. But only in a few passages is this preparation expressed explicitly.

Another well-known example of dramatic preparation, resulting less from individual passages than from the whole course of an episode and the dramaturgy involved in it, is in the reunion scene in Cyprus (II, i). The scene brings to an end the introductory phase which is particularly long-drawn-out in this play; it precedes the beginning of the actual conflict and is therefore itself part of the extensive dramatic preparation, and has even been described by Marco Mincoff as a 'separate playlet' because of its integrity and complexity.[1] In *Othello*, even more than in other plays, we can follow the conflict from the beginnings, seeing the situation out of which it arises. For Othello and Iago stand face to face long before the actual confrontation begins. We must become acquainted with them as they are, before seeing them as they will be during the conflict. It is part of this preparation that Iago, even before he carries out his campaign against Cassio and Othello, tries out his methods on Roderigo, an episode invented by Shakespeare and not found in the source, described by Coleridge as 'admirable preparation'.[2]

The scene in Cyprus shows us Othello and Desdemona once more at the height of their as yet unbroken trust and happiness. But Shakespeare has combined this climax of inner happiness with a climax in the external action, for everything that happens in this scene, and all our rising expectations, are directed towards the great moment of the reunion of Othello and Desdemona. The scene has been analysed a number of times,[3] and so it is sufficient merely to indicate the way in which Shakespeare builds up expectations at this point, rouses tension and leads us through various stages of delay and indirect preparation to that great climax. To begin with we observe the external overture to the scene: during a storm at sea a ship is awaited in the harbour of Cyprus,

[1] M. Mincoff, 'The Structural Pattern of Shakespeare's Tragedies', *Shakespeare Survey* 3 (1950), p. 62.
[2] 'The admirable preparation, so characteristic of Shakespeare, in the introduction of Roderigo as the dupe on whom Iago first exercises his art, and in so doing displays his own character'. S. T. Coleridge, *Shakespearean Criticism*, ed. T. M. Raysor, 1960, Vol. I, p. 40.
[3] Cf. H. Granville-Barker, *Prefaces*, Vol. II, *Othello*, 'The Arrival in Cyprus', London, 1930, pp. 13–23.

and it carries a valuable cargo. This is in itself a situation of expectation and tension. The anxious gazing out to sea, the apprehensive waiting while lines rich in associations give reality to the storm at sea and the coastal scenery, and while different pieces of news are brought in – all this presents dramatic preparation on several planes with the especial combination of imaginative poetry, stage business and fragments of information. The alternation between different levels of intensity in the language, rising from a simple report of events to poetic hyperbole, and falling again to everyday speech, in order to soar once more in Cassio's lines to poetic richness and vivid personification of natural elements until Desdemona's name is heard ('The divine Desdemona'), all this shows how the art of preparation is enhanced by diction and versification.

Shakespeare has Desdemona arrive first, to be followed considerably later by Othello. Thus Desdemona is drawn into the tension with which we wait for Othello; in the background, off-stage, Othello's ship approaches and reaches the land, and some of our attention is diverted to this. But the lively repartee which arises between Iago and Desdemona intrudes as a further delay before Othello's arrival (announced already in l. 90: 'A sail, a sail'), and creates an ironical contrast between the profound emotion and expectation which Desdemona must feel and the superficial gaiety of the apparently relaxed and frivolous conversation. This too is an aspect of Shakespeare's art of preparation, that beneath the surface of a playful chattering dialogue he maintains the tension and expectation. Desdemona's sudden question, interrupting the dialogue: 'There's one gone to the harbour?' (120) and her subsequent admission (described by some editors as an aside):

> I am not merry; but I do beguile
> The thing I am by seeming otherwise.
>
> (II, i, 122)

are indications to the audience of the clash between the playful foolish chatter continuing even now and her real apprehension. This clash is made increasingly clear to us.

But Shakespeare ventures to insert one more delay. In an aside he has Iago comment on the harmless exchange of friendly greetings between Cassio and Desdemona, which he watches closely, at once including this as material in his diabolic plan, with cynical villainy ('with as little a web as this will I ensnare as great a fly as Cassio'). So directly after the apparently merry interlude the audience receive a further warning. When Othello appears a little later to speak the beautiful lines of greeting, the audience see him with a certain foreknowledge of the danger which is approaching him. The situation of the audience at this point is similar to the situation before Othello's first appearance, except that in the meantime they have received more warnings. Othello's first words of premonition, with which at the height of fulfilment a new phase is introduced, carry even more meaning for us than for him and they prepare us for something of which he himself is not yet aware.

Thus in *Othello* we can again observe a relationship between the peculiar nature and construction of the play and its techniques of preparation. These are partly determined by Iago's central position within the intrigue, by his scheming, planning and disclosing his intentions to the audience. On the other hand, the process of gradual corruption going on in Othello's mind also requires careful dramatic preparation on several levels. Lastly the reunion of Desdemona and Othello in Cyprus could show us how Shakespeare leads us towards a climactic scene through several stages all of which serve as preparation of a great and moving encounter.

MACBETH

In *Macbeth* preparation is as it were personified in the witches and their prophecies and it becomes the axis of the whole play, without which some of the fundamental ideas could never find expression. Therefore a study of Shakespeare's art of preparation cannot afford to neglect *Macbeth*. But in this play the concept of preparation has so wide a meaning and is related so closely to the ultimate significance of the play and to its structure, its themes, its sense of tragedy, that we reach a point at which a detailed study of preparation would mean almost the same thing as an interpretation of the play in its entirety.[1] Some things which have been said by others would have to be repeated. But as

[1] Cf. for interpretations of this sort Roy Walker, *The Time is Free. A Study of Macbeth*, London, 1949; G. R. Elliott, *Dramatic Providence in Macbeth*, Princeton, 1960; J. R. Brown, *Shakespeare: The Tragedy of Macbeth*. London, 1963; J. Holloway, *The Story of the Night*, London, 1961; John Harvey, *Macbeth*, Notes on English literature, Oxford, 1960.

neither a detailed consideration of the basic ideas and problems of the play nor a detailed interpretation of the text can be attempted here, another method must be adopted. We shall consider the more important forms of preparation in this play and the possible ways of examining them, selecting a few examples only.

The witches and their prophecies will always remain the starting point for any discussion of preparation in *Macbeth*. In ancient tragedy an oracle and its fulfilment already formed the basic pattern for a dramatic sequence of events charged with powerful expectations. The prophecies of the witches are ambiguous: they raise expectations but they do not set clear goals towards which the characters and the whole course of the action might move in one direct line; as with the ancient oracle we are uncertain about its exact meaning and do not know in what form and with what prerequisites it will be fulfilled.[1] Thus the audience are stirred by that feeling of uncertainty which sometimes is an essential factor of dramatic preparation. This feeling is conditioned by the varying reactions of those affected by the oracles, and by their attitudes towards them. The audience know neither how the oracles will one day be fulfilled, nor how Macbeth and Banquo, and later on Lady Macbeth too, will act in the face of them. The prophecies of the witches are the point of departure for both the inner and the outer action, and they actually set it in motion, promising for the future the fulfilment of the hopes and desires but also of the fears and doubts of the main characters. So one might say that the events in the play are a continued reaction to the witches' oracles.

In Macbeth himself the prophecies are transformed into delusions that such and such a thing must happen so that nothing may stand in the way of these predictions. Thus first the murder of Duncan becomes a goal in the dramatic action for which we are prepared on different levels. Next, in a different sense, the murder of Banquo is planned by Macbeth in order to prevent the predictions from being fulfilled. Within the range of changing expectations leading up to the final clarification and fulfilment of the witches' oracles, shorter phases of preparation are worked in which lead up to these two murders but also to the second meeting with the witches, the murder of Lady Macduff and the ultimate fatal end of Macbeth. The way in which these events and actions depend on Macbeth's reaction to the prophecies and his interpretation of them,

[1] Cf. R. G. Moulton, *Shakespeare as a Dramatic Artist*, 1885/1929, p. 131.

as well as his initial blind trust and later attempt to prevent their fulfilment, make the audience ask over and over again: to what extent is it
a matter of destiny, or providence, or free will, or is it rather a matter of
compulsion? Do the witches have the power to enforce evil in the
world and in the actions of an individual, or do they just create the
potentiality?[1] The examination of dramatic preparation will have to
include these questions, in the course of which we shall see that they
continue to be questions which can receive no certain and immediate
answer. As early as the first scene, which is not only an important
'atmospheric preparation' for the whole play, we enquire into the
nature of the witches and the role of the supernatural.[2] The first meeting
between Macbeth, Banquo and the witches (already in itself a preparatory scene) deepens and extends these questions. From the different
attitudes of Banquo and Macbeth during this meeting, and their
different reactions to the witches' pronouncements, we receive some
indications of the future. In this scene we may look into the process of
'inner preparation' which is taking place in Macbeth's soul. Clearly only
a small incitement is necessary for Macbeth to conceive this monstrous
plan, which will gain increasing power over him. Almost all the words
spoken by Macbeth in this scene point towards the future. But the
future is seen from different viewpoints – for Macbeth may take the
prophecies 'As happy prologues to the swelling act/Of the imperial
theme' (i, iii, 127), or interpret their ambiguity as 'supernatural
soliciting', or shrink back from 'that suggestion' which he thinks he can
recognize in the prophecies, or again he may wish to commit his further
ascent to 'chance' (i, iii, 142).

However, the words of Macbeth reveal only a fragment of what is
taking shape within him. For his demeanour, his silence, his 'reactions',
all allow us to feel what is in progress beneath the surface of the spoken
word. We see that Macbeth is profoundly shaken (139), but we do not
know whether he has ever before entertained the thought of killing
Duncan, or whether this thought comes to him now for the first time.
The contrast with Banquo helps to make clear to us which path

[1] 'But the mode of evil they can create is potential only, not actual, till the human
agent takes it inside his mind and makes it his own by a motion of the will'. G. K.
Hunter. Introduction to *Macbeth*, New Penguin Shakespeare, London, 1967.
[2] Cf. the detailed discussion given by W. C. Curry in *Shakespeare's Philosophical
Patterns*, Baton Rouge, 1937.

Macbeth will choose. But at the same time we are prepared for Banquo's future role, or rather, we are made to wonder how Banquo will now behave, and how his sober critical attitude towards the witches and his testimony at this meeting will develop in the future. At the end of the scene we shall still be asking how Banquo will react to Macbeth's assurances of trust ('. . . let us speak/Our free hearts each to other' 154). In the first scenes of the second and third acts this development is continued, and each time a new element of expectation and anticipation is added.

The first meeting between Macbeth and the witches already makes it clear that Shakespeare's dramatic preparation does not emphasize the interlocking of external events (in spite of the skill with which this is done), but rather the processes within Macbeth himself. For we watch Macbeth's thoughts step forward and become decisions, and we watch imagination give way to action, and this process is reflected by recurrent turns of speech in the play.[1] But because it is accompanied by torments, and also by hesitation, horror, the desire to avoid the consequences, and by clear-sighted recognition of his own guilt, we watch this development, which 'prepares' us more than anything else does for the climaxes of the external action, fascinated and now without sympathy. In this progressive preparation, which leads first of all to the murder of Duncan, the part played by half-suppressed words, not quite admitting the murderous intent, and by Macbeth's words to Lady Macbeth (answering her question as to when Duncan intends to leave the castle): 'To-morrow, as he purposes' (I, v, 57), is just as important as the part played by the clear and candid consideration of the obstacles which will have to be removed from the path (cp. the aside in I, iv, 47).

With the introduction of Lady Macbeth a new element is added to the inner and outer preparation for the murder, and it is through this contrast that Macbeth's character emerges more clearly. Lady Macbeth, who says of herself 'I feel now/The future in the instant' (I, v, 54), has

---

[1] Cf. *Macbeth*.   Strange things I have in head that will to hand,
                                    Which must be acted ere they may be scann'd.

                                                                                                    (III, iv, 139)

Cf. also I, iv, 52.
This antithesis between 'head' and 'hand' threads its way in a modified form through the whole play. Cf. J. R. Brown, *The Tragedy of Macbeth*, London, 1963, p. 29. Brown's study contains many illuminating remarks on anticipation and preparation in *Macbeth*.

a quite different way of taking in hand the future which she is speaking of, even though we learn later, in retrospect (v, i), that she did not escape unscathed. So two people approach the murder and prepare for it – internally and externally – each in his or her own way so that we, the audience, are given a double perspective in our view of what is coming. Though certain agreements and arrangements for what is to be done are discussed between the two of them, they nevertheless remain alone and separate, even at this early stage in the play. The soliloquies are a means of revealing this isolation.

Macbeth's soliloquies have been admired by many critics for the unique way in which inner experiences and developments are brought to life in them. Here the soliloquy of reflexion and planning has been transformed into an imaginative presentation of ideas and modes of consciousness. The cool and calculating display of plans and machinations which we found in Iago's soliloquies has become a visionary picture of the immediate and distant future. Yet Macbeth's soliloquies too contribute in almost every line to preparation, with the difference that we now see preparation as something more far-reaching and complex, not restricted to the level of rational planning, but including the imaginative anticipation of imminent events and metaphysical issues.

It is from this point of view that we should interpret Macbeth's words in his monlogue 'If it were done when 'tis done' (I, vii, I), his thoughts of the life to come, his reference to the lethal knife which he carries on his own person,[1] his vision of divine plaintiffs taking their stand against his 'horrid deed', and also in the next soliloquy (II, i), his vision of the dagger showing him the way, his evoking of witchcraft and 'wither'd murder', his address to the 'sure and firm-set earth', whose stones are not to betray his footsteps, and his final words on the bell announcing Duncan's death. The images and visions of this second soliloquy, which directly precedes the murder, anticipate the deed and its circumstances, and evoke the 'forces of murder and stealth' which it will arouse.[2] But at the same time they represent the inner torment, the frenzy and the horror, which at this moment fill Macbeth's soul. So 'preparation' in these soliloquies also involves presentation of the moral

---

[1] This should be compared with the way in which the knife appears in Lady Macbeth's monologue (I, v, 53).
[2] Cf. the interpretation of the dagger soliloquy by Robert Langbaum, *The Poetry of Experience*, New York, 1957, p. 161.

dilemma, of the suffering and the compulsion to do what one knows is wrong. Because we have become acquainted with these features in Macbeth, we are also prepared to accept, as an imaginative vision of self-accusation, his apprehensive lines in the following scene ('will all great Neptune's ocean wash this blood . . .' II, ii, 60)[1] and we can understand the revealing function of Lady Macbeth's words 'A little water clears us of this deed./How easy is it then!' (II, ii, 67), although the irony of this passage does not become intelligible to us until much later – in the sleep-walking scene.

Macbeth's anticipation of the future and his own preparations for it are couched in language rich in symbols and in apostrophes, directed to the elements and to nature. But this should not be understood on a metaphorical level only. Macbeth is secretly in league with the supernatural powers. Therefore an enquiry into Macbeth's anticipation of the future (and into Lady Macbeth's) should include the significance of these apostrophes, both in early passages such as 'Stars, hide your fires' (I, iv, 50) and in passages such as 'Come, seeling night . . .' (III, ii, 46), where Macbeth contemplates the murder of Banquo (still concealed from Lady Macbeth). Equally important are Macbeth's imaginative gifts, which enable him to experience and interpret the natural events around him as if they were to reflect his evil intentions. Shortly after the apostrophe to the 'seeling night' quoted above come the lines:

> Light thickens, and the crow
> Makes wing to th' rooky wood;
> Good things of day begin to droop and drowse,
> Whiles night's black agents to their preys do rouse.
>
> (III, ii, 50)

This is a particularly effective example of symbolic and poetic preparation for the future, rich in meanings, transposing the 'interior' to the 'exterior'. A comparison with Lady Macbeth's soliloquy in I, v ('Come, thick night . . . ') would yield both striking similarities and characteristic differences.

Pursuing Macbeth's comments on his future actions right through the scenes following Banquo's murder, we are struck by the decline in

[1] Macbeth's prophetic lines in II, iii, 90 ('for from this instant/There's nothing serious in mortality') should also be considered in this connexion.

the imaginative poetic element and the ascent of a more direct and decisive mode of experience (e.g. III, iv, 136–40; IV, i, 146 ff.). In this way the language reflects the inner transformation which has taken place in Macbeth. The gap between thought and action has narrowed, deeds follow one another in rapid succession, for their 'inner preparation' has been curtailed.

So intense is the anticipation resulting from Macbeth's own words that Shakespeare can afford to postpone the usual reference to portents in the natural and animal world until after Duncan's murder (II, iii, 59 ff.; II, iv, 11 ff.). The function of this 'choric and foreboding scene' (II, iv)[1] should be compared with III, vi; IV, ii and IV, iii. In these scenes Macbeth does not appear. The portents give an additional perspective which will make an increasingly strong impression on the audience as the action nears its end.[2] The whole land is affected by the ever-increasing threat; but the countermovement against this threat gradually gains strength, so that by these two factors contrary expectations are kindled in the audience. The countermovement begins in the hurried conversation between Malcolm, Donalbain and Banquo shortly after the murder of Duncan has been discovered. Many of these words, spoken in the face of danger immediately before the flight from the murderous castle, prepare the audience for the stakes which the other side will set, and for their future line of action (cp. II, iii, 127, 130, 136, 144 ff., 147).

Because of the intensity with which the 'inner action' is used as a means of preparation in the play, the audience will scarcely notice the way in which 'outward events' are carefully prepared beforehand by informative hints and references. An example of this method may be seen in the arrangements leading up to the murder of Duncan. For almost every step and every detail are discussed by Macbeth and Lady Macbeth beforehand, and planned and arranged so elaborately[3] that in the murder scene itself Shakespeare can afford to do without the scenic presentation of the murder, and concentrate on the inner reactions of the characters involved. Although the observer is made acquainted

[1] More examples of 'choric comment' are quoted by J. R. Brown, *The Tragedy of Macbeth*, 1963, p. 22.
[2] Cf. in this connexion, v, i, 79.
[3] Cf. Kurt Schlüter, *Shakespeares dramatische Erzählkunst*, Schriftenreihe der Deutschen Shakespeare-Gesellschaft N.F. VII, Heidelberg, 1958, pp. 46 ff., 74 ff.

with the plan by the conversation between Lady Macbeth and Macbeth in an earlier scene (I, vii, 61 ff., 67 ff., 74 ff., 77 ff.), he does not notice that he is being prepared for a later scene. A similar preparatory indication is the repeated insistence of Lady Macbeth and Macbeth, that neither should let anything be discovered, and that they should look 'like the innocent flower' (I, v, 62). And this concerns not only the meeting with Duncan, but also the later scene when they wait for the guests at the banquet to which Banquo was invited.[1] Equally remarkable is the skill with which Banquo's invitation to the banquet and the murderous attack on him by night as well as the appearance of his ghost at the festive meal are prepared for.[2]

Similarly the preparation for the murder scene in the house of Lady Macduff deserves attention (IV, ii). For shortly beforehand the audience has heard from Macbeth's lips: 'The castle of Macduff I will surprise' (IV, i, 158), and now we listen to the whole dialogue between Ross and Lady Macduff and then between her and her little son with this consciousness of the *impending* disaster, and we listen with particular attention and suspense to the various unconscious ironies of this conversation. The gentle and innocent mood of this dialogue between Lady Macduff and her son is overshadowed for the audience by the knowledge that the murderers may break in at any moment, and this contrast constitutes expectation of a particular kind, which Coleridge pointed out.[3]

Lady Macbeth's sleep-walking scene presents an exception as far as preparation in this play is concerned. For here we see a completely altered Lady Macbeth, whose transformation has not been alluded to during the preceding scenes by any reference or intermediate appearance. Since the banquet, to which Banquo was invited, Lady Macbeth has not appeared. Macbeth has continued on his way alone. Even outstanding actresses have found it almost impossible to make the sudden transition from the Lady Macbeth of the third act to the Lady Macbeth

---

[1] Cf. I, v, 73; I, vii, 80; III, ii, 28 and 34.

[2] Cf. above all III, i, where Macbeth cleverly extracts from Banquo all the details he needs to know in order to carry out the murder (G. K. Hunter, Introduction to *Macbeth*, New Penguin Shakespeare, London, 1967, p. 17).

[3] 'How preparatory to the most horrid scene, the assassination of Lady Macduff, he at once gives variety, a pleasing relief, and yet heightens the after pathos, by the sweet scene between Lady Macduff and the child.' S. T. Coleridge, *Shakespearian Criticism*, ed. T. M. Raysor, 1960, Vol. I, p. 70.

of the fifth act convincing on the stage. But it is part of the singular construction of this tragedy that the basic narrative behind the plot has been condensed and that several explanatory episodes, which a lesser dramatist would certainly have expanded into effective scenes, have been left out. In this way a structure emerges where the art of the dramatist has been engaged not in 'a closely locked and logically coherent action that points irresistibly to a certain deduction, but in selecting those fragments of the whole that stimulate our imaginations to an understanding of the essential experience, to the perception of a nexus of truths too vast to be defined as themes, whose enduring power disengages a seemingly unending series of perceptions and responses'.[1] This method of composition, which Una Ellis-Fermor illustrates particularly from *Macbeth*, reflects on the ability of the audience to anticipate the course of the action. The gaps and the compression in the sequence of events make great demands on the imaginative response of the audience. For we are presented now and then with 'isolated situations' – which nevertheless convince us by their inner truth. The consideration of this scene therefore provides us with a new aspect of Shakespeare's art of preparation.

It is true that at the very last moment the audience is in fact prepared for Lady Macbeth's appearance[2] by the conversation between the Doctor of Physic and the Waiting Gentlewoman, and by their continued commentary which accompanies Lady Macbeth's appearance, giving the audience frequent pieces of information and explanation. What Lady Macbeth says and what she conveys to us through her gestures is, as was shown by Bradley, an echo of earlier words and situations, particularly of II, ii. Recent criticism has made additions to the correspondences pointed out by earlier critics.[3] With these correspondences the scene forms a significant response to earlier scenes, and the transformation and the fearful recognition which have come about in Lady Macbeth, and which seem to contradict her earlier speeches and actions, are made clear to us. But can we therefore say that this scene was 'prepared for' in the earlier stages of the play? The way in which earlier comments are taken up again with a different (negative) meaning

---

[1] U. Ellis-Fermor, *Shakespeare the Dramatist*, London, 1961, p. 95.
[2] This was emphasized by Otto Ludwig in his *Shakespeare-Studien*, 1901, p. 25.
[3] e.g. Roy Walker, *The Time is Free*, 1949, pp. 176 ff.

causes us to look back, and the especial brand of irony expressed in this way is 'retrospective rather than prophetic. It does not prepare the spectator for what is to come; but rather, when it comes, reminds him as by an echo that it has been coming all the while'.[1] Of this 'reminiscent irony', as Quiller-Couch called it, there are many other examples in *Macbeth*. It is in a sense the complementary aspect to Shakespeare's art of preparation.

Macbeth displays a wealth of irony and ambiguity, even though we may not be prepared to accept all the ironies and ambiguities which New Criticism has ingeniously sought to bring to light. But only some of these ironic comments, which we find on almost every page, could be classed as means of preparation, consciously accepted as such by the audience at the moment at which they occur. When Duncan addresses Macbeth in the fourth scene with the greeting:

> Welcome hither.
> I have begun to plant thee, and will labour
> To make thee full of growing
>
> (I, iv, 27)

the irony of these words and their significance for the future will strike every observer, as will Duncan's words spoken directly before Macbeth's entrance ('There's no art . . .'). But when, in the previous scene, one of the witches chants even before the meeting with Macbeth:

> Sleep shall neither night nor day
> Hang upon his pent-house lid, . . .
>
> (I, iii, 19)

the fate which will later overtake Macbeth is described and anticipated, but at this early stage the audience cannot be aware of it. So we would need to differentiate, and to ask to what extent the observer can appreciate the prophetic irony of a passage with the knowledge already at his disposal, and to what extent he is affected by it.

We might also describe as 'ironical' the way in which we are prepared for Macbeth's first entrance in the second scene of the play.[2] For the

---

[1] A. Quiller-Couch, *Shakespeare's Workmanship*, Cambridge, 1918, p. 73.
[2] This second scene, with its comparisons, imagery and 'ironical utterances', forms a complex preparation for later events. Cf. Roy Walker, *The Time is Free. A Study of Macbeth*, 1949; J. M. Nosworthy, *RES*, Vol. 22, April 1946; see the notes on

picture we are given of him there, in the report of the Sergeant (as 'brave Macbeth . . . disdaining fortune', as 'valour's minion', as 'Bellona's bridegroom, lapp'd in proof'), does not correspond to the impression made by Macbeth in the following scenes, though the objection could be made that Macbeth fights in this battle as a loyal ally of Duncan's and may therefore still appear as an uncontested hero. But the other piece of information which we receive about Macbeth before he himself appears in the third scene is that the witches want to meet him (i, i, 8). So two sets of expectations are aroused which do not conform to one another, and it is with the consciousness of this 'foreknowledge' that the audience will then take in the first meeting between Macbeth and the witches.[1]

Finally we may indicate a means of preparation which Shakespeare uses particularly frequently in this tragedy, but which operates on a subconscious level. We refer here to the numerous key-words and key-images, which, from the very beginning, create an atmosphere of threats, fear, darkness and crime. *Fear, blood, danger, darkness*, and a number of other words and phrases may be listed here. Together with the suggestive nature-imagery they impart to the vocabulary of the play a quite distinctive colouring which will impress itself upon us from the first act onwards, whether we read the play or see it in the theatre.

The consideration of the art of preparation in *Macbeth* thus reveals not only an extraordinary range and a great variety but also takes us to the very heart of this tragedy, its theme and its meaning being closely linked up with the problem of anticipation, predestination, and free will.

CONCLUSION

This discussion of *Macbeth*, the last play treated at some length, has again made it clear that the concept of 'preparation' in Shakespeare's

---

[1] 'It is fit preparation for this play that we do not meet Macbeth until the third scene; and that as he comes to meet us, we, with the witches, have more than mortal knowledge . . .' John Lawlor, *The Tragic Sense in Shakespeare*, London, 1960, p. 113.

this scene in Kenneth Muir's edition of *Macbeth* (New Arden Shakespeare, London, 1951) and the comments by Sylvan Barnet in his introduction to the play (*The Signet Classic Shakespeare*, New York, 1963, p. xxx).

great tragedies becomes so complex and ambiguous that it appears almost impossible to draw a dividing line between preparation as a definable dramatic technique and preparation as a motivating force or a feature of the play's thematic structure. In fact, preparation in Shakespeare's later tragedies constantly verges on motivation but it is also a manifestation of the cohesion of the play's structure as a whole. It would therefore be a vain endeavour to restrict the study of preparation to distinguishable devices, such as the planning of an intended deed of violence (like the murder of Duncan in *Macbeth*). Isolation of a 'device of preparation' for the sake of systematic investigation would result in a wrong approach because what goes towards preparing these turns of the action usually extends beyond the reach of distinguishable devices and is closely bound up not only with other aspects of Shakespeare's dramatic art but also with the play's central problems and its major themes.

It is with these considerations in mind that some suggestions are offered in the following pages of the way in which the study of preparation could be pursued further. For the preceding chapters on a number of individual plays have by no means exhausted the subject. But with each of these suggested approaches it will again become clear that preparation may mean different things in different plays and that it borders upon other aspects of dramatic art.

In *King Lear*, for instance, the study of preparation would have to focus on the inner development, the 'inner drama' of its main character rather than on the previous introduction and announcement of outward changes. Lear's madness, which forms the climax of this 'inner drama', is foreshadowed from the first scene. From Kent's warning 'Be Kent unmannerly/When Lear is mad' (I, i, 144) there is a series of subtle forebodings and anticipations[1] leading up to Lear's own poignant admittance 'O Fool, I shall go mad' (II, iv, 285). Edgar's feigned madness, for which he himself prepares us in a soliloquy of the conventional type (II, iii), acts as a parallel and also as an anticipation for Lear's madness. But besides these means of subtle acclimatization Shakespeare also has recourse to physical description in order to prepare us for the appearance of the mad Lear in the first great scene on the heath. Before this scene, which surpasses the potentialities of the stage and places a great demand on the imagination of the audience, Shakespeare has a

[1] Cf. I, iv, 233 f; I, v, 46; II, iv, 56; II, iv, 121.

'Gentleman' describe Lear's fight with 'the fretful elements' in a short scene with purely preparatory function (III, i).

However, if we were to understand 'preparation' in a wider sense, we would have to include also the verbal means by which Shakespeare makes us realize that an immense crisis will take place in Lear and that a complete break-down of his equilibrium is at hand. The complete change of Lear's speech, the disruption of diction and versification,[1] the transformation of his vocabulary and his imagery, give us indications of what is going to happen. On a different level, the sayings, proverbs and songs of the Fool contain many veiled prognostications pointing towards the coming disaster. Another forceful means of preparation is the repetition of a parallel situation which, by reminding us of what we have seen and heard already in a similar context, reinforces our expectations and premonitions. In this respect the fourth scenes of the first and second acts should be compared with one another. For the scene with Goneril (I, iv) serves as preparation for the parallel scene with Regan (II, iv), in which Lear reacts in a similar manner, and the Fool, too, plays the same role. The process of profound inner disturbance which takes place in Lear has a greater impact on the audience because we watch it 'stage by stage', each phase preparing for the next one. It would be worthwhile to enquire into the way in which the recurrence of scenes which display similarity of structure and theme serves the purpose of dramatic preparation in other plays.[2]

Another even more subtle effect of preparation emerges if we observe the interplay between imagery and symbolic gesture on the stage. When Lear, confronted by 'poor Tom', tears off his clothes (III, iv) or when Gloucester is blinded (III, vii), these central scenic moments have been long prepared for as Robert Heilman has shown,[3]

[1] Cf. W. Clemen in *Shakespeare-Jahrbuch (West)*, Heidelberg, 1969, S.10. Werner Sedlak, *Shakespeare-Jahrbuch (West)*, Heidelberg, 1969, p. 135. H. Granville-Barker, *Prefaces, First Series, King Lear*, London, 1946, p. 158.
[2] Matthew W. Black, 'Repeated Situations in Shakespeare's Plays' in *Essays on Shakespeare and Elizabethan Drama*, ed. R. Hosley (in Honour of Hardin Craig), University of Missouri, 1963.
[3] R. B. Heilman, *This Great Stage. Image and Structure in 'King Lear'*, University of Washington, 1948. For similar examples in *Othello*, see Heilman's book, *Magic in the Web. Action and Language in Othello*, University of Kentucky, 1956.

by a chain of phrases and images which underline one of the play's themes and form a 'pattern' made up of verbal hints, of images and dramatic situations. However, the occurrence of these verbal phrases and images does not mean that the audience is aware of their preparatory effect. No expectation surely is raised by them, and they do not point towards the future. Their impact on the audience must be sought in another direction. They impress on the minds of the audience a certain theme, a symbol, an idea, so that when this idea is being transformed into a gesture or a symbolic situation on the stage, the audience may recognize its meaning more clearly. Part of this process takes place unconsciously, as is the case with most of the foreboding images. The function of imagery to foreshadow and anticipate is particularly important in the tragedies.[1] A study of this foreboding function, however, would have to differentiate between varying degrees of awareness of this function in the minds of the audience.

In a similar manner dramatic irony can only in certain cases be included in a study of dramatic preparation, as the instances quoted above from *Julius Caesar* and *Macbeth* have shown. For in order to recognize dramatic irony as a means of preparation one must generally be familiar with the later parts of the play. These ironies reveal their preparatory or foreboding function only in retrospect. On the other hand, with plays of which the plot was well-known to the theatre-goer some of the more obvious dramatic ironies at least would have been clearly understood by the audience.

If for these reasons dramatic irony and foreboding imagery only partly come under the heading of preparation, this applies less to those scenes of the 'low comic kind' 'which serve the function of establishing probability for later important actions or sequences of actions'. The foreshadowing use of these scenes has been examined by Paul J. Aldus[2] who selected his examples primarily from the two parts of *Henry IV*, but also from *Julius Caesar* and *Antony and Cleopatra*. Preparation in these scenes is subtle and veiled rather than obvious, ironical allusions being a frequent means of foreshadowing. But if this approach were to be applied to further plays, more scenes of this type could certainly be discovered.

[1] Cf. W. Clemen, *The Development of Shakespeare's Imagery*, London, 1951.
[2] Paul J. Aldus, 'Analogical Probability in Shakespeare's Plays', *Shakespeare Quarterly* VI (1955).

Discussing *Richard III* and *Richard II* we came across short 'mirror-scenes',[1] the function of which was primarily preparatory (*Richard III*, II, iii; *Richard II*, II, iv). In Shakespeare's tragedies, too, one could discover this type of anticipatory mirror-scene which does not add any important new element to the action but by creating atmosphere, arousing expectation and reflecting something of the play's mood prepares us for what is to come.[2] A typical example is act IV, scene iii of *Antony and Cleopatra* which gives us the restless and quick exchange of short questions, exclamations and phrases between four soldiers the night before the decisive battle. Here unexplained rumours, false hopes, warnings and strange noises ('Music i' the air') combine with the nervous stirring, whispering and strained listening of the soldiers, who move about the stage, to create a mood of dark foreboding and uncanny expectation.[3] In the first part of the second scene of act II (1–40) of *Coriolanus* again minor characters bustle about (to lay cushions in the Capitol for the expected session with Coriolanus) and discuss in a casual manner Coriolanus' chances of being elected. The conversation reflects the feelings and expectations of the people; when Coriolanus appears himself a few moments later we are prepared for an important scene.

Minor characters of anonymous description, soldiers, citizens, craftsmen, servants are often used by Shakespeare in this preparatory function. While going about their business or meeting in the street or waiting for the arrival of the main characters they may discuss what is about to happen, thus not only reflecting the people's reaction but also preparing us for major issues. Shakespeare's technique of interposing relaxing scenes or scenes of comic relief, in which the action scarcely moves forward, between his more important scenes should be examined in relation to his technique of preparation and information.

---

[1] 'Mirror-scenes' have been examined by H. T. Price in his important article in *Joseph Quincy Adams Memorial Studies*, 1948 ('Mirror Scenes in Shakespeare').

[2] Apart from the two scenes discussed here, cf. *Antony and Cleopatra*, I, ii, 1–78; *Julius Caesar*, II, iii; *Macbeth*, v, ii.

[3] Cf. the interpretation of this scene by Raymond Williams who notes in the very first exchange between the soldiers 'a curious premonitory rhythm' (*Drama in Performance*, 1968, p. 69). The scene should also be compared to the much longer scene in *Henry V*, the night before Agincourt (Act IV, Scene i). Cf. Sir John Squire's reference to the 'premonitory hushes' of this scene (*Shakespeare as a Dramatist*, 1935, p. 119).

Preparation, as we have seen above, is closely tied up with Shakespeare's technique of characterization. Shakespeare as a rule gives us a previous portrait of his major characters but this portrait may stand in contrast to the actual appearance or conduct of this character. Certain expectations are roused which may partially be defeated or disappointed. But preparation, as we have seen in *Julius Caesar*, need not be limited to initial preparation. Some characters are further defined or we are given successive views of them from different angles, so that contrasting expectations are raised as to their bearing and further development. The running commentary (which we find in all plays) on what a character does or is and the evaluation of his actions are supplemented in Shakespeare's later tragedies by varying expectations and surmises of what will be (or should be) his conduct or his reaction in the forthcoming scenes. Part of the tension with which we watch these tragedies derives from our guessing the line of action the character is to choose, though this guessing may be moved by mixed and sometimes contrasting expectations. The play offering the best example of this interplay between changing expectations and their fulfilment or non-fulfilment with regard to the major characters is *Antony and Cleopatra*. As Ernest Schanzer has shown, in this tragedy 'the technique of "dramatic coquetry", consisting in an alternate enlisting and repelling of the audience's affections for a character . . . reaches its climax'.[1] If the study of Shakespeare's art of preparation were to be extended to *Antony and Cleopatra* it would have to show to what degree 'dramatic coquetry' involves raising expectations of a very different kind, and to what degree the 'opposed evaluations' which this play conveys to us are conditioned by contrasting expectations which may clash with the actual development of the characters themselves, or offer only one 'perspective' which will be modified or corrected later on. Of this technique the play makes use from its very beginning, Philo's opening speech exemplifying the 'oblique manner' of previous characterization which is contradicted by the following entry and dialogue of the two lovers themselves.[2]

[1] Ernest Schanzer, *The Problem Plays of Shakespeare*, London, 1963, p. 146.

[2] 'We were prepared for baseness, and we see magnificence; and both emotions are important' (Raymond Williams, *Drama in Performance*, London, 1968, p. 63). Cf., too, A. P. Riemer, *A Reading of Shakespeare's 'Antony and Cleopatra'*, London, 1968, p. 26; W. Rosen, *Shakespeare and the Craft of Tragedy*, Cambridge, Mass., 1960, p. 108.

This technique of preparing us for a character by differing portraits or varying expectations may be found in other 'problem plays' too, (*Julius Caesar* and *Measure for Measure* being illuminating examples) but it may be traced back to the histories. Comparing the portraits given of Prince Hal and Hotspur by King Henry IV and Westmoreland[1] with their actual character, and looking at other later passages which raise expectations as to the conduct of Hotspur and Hal, we also find contradicting evaluations and differing perspectives which will stimulate the feelings with which we watch the further progress of the play.

But this oblique and sometimes deliberately contradictory method of preparation does not pertain to character-portrayal alone. It would be worthwhile to enquire how often Shakespeare puts his audience on 'a false track' regarding the further course of things. Again *Henry IV* could yield an instance of this device.

As a rule, however, Shakespeare does not raise expectations which are not fulfilled in some way or other. And rarely does he contrive effects which take us completely by surprise and have not been prepared for at all. One of these instances is Hermione's reappearance in the last act of *The Winter's Tale*. This contradicts the information of Hermione's supposed death propagated in previous acts. Neither the audience nor any character in the play has been let into the secret of Hermione's survival, and this is unique in Shakespeare's work.[2]

There are other cases in which Shakespeare deliberately does not make use of preparation and motivation although his source did so (for as a rule we find the reverse process). A famous instance is the 'love-test' arranged by the king in the first scene of *King Lear*. Whereas in the old play *King Leir* the king motivates this stratagem by some positive considerations in Cordelia's own interest so that we are prepared for the situation when it is enacted, this strange request appears in Shakespeare's tragedy all of a sudden as an afterthought[3] and contri-

---

[1] *1 King Henry IV*, I, i.
[2] Cf. Clifford Leech, 'The Structure of the Last Plays', *Shakespeare Survey* 11 (1958), p. 24.
[3] Cf. Kenneth Muir, *Shakespeare's Sources*, London, 1957, I, p. 145; Leir's motivating speech in the old play *King Leir and his Three Daughters* is also quoted and commented upon by John Dover Wilson in his edition of *King Lear* (The New Shakespeare, Cambridge, 1960), p. xvii.

butes to the effect of inconsiderate rashness and blind irrationality with which Lear's demeanour in this scene leaves us.

Comparison with Shakespeare's sources enables us to appreciate another aspect of Shakespeare's art of preparation. For he often inserts a narrative which he then uses in order to prepare a new development, a new intrigue, or phase of the plot. Some instances are considered in the chapter 'Past and Future in Shakespeare's Drama' (p. 137 ff.) under the aspect of retrospect linked to anticipation. But it would be worth-while to examine the way in which Shakespeare makes use of narrative for the specific purpose of preparation. These retrospective narratives either form part of the story which Shakespeare used for his play or they are taken from some other source, or they are invented in order to serve the mechanics of the plot. Thus Shakespeare took from North's Plutarch the famous account of Cleopatra's first meeting with Antony on the river Cydnus.[1] However, this passage describing Cleopatra in her barge is given quite another position; it is put into the mouth of Enobarbus at a critical moment in the play, for Antony is to marry Octavia and appears to be about to leave Cleopatra for ever (II, ii). But this magnificent and colourful vision of Cleopatra, besides prepar-ing us for her next appearance, serves an important dramatic purpose, for it changes the prospect of the future: There will be no marriage with Octavia, no agreement between East and West. 'Never, he will not' is Enobarbus' determined answer to Maecenas' false assumption 'Now Antony must leave her utterly' (II, ii, 233). In *Measure for Measure* the Duke's account of Mariana,[2] who is introduced into the play at this late moment (III, i, 202), serves as preparation for the stratagem practised in IV, i. In *The Comedy of Errors* it is not until the fifth act that the story of the abbess Aemilia is disclosed which now precipitates the final dénoue-ment. In *Cymbeline* Belarius' account of his banishment and of the abduction of the two princes (III, iii) introduces the subplot and pre-pares a new strand of the action. More examples of this specific preparatory use of narrative can easily be found. They would con-firm the basic law that whatever is absorbed in the process of play-writing comes under the influence of 'forward movement' (Thornton Wilder).

[1] Cf. K. Muir, *op. cit.*, p. 202.
[2] For a parallel in Cinthio see the introduction by J. W. Lever to his edition of *Measure for Measure* (New Arden Shakespeare, London, 1965), p. xl.

But preparation pertains not only to words, to what is spoken on the stage, it pertains also to other means of dramatic performance: music,[1] off-stage sounds, stage-business and spectacle.[2] Sometimes even a certain grouping of characters on the stage as suggested by the text serves as preparation for a following event. As every theatre-goer will confirm from his own experience of a successful production, Shakespeare contrives to make our imaginative vision include the space behind the stage. With a mixture of uncertainty and expectation we take into account what is going on behind the stage, awaiting previously announced new-comers or those who have been sent away on an errand and are due to come back. The impending arrival of friends and enemies puts us into a state of expectancy and directs our imagination towards that hidden area behind the stage which Shakespeare brings to life through many subtle and suggestive hints. It is up to the producer to realize these potentialities.

In order to prepare us for a climax or a decisive turn of the action Shakespeare sometimes also makes use of silence. The dramatic tempo slows down and there comes a moment of suspense or of interruption, the attention of the audience is arrested and we eagerly listen and watch out for what may come. The moments preceding the murder of Duncan (II, ii), the seconds elapsing between Claudius' prayer and Hamlet's arrival (III, iii), Othello entering Desdemona's bedchamber after she has fallen asleep (v, ii), are instances which could be multiplied. On the two 'pregnant nights' in *Julius Caesar*, the night before Philippi and the night before the murder of Caesar, it is worth quoting Sir John Squire 'In both is a great event prepared by whispers amid the darkness that awaits the inevitable and relentless dawn, which brings once the prepared and deliberate slaying, and once its retribution.'[3]

Preparation understood in this wider sense as something not ex-

---

[1] For examples of the preparatory function of music in Shakespeare's plays see my article 'Shakespeare und die Musik' in *Shakespeare Jahrbuch (West)*, 1966.
[2] Cf. J. L. Styan, *Shakespeare's Stagecraft*, Cambridge, 1967. Nevill Coghill, *Shakespeare's Professional Skills*, Cambridge, 1964.
[3] Sir John Squire, *Shakespeare as a Dramatist*, London, 1935, p. 121. For further examples of Shakespeare's use of silence see J. L. Styan, *Shakespeare's Stagecraft*, Cambridge, 1967.

pressly stated in the text but suggested as it were 'between the lines' in a combination of stage-business, dramatic tempo, gesture, spectacle and atmosphere will be a concern of the producer rather than the scholar. It would carry us still farther and prompt us to explore fields beyond the scope of the present study.

2

Shakespeare's Use
of the Messenger's Report

Shakespeare's achievement as a dramatist lies in different directions and may therefore be looked upon from different angles. Part of this achievement certainly is due to the extraordinary way in which Shakespeare – on all levels of dramatic art – makes use of existing conventions and devices which had been handed down to him by theatrical tradition. His indebtedness to this rich dramatic tradition which goes back to the medieval as well as to the classical drama of antiquity has been the subject of quite a number of illuminating studies and has proved a help for the understanding and interpretation of his plays.[1] Sometimes an endeavour has also been made to examine one single dramatic convention, tracing its use throughout Shakespeare's work. This kind of approach could integrate the historical perspective into a critical appreciation of Shakespeare's artistic development. For Shakespeare's dramatic art is too complex a subject to be tackled by an overall study, and consequently our notions about it tend to be rather general and vague. Singling out certain aspects from this comprehensive concept 'dramatic art' for individual treatment would, however, enable us to arrive at concrete findings and to apply more successfully the tools of analysis and comparison which according to T. S. Eliot form the indispensable equipment of the critic. By following up the development of certain devices or conventions in Shakespeare's plays we shall see that the way in which Shakespeare transforms and revives these conventions, enriching them with new functions and turning them to new dramatic uses, is a key to the steady growth of his craftsmanship and his

[1] Only the following titles are mentioned here: M. C. Bradbrook, *Themes and Conventions of Elizabethan Tragedy*, Cambridge, 1935. W. Farnham, *The Medieval Heritage of Elizabethan Tragedy*, Oxford, 1936. S. L. Bethell, *Shakespeare and the Popular Dramatic Tradition*, London, 1944. A. Harbage, *Shakespeare and the Rival Traditions*, New York, 1952. R. Weimann, *Shakespeare und die Tradition des Volkstheaters*, Berlin, 1967. G. Wickham, *Shakespeare's Dramatic Heritage*, London, 1969.

artistic perfection. Even the examination of a minor convention such as the Messenger's Report, inconspicuous though it may seem at first, can give us some insight into this fascinating process of transformation and dramatic integration.

The Messenger's speech in Greek tragedy and Senecan drama

One of the rules laid down by poetics (formulated by Horace in his *Ars Poetica* 182–4) had recommended that certain events which can be represented only imperfectly on the stage should take place off-stage and be reported subsequently in the form of an eye-witness account. This has been taken to be the main reason for the prominence of the messenger's speech in ancient tragedy, but it provides only an external motivation, though an important one. Similarly unconvincing is the argument that narrative as a form of dramatic representation was appropriate to the Greek drama with its relative scarcity of outward events and that this method was also prompted by the limited number of actors available in a Greek theatre. For even with Aeschylus, Sophocles and Euripides the messenger's speech served a wide range of purposes.[1] The great variety of functions which may be fulfilled by the messenger within the dramatic structure makes it impossible to limit his role to one or two definitions. The same would apply to the chorus in ancient tragedy.

However, Shakespeare must have had in mind not so much the messenger in Greek drama (which was largely unknown to his generation) as the use of this convention in Senecan plays and in the so-called classical tragedies of his own time.[2] In Senecan drama the messenger's speeches take up more space than in the Attic tragedy, while their function is less subtle and varied and indeed less 'dramatic'. But in Senecan drama which largely dispenses with movement and action on the stage and favours long speeches, the lengthy messenger's report fits in quite appropriately,[3] tending as it does towards narrative and epic form. For Seneca the messenger's report was all the more necessary as his plots are built around sensational horrifying deeds which were

[1] Cf. Joh. Fischl, *De nuntiis tragicis*, Diss. Wien, 1910.
[2] Cf. *Early English Classical Tragedies*, ed. John W. Cunliffe, Oxford, 1912 (Introduction).
[3] Cf. Clarence W. Mendell, *Our Seneca*, New Haven, 1941, Ch. V.

not permitted to be shown on the stage but had to be related in retrospect. Thus the messenger's reports in Senecan drama often form the climax in the play. In *Thyestes*, for example (well known to the Elizabethans in Heywood's translation), the messenger's report of the frightful feast at which Thyestes devours his own sons takes up the whole of the fourth act (623–788), and forms the actual climax of the play. Similarly in Renaissance plays written after the model of Seneca (first in Italy and then in France and England) the messenger's speech plays an outstanding part.[1]

The messenger's speech in the English classical plays of the sixteenth century

The attempt to conform to Scaliger's *Poetics* (1561) led to an even greater preponderance of the role of the messenger and that of the confidant. Action was replaced more and more by retrospective report. Scaliger would allow on the stage only those actions which according to the laws of probability could have taken place within the span of time covered by the performance. The demand for unity of time and place which was added to the Aristotelian principle of unity of action led to a further curtailment of the action on stage. Thus in 'classical plays' such as *Gorboduc* (1562), *Gismond of Salerne* (1567–8) and *The Misfortunes of Arthur* (1588) we find as a rule not the events themselves, not what we generally call 'the action', but rather its 'before' and 'after', including reflexions on the action and the emotional reactions of the characters. The events themselves, however, are merely reported. In imitation of Seneca, the messenger's speeches in *The Misfortunes of Arthur* and *Gismond of Salerne* take up whole scenes, sometimes of considerable length.[2] The characters reporting need not always be messengers; they can just as well be principal or subsidiary figures in the drama. However, this has no effect on a more organic integration of the report into the interplay between the characters.

[1] Cf. W. Clemen, 'The Set Speech in Renaissance Drama' in *English Tragedy before Shakespeare*, London, 1961.
[2] Cf. act IV, scene II of *Misfortunes* where the messenger is given 213 lines.

The messenger's speech in popular drama and in the Mysteries

The development which goes back to Seneca and English classical drama is only one line of tradition leading up to Shakespeare's use of the messenger's speech. For in the popular plays deriving from the native tradition, action and movement are brought on to the stage, lively dialogue replaces lengthy speech and rhetoric gives way to colloquial language. In these plays which may be represented by dramas of such different character as *Horestes* and *Appius and Virginia* there is no place for elaborate retrospective narrative. Instead we find the short message, sometimes consisting of only a few words. These brief reports may bring the news of the issue of a battle, of approaching enemy armies, of deaths and conspiracies, in short they establish links between the different strands of the plot, building a bridge between the changing scenes of action in the progress of the play. Through this news and information the dramatist supplements his exposition, and puts across to the audience facts and events which belong to his plot.

There is yet a third model for the use of the messenger and the messenger's speech in drama, a model which had been influential up to Shakespeare's time: the Mystery and the Morality Play. In the Mysteries angels appear as heavenly emissaries, as bearers of commands, warnings and sometimes even 'news'. Noah may be ordered to build the ark or Abraham to sacrifice Isaac. But there are also instances of the earthly messenger, the 'nuntius',[1] who may, for example, inform Herod of the flight of the three kings. In the Moralities these celestial and terrestrial messengers have made way for personifications. In *Everyman*, for instance, it is Death who is sent down by God as a bearer of warnings.[2]

The purpose of this short historical survey was to show that at the time when Shakespeare was beginning to write his first plays there were in existence several distinct traditions as to the use of the messenger and the messenger's report. There was, in particular, the striking contrast between the long detailed messenger's speech and the short message. Thus the question arises as to how Shakespeare will combine these

---

[1] The nuntius, in these plays, also acts as Prologue or Epilogue, or assumes a choric function, as pointed out by Howard Baker (*Induction to Tragedy*, Baton Rouge, 1939).

[2] Cf. R. W. Zandvoort, 'The Messenger in the Early English Drama', *English Studies* 3 (1921).

two traditions, how he will integrate the epic and narrative elements, of which the messenger's speech is a typical expression, into his dramatic structure.

The messenger's report in Shakespeare's early histories

Dramatization of the chronicles, with their wealth of events and persons, of political and historical details, is achieved in Shakespeare's early histories at the cost of dramatic cohesion and unity. Shakespeare takes over too many events and episodes from his chronicles and tries to transform them into drama. Consequently the messenger's report has to replace the acted scene and has to fill the gaps in the sequence of events.[1] Being primarily a device for linking events and supplying information, the messenger's report is not much more than a technical expedient. Even a dramatist at the very height of his achievement cannot dispense with such technical devices, but he will integrate them in the texture of his play so that the mechanics become invisible. In Shakespeare's early histories, however, the messenger's speeches are not yet sufficiently integrated and adapted to the needs of the dramatic situation. The messenger's report is as a rule given *en bloc*, whereas in later plays it is divided up into dialogue, and in these early plays it lacks the emotional quality and the characterizing touches which we shall find later on. It is sprung on us without warning and we are not prepared for it. As to the messengers themselves, they are neutral figures without individuality whereas in later plays they are made into sympathetic characters who may be weighed down by the fateful news they bear.

Apart from their expository and informative function the messenger's reports act as an impulse from outside, propelling the action. They prepare the way for new decisions or serve as harbingers of coming events. Thus they sometimes relieve the dramatist from working out an inner motivation. In *Henry VI* the action is moved forward primarily by external factors and among these external factors alarming

---

[1] The valuable article by Gary J. Scrimgeour, 'The Messenger as a Dramatic Device in Shakespeare' (*Shakespeare Quarterly* XIX, 1968), which appeared some years after the publication of the German original of this chapter uses a somewhat different approach and helps to supplement and modify my own findings in several respects. His remarks on Shakespeare's histories are particularly illuminating.

news of disaster ranges foremost. In Shakespeare's tragedies, too, such news, such outward impulses, are indispensable for keeping the action in motion. However, in these later plays, they are no longer the motivation for the resulting action, they merely trigger it off. Action becomes partly a result of characters reacting to an external event, and, in doing so, facing a choice. In the early histories, however, the news delivered by messengers on the loss of territory, on treason, on approaching hostile armies rarely places the recipients in a situation of choice and decision. The character does not yet reveal itself.

The very first scene of *1 Henry VI* serves as an illustration. Here three messengers succeed one another, the third reporting at length on Talbot's capture and defeat. The fatal news brought by these messengers (about the loss of the French provinces, the coronation of the Dauphin, the revolt of English Dukes, etc.) is a means of exposition, it describes the situation which is now menacing England and thus summons the Lords mourning over the past at the bier of King Henry V to immediate action. Nevertheless the dramatic possibilities inherent in this contrast have not been exploited. For these messengers' reports are nothing but mechanical levers to set the action in motion. Moreover, the report given by the third messenger is far too lengthy for the occasion. The second messenger, in exhorting the Lords to noble action ('Awake, awake, English nobility!') does not speak 'in character' but serves as a mouthpiece for the dramatist to point the moral.[1] The theme suggested by the situation as it develops in this scene is 'call to action'. But the speeches and the long epic narrative (about Talbot) are like leaden weights which slow down the dramatic tempo where lively action would be more appropriate.

The histories from *Richard III* onwards show how the messenger's report assumes new functions within the dramatic structure. In the first scene of *1 Henry VI* we noted the accumulation of messengers' reports in one single scene. The same quick succession of reports occurs in the fourth act of *Richard III*, but this time with high dramatic significance. The fourth scene of act IV is one of the longest scenes ever written by Shakespeare (540 lines).[2] It opens with the great choric imprecation

---

[1] This 'departure from realism' is seen by A. C. Sprague as typical of messenger's speeches (*Shakespeare and the Audience*, Camb. Mass., 1935, p. 179).

[2] For a more detailed interpretation see my *Commentary on Shakespeare's Richard III*, 1968.

spoken by the two queens and the Duchess of York. This episode with its melodramatic rhetoric and its static manner of dramatic presentation is marked by that 'ritual' style[1] used by Shakespeare for certain kinds of scenes and situations. The wooing of Elizabeth by Richard which follows is still in the rhetorical-static mode. But then towards the end of the scene the rigidity of confrontation, the almost symmetrical exchange of speech, is broken up and resolves itself into action. The outward world with the impact of new events breaks into the closed circle of the rhetorical debate. Seven messengers, hard on one another's heels, tell of events which presage the downfall and defeat of Richard; namely the approach of Richmond and the falling off of his last friends. These messages constitute reality's reply to the maledictions and curses invoked by the three women at the beginning of the scene. Thus the beginning and end of the scene fit together like two complementary halves; the structural principle of inner correspondences – employed all through the play – finds expression here in the architectonics of a single scene. If in the first part of the scene we have the impression that time is standing still, we experience towards the end of it a violent acceleration of tempo, due to the rapid succession of messengers bursting in one after the other. With bated breath we witness the catastrophe descending upon Richard. Within the structure of the play this series of messages is a token of the inevitability of the fate which now overtakes Richard, of the inexorable course of Nemesis. His destiny had taken a downward course two scenes earlier, and this moment had also been marked by a fateful message (the flight to Richmond of Dorset, whose name is mentioned here for the first time, IV, ii, 47).

However, the messengers' speeches not only function as a constituent part within the structure of the plays, Shakespeare uses them as a means of characterizing the recipient of the news as well. An early instance of this technique occurs in *Henry VI*. In *2 Henry VI* the murderers hired by Suffolk to kill Gloucester report to him on the success of their mission. The king enters and sends Suffolk to fetch Gloucester who presently returns with the news of Gloucester's death. The king's response to this sad message is, however, no longer a well-organized speech. For he swoons and his first words upon awakening are:

[1] Cf. A. P. Rossiter, 'The Structure of *Richard III*', *Durham University Journal*, 1938.

O heavenly God!

It is only then, after another interruption, that a more lengthy utterance follows:

> What, doth my Lord of Suffolk comfort me?
> Came he right now to sing a raven's note,
> Whose dismal tune bereft my vital pow'rs;
> And thinks he that the chirping of a wren,
> By crying comfort from a hollow breast,
> Can chase away the first conceived sound?
> Hide not thy poison with such sug'red words;
> Lay not they hands on me; forbear, I say,
> Their touch affrights me as a serpent's sting.
> Thou baleful messenger, out of my sight!
> Upon thy eye-balls murderous tyranny
> Sits in grim majesty to fright the world.
> Look not upon me, for thine eyes are wounding;
> Yet do not go away; come, basilisk,
> And kill the innocent gazer with thy sight;
> For in the shade of death I shall find joy—
> In life but double death, now Gloucester's dead.
>
> (III, ii, 37)

Here the imparting and receiving of the sorrowful news has been transformed into a complex dramatic situation, in which several elements combine to rouse feelings of tension and sympathy in the audience. First we are let in to Suffolk's plot to kill Gloucester; then the same Suffolk is sent to fetch Gloucester, a stroke of fine dramatic irony; then, as Suffolk returns, we hear the foreboding words of the king, followed by his violent physical reaction to the news of Gloucester's death; and lastly as a conclusion there is his speech addressed to Suffolk and those standing round half guessing who the murderer is, and half shrinking from him. Though this long speech with its artificial antitheses and its rhetorical diction still bears the mark of Shakespeare's early style, it is no longer stiff and monotonous declamation. For we never lose sight of the person it is directed to, even his gestures and looks are mirrored in the king's speech. Furthermore: it is not arguments or abstract reflexions which make up the subject matter of this speech, but rather feelings experienced in the act of speaking, feelings which even force their way through the fence of the antithetical and artificial diction ('forbear, I say'). Here then a piece of news has struck closer to the core than usual and has produced an immediate dramatic effect which is reflected in the language.

The messenger-scene as a means of characterization

It is not, however, until *Richard III* that we can speak of actual characterization through the device of the message. For the messages which throng on the king in the second scene of the fourth act shatter his confidence and destroy his self-discipline: he gives confused and contradictory directions to Ratcliff and Catesby, his speech becomes distracted (455, 470 ff.); uncontrolled, he strikes out at the only one of the seven messengers who is the bearer of good news before he can even open his mouth. Though these are as yet momentary lapses followed by a display of his former firmness, they leave a strong impression on the audience, which becomes aware that a change is taking place in Richard Gloucester.[1]

In *King John*, too, Shakespeare uses messengers' reports which follow one another in quick succession in order to portray the growing uncertainty of the king. But instead of the 'cumulative technique' of seven messengers' reports rigidly following one another without much differentiation we now find a more varied method of dramatic presentation. The very first piece of news we do not hear at all though we witness its communication: King John takes Hubert aside and they whisper together (IV, ii, 68). The audience, however, knows that the subject of their whisperings is Hubert's report on the murder of Arthur (which in fact has not taken place). This is also guessed by the lords who stand by in silent opposition commenting on what is going on between Hubert and the king. They refuse to believe the king when he tells them that Arthur has died from illness and they leave him in open rebellion. The king, however, left on his own, expresses his first feelings of remorse. Thus a message which is not spoken aloud, and which is moreover not in accordance with the truth, has its impact on a whole train of events and leads to quite different reactions. But before Hubert gives the true facts of the case at the end of the scene, new tid-

[1] Cf. my *Commentary on Shakespeare's Richard III*, 1968.

ings of woe hail down upon the king. The overwhelming effect on the king of this calamitous news[1] is reflected by powerful language and suggestive imagery as the following quotations may show:

Enter a Messenger

King John. A fearful eye thou hast: where is that blood
That I have seen inhabit in those cheeks?
So foul a sky clears not without a storm:
Pour down thy weather: how goes all in France?

(IV, ii, 106)

Withhold thy speed, dreadful occasion!

(125)

Thou hast made me giddy
With these ill tidings.

(131)

In the following scenes the series of messengers' news which gives a new impulse to the action and makes us aware of the impending downfall is continued (v, i, 30; v, iii, 5; v, vi, 22; v, vii, 59). It is significant that the king should die just as the Bastard divulges the final disastrous piece of news (v, vii, 64). Thus in the initial scene of the third act the emphasis is again shifted from the message itself to the reactions it provokes. Here we see Constance passionately shaken and deeply disturbed by the news that the French and the English have been reconciled. However, we are not shown the scene in which this news is reported, for the third act begins after this has already happened, although the bearer of this message, Salisbury, remains on stage as an almost silent partner to Constance's monologue-like complaint. We are thus given only what comes after the delivery of the message, its repercussion in the mind of the recipient.

Richard II

In *Richard II*, Shakespeare's manner of using the device of the message

---

[1] In *The Troublesome Raigne of King John* at this point only one piece of news is brought (the landing of a French army). Shakespeare adds the news of Constance's death and of the death of King John's mother. But in a later messenger's scene (*Tr. Raigne* II, vii, 22) he uses the inverse method, replacing the successive arrival of three messengers by only one messenger for all the pieces of news.

as a means of characterization becomes even more manifest. The king lightly passes off the news of Gaunt's death which Northumberland has just brought with the words

> The ripest fruit first falls, and so doth he;
> His time is spent, our pilgrimage must be.
>
> (II, i, 153)

These lines are marked by dramatic irony and disclose the inadequacy of the king's attitude. Then, in the second scene of the third act the king receives a series of reports of which we already know the contents. Thus Shakespeare no longer uses news and messages to bridge the gaps of the action or to cope with the wealth of information which is to be conveyed. The function of this news clearly is to characterize the king. Thus the first piece of news delivered by Salisbury (reporting the desertion of the Welsh troops) provokes the famous conceit by which the king interprets the pallor of his own cheeks in theatrical and posing fashion (III, ii, 75–9). Richard's reaction to the appearance of Scroop who bears another piece of bad news is characteristic in another way: for the king at first refuses to let him speak at all, indulging in high-flown reflections on the present situation. Typical, too, is his reaction to the news that Bushy, Bagot and Green have betrayed him (129) as is his famous long speech

> No matter where – of comfort no man speak.
>
> (III, ii, 144)

a patent attempt to avoid hearing any further news, although Aumerle's pointed question 'Where is the duke my father with his power' is an invitation to Scroop to continue his tale (for which he must wait until much later in the scene). Thus all these messages do not move the king to action but rather to eloquent self-portrayal and indeed to the abandonment of the last vestige of active resistance (211 ff.). But at the same time they help Richard towards an acceptance of the human existence which he shares with all others

> I live with bread like you, feel want,
> Taste grief, need friends; subjected thus,
> How can you say to me I am a king?
>
> (III, ii, 175)

Within the process leading him from self-deception to self-knowledge the news and messages reaching the king's ear can be said to act as an incentive for self-probing introspection.

Henry IV

The two parts of *Henry IV* contain further instances of the way in which the messenger's report is more closely integrated into the play's structure and turned to new uses. In the very first scene, for instance, three different messages (36, 50, 66) are no longer delivered by special messengers but are incorporated in Westmoreland's conversation with the king. Thus our whole attention can be focused on the king – without being interrupted by messengers entering – and we listen intently to his lines about Prince Hal and Hotspur which introduce us to the central theme of the whole play.

The first scene of *2 Henry IV*, however, presents somewhat the reverse process. For here a single piece of important news is split up into three different 'messenger's scenes' which contain contradictory reports and let the facts of the case emerge only gradually. Each time the messenger's scene grows organically out of the dramatic action and is not a mere repetition but a lively variation on the preceding one.

To begin with, the arrival of the messenger, whose role this time is taken over by Lord Bardolph, has been turned into a lively scene in its own right. The messenger knocks at the gate which is opened by the porter, and Northumberland, who is anxiously awaiting the news, is summoned. The delight at the good news he bears sounds through Lord Bardolph's speech ('O such a day/So fought, so followed and so fairly won . . .'), and his report is broken up into dialogue, for it is in answer to Northumberland's questions that he confirms the victory. The two other messengers are also presented as characters of feeling. Travers adds a lively dramatic touch by introducing to his tale the figure of the rider who catches up with him and gives him the latest news:

> After him came spurring hard
> A Gentleman, almost forspent with speed,
> That stopp'd by me to breathe his bloodied horse.
>
> (I, i, 36)

The information itself, fragmentary though it is, is contained in the short space of two lines

> He told me that rebellion had bad luck,
> And that young Harry Percy's spur was cold.
>
> (I, i, 41)

But these lines are framed by the account of the exciting meeting of the two riders – obviously this has taken away the time for a more detailed report on the actual event. The ambiguous phrase 'Harry Percy's spur was cold', casting doubt on the first optimistic version[1] and the subsequent conversation between Northumberland and Lord Bardolph, acts as a forewarning and paves the way for the third message which contains the real news of the disaster. The fatal effect of this final news is heightened by its contrast to the first 'good' news. But Morton, who is the bearer of this news, scarcely needs to speak at all, for Northumberland, whom he has to inform of the death of his son, guesses what the messenger is going to say from his mien and gestures as well as from his halting words. He literally anticipates Morton's disclosure ('This thou wouldst say . . .'). Intuition and guess-work have taken the place of explicit narrative. Northumberland's speech mirrors the as yet unspoken message brought to him by Morton. The message has been, as it were, transferred from the messenger to the recipient. The bare fact of death is so overwhelming here that only much later are we given the actual report of the circumstances surrounding it. But this report itself (105–35) no longer constitutes the centre of this 'messenger's scene'. For the central interest lies in the reaction it provokes and in the way in which its chief contents (Hotspur's death) had intuitively been guessed beforehand. Thus this scene, in which a fatal message is delivered, shows a new form of communication which relies on gesture, acting and implicit statement more than on explicit report.

The difference becomes clear when one compares a similar scene in *3 Henry VI*, in which, too, news of a death is brought (II, i, 43 ff.). Here the detailed account of the circumstances is what matters most, whereas in *Henry IV* this is very much kept in the background. Although in the scene from *Henry VI* the greeting of the messenger and

---

[1] The audience, however, already knows that the first piece of news is not true. A. C. Sprague (*Shakespeare and the Audience*, 1935, p. 178) cites this scene together with two others as examples of messengers reporting something which is untrue.

the brief anticipation of the fatal news may suggest a parallel to the scene with Northumberland, it is only in this later scene that the full human impact and the dramatic potentialities of this tragic situation have been realized.

The messenger in farewell scenes

The role of the messenger in the scenes we have discussed has often been the role of someone who breaks into a closed situation disrupting or disturbing it. His voice may be called the voice of reality reminding those 'inside' of the relentless course of events in the 'outside' world. This holds true of the farewell scenes in particular. The messenger interrupts the intimacy of two people taking leave of each other and brings with him a breath of the hostile world outside. Again a comparison between early and later scenes may be illuminating. Whereas in the two earliest farewell scenes, in 2 *Henry VI* (Gloucester's farewell from the Duchess of Gloucester II, iv; Suffolk's farewell from the queen III, ii) the messenger is a shadowy figure whose only function is to interrupt the lovers' meeting, Northumberland, on the other hand, who appears as a messenger in the farewell scene between the King and Queen in *Richard II* (v, i, 50), acts as a hostile intruder. With him a discordant note of betrayal and insensibility is introduced into the scene. Richard, in the prophetic words he addresses to him, foresees his later role of treachery and thus makes us doubly aware of the dissonance created by Northumberland's entry.

In *Romeo and Juliet* it is the nurse who hastens the leave-taking between the lovers with the news that Lady Capulet is approaching (III, v). Her intrusion, because of the unmistakable individuality of her person, creates that peculiar contrast which is one of the recurring keynotes in this play. A similar type of contrast, but at a higher level, is achieved by Pandarus in *Troilus and Cressida*. As 'messenger' he interrupts on several occasions the lovers' meeting, his pointed comments adding to the note of satire and irony which pervades the whole play.

The messenger's report in double perspective

A characteristic feature of Shakespeare's dramatic art is the way in which he makes us see events or decisions in a double perspective.

Things, characters, situations are looked at from different view-points, so as to present every phenomenon to us in its complexity and to demonstrate that truth has various aspects according to the angle from which one views it. How is this principle of dramatic presentation applied to the messenger's report?

One of the first instances occurs in *Richard III*. In IV, iii Tyrrel gives his royal master an account of the murder of the two princes which he has carried out at the King's behest.[1] For Richard this is good news and he reacts to it with the cynical remark that Tyrrel should come to him again after dinner to give him a more detailed account of the murder, as 'dessert', so to speak. This scene, however, is not shown on the stage, but Tyrrel is given a monologue before his short scene with the king. In this monologue the hangman is shown in quite a different light; with genuine horror and remorse he gives a moving account of the death of the two princes. This 'messenger's speech' is obviously meant for the audience, which thus is in a better position to share the emotion roused by the princes' murder and to sense the cynical anticlimax of Richard's reaction. Comparing the role played by Tyrrel to that of the hired murderer in pre-Shakespearian drama (who also acts as messenger to report on the execution of the deed) the new development is manifest. This art of casting light on the messenger's report from various angles is exemplified also in *Richard II*. In II, ii Green brings the Queen the news of Bolingbroke's approach and the defection of the Lords. But this information is in effect only the confirmation of the Queen's vague presentiment expressed at the beginning of the scene.[2] The message is thus linked to the preceding forebodings of its recipient, but we have also been prepared for it by the information in the previous scene.

There is a similar correspondence between the inner mood of a character and the news from outside a little further on in the same scene. When York appears (77) his figure and his words convey an atmosphere of anxiety and hopelessness. Shortly afterwards (97) a servant brings him the news that his wife has died. Even in the very rhythm of his lines his despair at this message, the saddest of all, is expressed:

[1] For more detailed comment see my *Commentary on Shakespeare's Richard III*, London, 1968, p. 171.
[2] Cf. Chapter I. p. 33.

what a tide of woes
Comes rushing on this woeful land at once!
I know not what to do.

(II, ii, 98)

Once again in *Richard II* the Queen is the recipient of fatal news, although this news reaches her in an unusual manner. In the famous garden-scene (III, iv) she involuntarily overhears the talk between the gardener and his men which contains – among other things – the news of the impending deposition of the King. The Queen thus receives this information not through the direct medium of a messenger but as an unseen witness to a conversation.

The messenger in the tragedies

In the tragedies one is struck by the different treatment of messengers and messengers' reports according to the degree of importance and dramatic relevance. Whenever Shakespeare needs the message merely to convey some relevant facts he slips it in almost unnoticed. Thus in *Othello* he disposes of the Turkish war intentions once they have fulfilled their function in the exposition with remarkable brevity (II, i, 20).[1] In other places, however, where he could use the messenger's report for dramatic purpose, he turned it into an effective element by which the whole scene gains in meaning.

Thus at the end of the scene in which Caesar is murdered on the Capitol a servant arrives to bring Antony the news of Octavius' approach (III, i, 277). Seeing the corpse he breaks off in the middle of his message and tears come to his eyes. What Antony had expressed beforehand through words is now, at the end of this memorable scene, conveyed again by means of a simple gesture and a telling silence.

At other times, however, the use of the messenger in *Julius Caesar* is not much different from what we often find in pre-Shakespearian plays. Thus at the beginning of act v a messenger arrives to tell the two generals, Octavius and Antony, who are waiting with their troops armed for battle, that the enemy is close at hand. Directly afterwards the opposing army makes its appearance. This use of the messenger to

[1] Cf. H. Granville-Barker, *Prefaces to Shakespeare, Fourth Series, Othello*, London, 1942, p. 2.

give advance notice, as it were, of approaching people, heralding the entry of princes or announcing the arrival of important persons, may be regarded as a convention of the Elizabethan stage[1] and ranks among the obvious devices of preparation. Shakespeare adopts this device and in the early histories and even here in *Julius Caesar* these advance messages contain little more than the mere facts. However, looking at *Hamlet* we find this device of an 'advance message' used with deliberate art as a means of heightening the audience's keen expectation.[2] There are two instances in IV, v. Shortly before Ophelia appears on the stage in her mental derangement, a 'Gentleman' arrives to give the queen an account of Ophelia's altered behaviour, an appropriate preparation for her ensuing tragic appearance. A little later in the same scene Laertes forces his way into the palace with a band of outraged Danes. Again a 'Gentleman' heralds the event shortly beforehand, but he does not limit his announcement to the bare fact. Vividly describing Laertes with his companions he creates an atmosphere of excitement and anxiety, preparing the way for the agitated dramatic scene which follows.

A number of similar instances of Shakespeare's 'art of preparation' could be quoted in which a 'Gentleman', a servant, or a neutral minor character is employed to give a preliminary report or announce a forthcoming scene. But the most remarkable example of this occurs in *Othello*, II, i, where no less than four 'Gentlemen' report on what they can make out on the high seas and in the harbour below, thus heightening the expectation for the arrival of the ships carrying Desdemona and eventually Othello.[3] Their words again are much more than factual information, for they convey a vivid picture of the sea, the storm and the approaching ships, providing a colourful and significant background for the conversation which is going on among those waiting. Shakespeare has here brought to perfection the device of linking one scene which is taking place on stage with another one off-stage. The theatrical convention of 'teichoscopy' used as early as in Aeschylus' *Persians* is revived here in a dramatically effective manner. For in the *Persians* the account of the naval battle was given in one lengthy messenger's speech, complete in itself, while the action on the stage was

[1] Cf. e.g. *Troublesome Raigne*, Part II, III, 151; VIII, 110.
[2] For further examples see p. 63.
[3] Cf. the discussion of this scene in Chapter 1.

completely suspended. In *Othello*, however, by breaking up the report on what happens on the sea into fragments which are inserted into the conversation on the stage Shakespeare has contrived to combine two parallel actions into one simultaneous process.

The delivery of letters by messengers

Likewise in *Othello* we can observe a new development in the use of another variation of the message, namely the delivering of a letter by a messenger. The device of a letter delivered and read aloud or silently frequently occurs in Shakespeare's plays, particularly in his comedies. But this would deserve a study of its own, for a number of new problems which lie outside the scope of this essay would have to be dealt with. In this connexion the instance to be found at the beginning of act IV of *Othello* must be sufficient. For here the message addressed to Othello in the form of a letter is not read aloud at all but is shown in its shattering effect on Othello. The opening and reading of this letter is skilfully blended with the conversation which develops between Desdemona and Lodovico. Our only intimation of what this letter has to say is gathered from a single disconnected sentence which Othello reads out at one point (223) and an explanatory comment on the part of Lodovico (232). The letter prompts Desdemona to make another unfortunate remark in Cassio's favour and this, together with the hurtful effect which the letter has on him, incites Othello to that inconsiderate outbreak of wrath in which he strikes Desdemona. As with the messages which are much shortened, or not even conveyed in words at all, this scene again shows that it is the effect rather than the actual contents of a message which Shakespeare is interested in for his dramatic purpose.

Messenger-scenes in Macbeth

Even more illuminating for the way in which earlier uses of the messenger's report reappear in a more integrated form is *Macbeth*. In *Richard III* and in *King John* (see p. 105) we observed the function of messengers' news to indicate the downward trend in the hero's tragic career. In *Macbeth*, there are three messengers' reports (one in v, iii; two in v, v) which mark the turning-point of Macbeth's career. But compared to the histories the impact of these reports on Macbeth's inner mood is portrayed with much greater intensity. The news (of the approach of the English army v, iii; of the moving of Birnam Wood towards Dunsinane v, v) not only shatters Macbeth's self-confidence, it also makes him foresee his own final downfall and makes him 'to be aweary of the sun' (v, v, 49). His reaction to the news of his wife's death (of which we hear at the beginning of this scene v, v, 17) reveals to us the empty hopelessness into which his soul has fallen ('To-morrow, and to-morrow, and to-morrow'). In each case then the message leads to a self-revelation which discloses to us the tragedy which is evolving in Macbeth himself.

Another function of the messenger's report had been to interrupt a 'static scene' by news from outside, acting as a new impetus for the action which had come to a standstill (see p. 101). In *Macbeth* the long conversation between Malcolm and Macduff (IV, iii) is interrupted first by the 'Doctor' who reports on the miraculous cures effected by the King;[1] and shortly afterwards by Ross who – in striking contrast to this 'good' news – brings the deadly news of the murder of Lady Macduff and her children. Even more than in earlier plays the very act of delivering tragic news has been turned by Shakespeare into a moving scene in which silence and gesture partly take the place of communication by words. The messenger at first does not have the courage to tell the truth. Twice he evades the issue, saying something else which appears reassuring although the truth is already concealed in the irony of his words ('No, they were well at peace when I did leave them', IV, iii, 179). But it is only after he has expressed his horror at what he does not dare to tell that the message is eventually conveyed. For the audience, however, who had witnessed the murder of Macduff's children shortly before (IV, ii), these intimations and evasions on the part of the messenger are fraught with particular meaning and tension. This then is a message of which the audience already not only knows the full contents, the reported event has even been witnessed in the preceding scene. The message thus does not replace an off-stage scene but mirrors what had

---

[1] John Dover Wilson in his edition of *Macbeth* (Cambridge, 1947, p. XXXII) assigns this passage only 'slight dramatic relevance' and takes it for a later addition. But the passage becomes dramatically meaningful if we take into consideration its contrast with what follows and the resulting comparison between the 'true prince' and the tyrant.

already been shown to us, the emphasis, however, being again on the reaction of the recipient and the feelings of the messenger. In these scenes then (to which others could be added – e.g. *Antony and Cleopatra* IV, xiv, 27) the messenger has ceased to be the neutral bearer of news and has become a sensitive human being, who conveys the bad news as sparingly and tactfully as he can, is himself affected by the import of the message and plays an active part in the scene in which he appears. Seneca, it is true, had also depicted the messenger as being moved by ill tidings (e.g. *Thyestes* IV), but the message itself, which with him was the chief concern, was in no way attuned to the sensibilities of the recipient, nor was the 'act of delivery', the confrontation of messenger and recipient, turned into a dramatic scene in its own right. Shakespeare appears to have been the first to do this.

The second scene of *Macbeth* contains a messenger's report which poses a new problem which we have not so far discussed. For the bombastic and stylized diction of this messenger's speech has given rise to criticism of various kinds.[1] Did Shakespeare deliberately use this style in order to colour this report and to mark its epic mode? Or did he not write this scene at all? The Cambridge Editors had in fact doubted the authenticity of the whole scene: 'The bombastic phraseology of the sergeant is not like Shakespeare's language even when he is most bombastic', they wrote in 1869, whereas Cuningham, the editor of the Arden Edition (1912) called it 'a corrupt piece of bombast'. However, more recent criticism[2] has justified the passage on the very grounds that Shakespeare used this heightened artificial style as an appropriate medium for this particular messenger's report which is thus set off from its context. Shakespeare availed himself of the conventional pattern of antiquated epic diction, including exaggerated bombast, to bring about an ironic contrast between the first occasion when Macbeth is mentioned at any length *in absentia* and his personal appearance in the next scene.[3]

But the *Macbeth* scene is not the only instance of a 'report' which

---

[1] Cf. the notes in the editions of *Macbeth* by Kenneth Muir (New Arden, London, 1951) and J. Dover Wilson (1947).

[2] Cf. the important article by J. M. Nosworthy 'The Bleeding Captain Scene in *Macbeth*', *Review of English Studies*, 22 (1946).

[3] A similar case of the use of an antiquated epic style suited to the occasion occurs in the famous Player's Speech in *Hamlet* which has also found favourable explication only in recent years. Cf. Harry Levin in *The Kenyon Review* XII, 1950.

bears marks of conscious stylization.[1] In *1 Henry IV* Vernon brings
Hotspur the news that the royal army is approaching:

> All plum'd like estridges, that with the wind
> Bated like eagles having lately bath'd;
> Glittering in golden coats, like images;
> As full of spirit as the month of May
> And gorgeous as the sun at midsummer;
> Wanton as youthful goats, wild as young bulls.

(IV, i, 98)

This extravagant display of imagery is certainly intended to lend ironic
overtones to the glaring and boastful approach of the enemy army.
Apart from that the passage tends to resemble the exuberant diction,
rich in hyperbole and metaphor, used by Hotspur, one of those characters in *Henry IV* to whom Shakespeare has given an unmistakable
individual style of speech.

Other kinds of 'report' in Shakespeare's plays

The messenger's report is by no means the only kind of report to be
found in Shakespeare's plays. Even with the instances discussed so far
it has not always been a messenger, a 'Gentleman', a servant, who
carried the news or gave the report but it has sometimes been one of the
play's regular characters who took over this role. These gliding transitions between a message delivered by a neutral person and an account
of an off-stage event given by one of the characters involved make it
difficult to draw a sharp dividing line and to define the messenger's
report properly. The messenger's report, as we have already seen,
easily develops into dramatic narrative which is used by Shakespeare
in many places for retrospective accounts or for building up, in the
audience's imagination, the background of dramatic impressions which
accumulate behind the foreground of the stage-action. Dramatic
narrative, however, is a complex phenomenon which would call for
special treatment.[2] Nevertheless the development of the messenger's
report must be seen within this wider context. For both messenger's

---

[1] Cf. too, *Richard II*, III, ii, 104.
[2] See the illuminating study by Kurt Schlüter, *Shakespeares dramatische Erzählkunst*; Schriftenreihe der Deutschen Shakespeare-Gesellschaft, Band VII, 1958.

report and 'narrative' make us ask how Shakespeare incorporates epic elements, how he makes characters given an account of off-stage events of past episodes. The striking preponderance of epic, descriptive and narrative elements in the early histories compared to the later plays must not lead us to the false assumption that Shakespeare simply excluded these epic elements and narrative passages from his tragedies and later histories. In fact he retained the art of relating past events or off-stage happenings which had been one of the main features of Senecan drama. But he dramatized these elements to such an astonishing degree that they become an organic part of the play in performance. In order to supplement our study of the messenger's report by a short digression into this related field of enquiry, it may be worthwhile to pick out from numerous instances a few passages illustrating this development which, as it were, runs parallel to the evolution of the messenger's report.

As early as *Richard II* we find an illuminating example of 'dramatized narrative'. In v, ii, York gives the Duchess an account of Richard and Bolingbroke's arrival in London. This lively narrative, once again towards the end of the play, epitomizes the contrast between the two great antagonists, expressing it this time by depicting an unforgettable scene which we experience with dramatic intensity although it is 'merely narrated'. Only the first twenty lines of the whole passage are quoted here:

Duchess.	My lord, you told me you would tell the rest,
	When weeping made you break the story off,
	Of our two cousins' coming into London.
York.	Where did I leave?
Duchess.	At that sad stop, my lord,
	Where rude misgoverned hands from windows' tops
	Threw dust and rubbish on King Richard's head.
York.	Then, as I said, the Duke, great Bolingbroke
	Mounted upon a hot and fiery steed
	Which his aspiring rider seem'd to know,
	With slow but stately pace kept on his course,
	Whilst all tongues cried 'God save thee, Bolingbroke!'
	You would have thought the very windows spake,
	So many greedy looks of young and old

> Through casements darted their desiring eyes
> Upon his visage; and that all the walls
> With painted imagery had said at once
> 'Jesu preserve thee! Welcome, Bolingbroke!'
> Whilst he, from the one side to the other turning,
> Bareheaded, lower than his proud steed's neck,
> Bespake them thus, 'I thank you, countrymen'.
> And thus still doing, thus he pass'd along.

Duchess. Alack, poor Richard! where rode he the whilst?

(V, ii, 1)

The description of the scene begins when York's report is already half over so that we join the speakers in the middle of a conversation. Many small details betray the emotion and interest of the speaker and the listener, although this is conveyed to us indirectly, by the rendering of the gestures, movements and words of those who appear in this scene. We ourselves become spectators of this scene in the street but our own perspective clashes with the perspective of the spectators within the picture, those young and old onlookers whose 'many greedy looks' and 'desiring eyes' are described by York. The way in which the typical bearing of horse and rider have been caught, with a sharp eye for detail, the way the whole street comes alive, the sparing use of direct speech and, in particular, the manner in which the emotional impact and significance of this 'symbolic scene' is brought home to us by means of visual description – all this betrays a master's hand.

York's report was the account of a scene which could not have been acted on the stage. In the tragedies, however, we sometimes come across cases where the narrative method was chosen although the happenings related could have been turned into an effective dramatic scene. To account for this by arguing that Shakespeare wanted to shorten the play is not a satisfactory explanation, especially as it would scarcely have taken longer – in some cases at least – to present the scene in dramatic form than in narrative. These and other explanations[1] silently assume that narration of events in a play is merely an expedient.

---

[1] Cf. the explanation given by Janet Spens (*Elizabethan Drama*, London, 1922, p. 18): 'In Shakespeare's theatre boys acted the women's parts and he seems to have become increasingly conscious of their inadequacy to the great moments. The messenger's speech used with greater frequency as time went on is probably partly to be accounted for in this way.'

However, Shakespeare has used narrative in such a way as to achieve special effects which the enacted scene could not offer.

We find an excellent example in the second scene of *Julius Caesar*. Part of the tension and the dramatic effect in this scene derives from its being linked to an off-stage scene which takes place simultaneously. For after his first short appearance Caesar leaves the stage to render himself to the Capitol where the crown is offered to him. We have some inkling of this event as the cheers of the crowd can be heard in the distance while on the stage a dialogue between Brutus and Cassius goes on. Then Caesar reappears and the feeling grows that something important has happened behind the scenes. After Caesar has left again the account of what has happened is gradually coaxed out of Casca who remains behind. The questions put to him by those who want to hear the whole story contribute to the fragmentation of the account and its integration in the current dialogue. The first part of Casca's report is quoted here:

> *Brutus.* Tell us the manner of it, gentle Casca.
>
> *Casca.* I can as well be hang'd as tell the manner of it: it was mere foolery; I did not mark it. I saw Mark Antony offer him a crown — yet 'twas not a crown neither, 'twas one of these coronets — and, as I told you, he put it by once; but for all that, to my thinking, he would fain have had it. Then he offered it to him again; then he put it by again; but to my thinking, he was very loath to lay his fingers off it. And then he offered it the third time; he put it the third time by; and still as he refus'd it, the rabblement hooted, and clapp'd their chopt hands, and threw up their sweaty night-caps, and uttered such a deal of stinking breath because Caesar refus'd the crown, that it had almost choked Caesar; for he swooned and fell down at it. And for mine own part I durst not laugh, for fear of opening my lips and receiving the bad air.

Even this short quotation can show that Casca's account fulfils several functions at one time. The blunt, straight-forward prose,[1] the baldness and directness of description, is in keeping with Casca's character and

---

[1] For Shakespeare's use of prose in this passage cf. Milton Crane, *Shakespeare's Prose*, Chicago, 1951, p. 142; Brian Vickers, *The Artistry of Shakespeare's Prose*, London, 1968, p. 246.

his way of looking at the world, but the report also conveys the over-tone of contempt and disrespect towards Caesar which had been expressed earlier on by Cassius and is now taken up by Casca. It thus affects Brutus and Cassius, for it incites them to continue what they had hinted at in their earlier conversation. The account contains, too, some significant details which a dramatic presentation could not have pro-vided. The audience is invited here to look at the scene described by Casca through the eyes of one of the future conspirators, and the cold and cynical light it sheds on his personality will be an important factor in the forthcoming conspiracy. As to Caesar himself, this account modifies the preparation for his second appearance (see p. 50). Caesar is deliberately kept in the background, but the reports and comments about him given while he is absent, supplement to a considerable degree the method of direct presentation and are an essential means of characterization.

Our last example of a 'reported scene' is the account given by the Gentleman in *King Lear* (IV, iii) of his visit to the French court (where Kent had sent him in III, i, to take a letter to Cordelia). This scene described by the Gentleman could also have been realized with great effect on the stage, and at first sight it may even seem surprising that Shakespeare relinquished this chance of showing Cordelia's reaction to the news of her father's fate. For Cordelia, though one of the tragedy's main characters, appears only seldom and then briefly – indeed she does not speak more than a hundred lines in the whole play. The Gentleman's report contributes to the particular effect of Cordelia's rare appearance. For during his account Cordelia's presence is felt and yet she is far away; after this moving description of her reaction on receiving the letter we long all the more for her to appear on the scene as a good angel bringing help. The Gentleman's report therefore paves the way for the reappearance of Cordelia who has been excluded for quite a long time from the action. Through this report our sympathy and regard for Cordelia are revived and a new and full vision of her is imprinted on our imagination. For the Gentleman's descrip-tion is given with partiality, vividness, and precision of detail, convey-ing to us her every change of expression, every gesture, every word. Indeed his account comes near the detailed sketch of a dramatic scene, but it succeeds in conveying some things which the scene if it had been acted out could not have included, such as the reaction of those listening to this report. Shakespeare gives us here, as it were, a three-dimensional rather than a two-dimensional picture. Kent's important comment 'It is the stars,/The stars above us, govern our conditions;' (IV, iii, 32) also fits naturally here, and his account of Lear's change of mind with regard to Cordelia can be added as a reply to the 'Gentleman's' story, thus preparing us for Lear's recovery and the loving reconciliation which will take place at the end of this act.

Reviewing Shakespeare's tragedies with the aim of establishing principles for the occurrence and the classification of certain types of the 'narrated scene' and of the messenger's report we shall constantly be thwarted in our efforts by Shakespeare's inventiveness and the wealth of variations he uses. There are many transitions between the various types and he constantly enriches and modifies the traditional patterns. It is not possible (*fortunately* not possible we ought to add!) to lay down definite rules. If, for instance, one were to point out that in *King Lear* Shakespeare seems to follow the principle of classical drama whereby messengers report atrocities instead of showing them on the stage, one would be forced at the same time to mention that the terrible blinding of Gloucester is shown to us without restraint (III, vii) but is also subsequently reported by a 'Messenger' (IV, ii). And there are reasons for both, just as arguments can be adduced for not presenting on the stage Goneril's murder of Regan and stabbing of herself, or the hanging of Cordelia in prison.

Similar problems arise if we look in conclusion at two late tragedies in which messengers' reports are fairly frequent, *Antony and Cleopatra* and *Coriolanus*. For again it is unsatisfactory to explain the frequency of messenger's reports in both tragedies by the fact that the several scenes of action of each play are far removed from one another so that the messenger has to act as go-between. Likewise the explanation that warfare in these plays takes on larger proportions and cannot be coped with dramatically without the old device of the message would be an over-simplification. Both explanations, though not false, touch on extraneous motivation only. For we would have to consider above all the dramatic function and integration of these messengers' reports which contribute considerably to the pace, tension and movement of the action in both plays, so that in each case they mean more than just the imparting of some necessary piece of information or the supplying of a link in the chain of events. Especially in *Antony and Cleopatra* the messengers going to and fro between the lovers help to convey the sense of their unique relationship, the tension, the longing, the intensity of feeling which exist between them.

An illuminating example which must stand for several others occurs in II, v, for this scene, in which the messenger from Italy brings Cleopatra the news of Antony's marriage to Octavia, represents a climax in the dramatization of a simple message. The news is drawn out over eighty-five lines of hasty dialogue, of stormy questioning and attempted answers which are cut off again to give way to invective, threats and bribes. Of these eighty-five lines Cleopatra herself, the recipient of the message, speaks no less than sixty-one. The whole range of violent and contradictory emotions, of ardent passion and unbridled rage is put across in word and action in the course of this messenger's scene. In this episode the transformation of what was once the messenger's report almost reaches the point of dissolution. For the message has become part of an exciting exchange between two partners, a small drama in its own right. If, to complete the picture, we take III, ii (in which the same messenger describes Octavia) and IV, xiv, in which Antony receives the news of Cleopatra's death (which is shortly afterwards recanted by Diomedes arriving in breathless haste but all too late), then we have in *Antony and Cleopatra* alone material of sufficient scope to illustrate the characterizing function of the message, and its role as a focal point within a new pattern of dramatic situations. For in *Antony and Cleopatra* the message of the histories, bringing news of battles, conspiracies and approaching troops, has developed into a means of communication not tied to political events which enables two lovers to reach out to one another in moments of crisis and of decision. The messenger and the message serve here to express spiritual presence despite physical absence, one of the play's recurring motifs. The brief words of the messenger suffice to conjure up in the mind of the recipient a vivid image of the absent beloved, and they may bridge the distance between east and west which is again and again evoked as the spatial dimension peculiar to this play.

The use of messengers and messages in Shakespeare's comedies and in his romances would offer some additional interesting viewpoints[1]

[1] For examples chosen from Shakespeare's comedies see the illuminating article by Gary J. Scrimgeour 'The Messenger as a Dramatic Device in Shakespeare', *Shakespeare Quarterly* XIX, 1968.

but our study has deliberately been limited to Shakespeare's histories and tragedies, for it is here that we can trace the development of a device which becomes a subtle instrument of Shakespeare's dramatic technique. As we have seen, Shakespeare not only assigned to the messenger's report new functions, integrating it into the dramatic texture by various methods, he also used it as a means of revealing human qualities and reactions in poignant dramatic situations. A technical device for imparting information has become a mirror of human relationships.

3
Past and Future
in Shakespeare's Drama

When Hamlet refers to the nature of man as 'looking before and after' Shakespeare here epitomizes a characteristic feature which can be detected on almost every page in his plays. For Shakespeare's characters though acting in the present invariably glance back to what has happened and look ahead to what is coming. What, in our daily existence, remains closed up within the mind and rarely reaches the level of spoken utterance, the constant flow of our thoughts either into the future or the past, becomes explicit and articulate in Shakespeare's dramatic characters. This applies to be sure in varying degree to most plays of the dramatic literature of the world. There is almost no drama without some reference to past and future. But the way in which the dramatists have made use of past and future for the structure of their plays differs widely and is often in many respects revealing. For the understanding of Shakespeare's plays, too, the relationship between past and future is of the greatest significance. It opens up an approach to the time structure in the plays; it is closely connected not only with the art of preparation, of exposition and of suspense, but also with the fundamental principles of composition. As in so many other respects Shakespeare displays 'infinite variety' in this field. For the specific function of retrospect and foreboding, of past and future, changes almost from play to play. Followed up throughout his work, however, Shakespeare's changing treatment of past and future could not only serve as a measure for the evolution of his dramatic art, but could also disclose to us some of his fundamental attitudes.

For with this subject there are always two sides involved, an element of dramatic technique and a problem of meaning and attitude. For one thing, retrospect and preparation are indispensable dramatic devices, important means of linking together separate situations, of giving unity and coherence to a play, of arousing expectation and tension, of creating contrasts and parallels within the play. References to the past, in particular, are absolutely necessary for the purpose of exposition. It was only a few years ago that a contemporary playwright, Arthur Miller, called this technique of 'how to dramatize what has gone before' 'the biggest single dramatic problem'.[1]

But Shakespeare never stopped short at mere devices. Out of procedures which were required by dramatic technique he created relationships which are conditioned by character and theme. We can watch a device becoming an attitude, a dramatic mechanism being transformed into meaningful utterance which grows out of the character's own inner life. The study of past and future in Shakespeare's plays, if carried out on a larger scale, could indeed teach us something about the connexion between dramatic technique and the expression of inner meaning. In each drama we discover a network of references to past and to future, but these fall into many different categories and operate, as it were, on several levels. Such passages and references range from merely informative hints, recapitulations, and announcements to retrospective narratives of some length or visions of the future which open up new vistas and take us to the very core of the play through their imaginative richness and their meaningful implications.

In short, we are faced with a vast and complex subject which cannot possibly be treated extensively in a single lecture. I shall therefore not examine the individual examples of retrospect and preparation or the roles of past and future separately, but shall restrict myself to the question of how Shakespeare links past and future in a particular situation or in the consciousness of an individual character. For there are, in some plays, key-scenes or crucial passages in which past and future are juxtaposed, and we also find certain characters who possess an intense awareness of both past and future. In such focal scenes and in such characters the relationship between past and future is sometimes crystallized and we may take them with some assurance as a starting-point from which a few general outlines as to the treatment of past and future in that particular play can be drawn.

In doing this we shall have to distinguish between the objective past anterior to the play's beginning, the past within the span of the drama, and the subjective manner in which this past is reflected in the minds of characters. If, first of all, we consider the past which is prior to the play's beginning we arrive at a conclusion that sounds almost

[1] Arthur Miller, Preface to *Collected Plays*, 1958, p. 21.

paradoxical in view of our subject. For, except for the histories, only very few of the plays are preceded by a past that is of decisive importance for the further course of the action, a past that could act as a pressure on the present and as a momentum for the future. Contrary to what we see in Greek drama and contrary, too, to the structure of Senecan drama, which constantly dwells upon the past, Shakespeare makes us watch the conflict leading up to the catastrophe (or to the happy end) from its inception.[1] Sometimes the hero in the first scene (as in *King Lear* or in *The Winter's Tale*) creates his own past from which not only his tragic course but also the fatal actions of others derive. This early and decisive event may then become in the mind of the hero a past which reverberates in his memory and towards which his own attitude may eventually change. But this past does not precede the play. And where we have in some plays events or conditions prior to the first scene, they are not of vital importance but just one of several important factors. For neither Othello's abduction of Desdemona, nor Antony's 'dotage' on Cleopatra, nor Caesar's rise to power nor the ancient grudge between the two houses in *Romeo and Juliet* are events that would necessarily constitute a conflict and lead up to a catastrophe. Apart from the histories there appear to be no more than three plays, *The Comedy of Errors*, *Hamlet*, and *The Tempest*, which are preceded by a past that would cast its shadow over the whole course of the action and determine the future.

We find this linking of past and future, however, most conspicuously in the histories and we shall therefore treat them first. In these plays Shakespeare not only handled episodes from the historical past but he translated into drama elements inherent in history itself. For history demonstrates to us how the past grows into the present and leads on to the future. And as the heroes in Shakespeare's histories are kings, princes, and statesmen, they must necessarily act as agents of their country's history; they are carried along by the current of history that flows from the past towards the future and to some extent it is they who guide this current. In Shakespeare's histories an unfulfilled past calls for fulfilment in the future; guilt from the past will cast its shadow for a long time over the present and even over the future. But this future will nevertheless contain a potential new beginning. To a greater extent than his contemporaries in the field of historical drama, but also with

[1] Cf. M. Mincoff, in *Shakespeare Survey* 3 (1950), pp. 59 ff.

more explicitness and cogency than the chronicles of Hall and Holinshed (as Paul Reyher has shown),[1] Shakespeare, in his histories, estab-
lishes a close connexion between past and future. He makes us see how
an inescapable line of development arises from the pressure of the past
on the future. The future is forestalled and foreshadowed in many
ways; it is linked to the past by the inexorable workings of destiny and
necessity, but so it is also by clear planning and purposeful intention.
'The Shakespearean characters are never allowed to forget that they
stand between a remembered past and an anticipated future.' Thus a
recent critic, Mr Driver, has summarized this particular connexion.[2]

The various conceptions underlying the dramatic presentation: the
notion of Nemesis, of divine providence, of punishment and redemption, but also the cyclical nature of history as represented in the two
tetralogies, invariably affect the connexion between past and future.
Moreover, Shakespeare has used the past to illuminate the contemporary present. He makes his audience recognize their own political
problems in the issues of his historical plays, and he brings home to
them the fact that the past episode mirrors the contemporary scene in
the same way as it repeats what has happened in an earlier part of the
cycle of histories. In Shakespeare's histories, the audience is expected
to look beyond the end of the play, just as it is taught to glance far back
to earlier times. 'With an instinctive propriety Shakespeare provides his
English histories with a conclusion that is yet to be concluded' as Peter
Alexander has put it.[3]

But how does this over-all pattern (which has often been commented
on by critics such as E. M. W. Tillyard, John Dover Wilson, Lily
Campbell, M. M. Reese, Clifford Leech) crystallize in a single figure or
a single scene? How is it turned to dramatic account? We take as our
first example the figure of Margaret in *Richard III*. In order to make
her appear in this play Shakespeare has altered the chronology, for
according to history she would have been dead long before. But Shakespeare obviously wanted her to step into this play as an embodiment of a
remote past to prophesy the impending future. Thus she is herself a
link between past and future. Margaret does not take part in the action

[1] P. Reyher, *Essai sur les idées dans l'œuvre de Shakespeare*, Paris, 1947.
[2] T. F. Driver, *The Sense of History in Greek and Shakespearean Drama*, Columbia
U.P., 1960, p. 97.
[3] *A Shakespeare Primer*, Welwyn, Herts., 1951, p. 70.

of the play, but looks at it from a distance, surveying and commenting on the course of things as if she were an onlooker. She thus resembles the chorus in Greek tragedy. In her indictments, imprecations, and prophecies Margaret includes almost all characters who have been guilty in the course of time, she recalls the curses and the crimes of the past, looks through the entanglements of the present and foretells the future.

> Let me put in your minds, if you forget,
> What you have been ere this, and what you are;
>
> (I, iii, 131–2)

These lines introduce us to her method. For by weighing past guilt or past greatness against the present state of misery or false security she can predict the future. From Margaret we learn that the faculty of prophecy grows out of an awareness of the past and a clear perception of the present, an idea which is most clearly formulated in *2 Henry IV* (where Warwick comments on Richard II's prophecy about Northumberland).

> There is a history in all men's lives,
> Figuring the natures of the times deceas'd;
> The which observ'd, a man may prophesy,
> With a near aim, of the main chance of things
> As yet not come to life, who in their seeds
> And weak beginning lie intreasured.
>
> (III, i, 80)

The two great scenes in which Margaret plays this role of prophetess and commentator (I, iii; IV, iv) are scenes of incantation and lamentation. The action comes almost to a halt while the pressure of the terrible guilt in the past and the imminent punishment or impending doom in the future are brought home to us. This static quality is also evident in the choric scene in which three citizens bemoan the past and express their apprehension as to the future (II, iii). In his later plays Shakespeare abandons this static method of surveying past and present, he weaves retrospect and prognostication into the action as it advances, into the dramatic discourse and conflict. The systematic manner in which Margaret metes out her curses and predictions, balancing past guilt, present misery, and future retribution in symmetrically built lines, suggests a kind of inevitable logic; her arraignments sometimes resemble balanced accounts. This corresponds to Shakespeare's characteristic mode in this play, which aims at explicitness, systematization, fullness, and recapitulation. The same systematic treatment of past and future recurs in the fifth act where the ghosts of all the victims murdered by Richard appear one after the other before him (and before Richmond). Their pronouncements alternately recall Richard's crimes and predict his ruin, while they promise a victorious future to Richmond. Again the linking of past and future is condensed into recurring formulas (just as in Margaret's curses) which are arranged in symmetrical pairs.

Clarence's dream narrative can, however, be quoted as an exception to this rather rigid systematization of past and future. This dream is both a recapitulation and a foreshadowing, but it is conveyed in an imaginative symbolic manner, rich in poetic suggestiveness and not by direct statement.

The wealth of references to past crimes or past guilt and their ensuing retribution, scattered all over the play, brings home to us with an almost insistent explicitness the 'moral lesson' of *Richard III*. But the range of these many references is nevertheless narrow, for the link between past and future is restricted – with only few exceptions – to the crime-punishment pattern. Of all plays by Shakespeare *Richard III* has been held (and in particular by Friedrich Schiller) to come nearest to Greek Tragedy, since the working of nemesis is shown here with the same unrelenting logic. This gives rise to the question as to whether Shakespeare intended to demonstrate the idea of predetermination in this play. But the course of action here has not been previously laid down by a divine oracle which, regardless of individual responsibility, determines the future course of destiny as in Sophocles' *Oedipus Rex*. For in *Richard III* we can see how each character becomes guilty (or how he became guilty in the past), and we can often see the cross-ways at which a character must make his choice. The future in this play is forecast but not inexorably pre-determined. We must, however, admit that the problem of the secret interplay between man's free will, God's divine providence, and the predictability of the future is more convincingly dramatized in the later tragedies than in this early history.

But the abundance of references to past and future[1] in *Richard III*

---

[1] For further examples see my *Commentary on Shakespeare's Richard III*, London, 1968.

provokes criticism in yet another respect. For a past and a future which are evoked incessantly and on every conceivable occasion cease to be dimensions of remoteness. The past no longer resides in the depths of the mind from which it has to be resuscitated by a special act of remembrance. It is altogether too present, too obtrusive, too much a matter of course; there is too much of it. And we realize that the art of the dramatist is to strike a balance between the pressure of the past and the instantaneousness of the present. The future in this play, too, is computed rather than divined, or sensed a remote distance away. Moreover, past and future are not much differentiated according to character and situation, to individual mood and the changing rhythm of the play. They belong to an over-all scheme which serves an obvious purpose. Past and future are, as it were, an objective frame of reference, applicable to all the characters concerned, but narrowed down to the moral issue of guilt and retribution.

In *Richard II*, however, this is different. Here past and future are related to the individual consciousness of single characters, but they are also viewed in varying and more complex perspectives. We may take King Richard's later speeches in the play as a focal point for the juxtaposition of past and future. When his own position is endangered he tends to evade the demands of actuality by escaping into the past or into the future. Confronted by a chain of fateful news which predicts the loss of his kingdom, he does not act but allows his imagination to fly back to the 'sad stories of the death of Kings', and these lead him on to a prophetic vision that might also suggest his own death:[1]

> for within the hollow crown
> That rounds the mortal temples of a king
> Keeps Death his court; ...
>
> (III, ii, 160)

In the next scene, faced with the necessity of submitting and abdicating, Richard still more fully exploits the poetic and imaginative potentialities of the situation, drawing comparisons between his former and his present state:

> Or that I could forget what I have been,
> Or not remember what I must be now!
>
> (III, iii, 138)

[1] Cf. Chapter 1, p. 36.

In a set of elaborate symbols he offers up his own royal past ('my jewels/My gorgeous palace/My gay apparel/My figured goblets/My sceptre') in exchange for the humble requisites of a poor hermit which would suit his future state. But these reflections, too, end up in lines which imply the vision of his own future grave 'A little, little grave, an obscure grave' (III, iii, 154). The most telling moment, however, which joins together past and future, occurs in the abdication-scene itself (IV, i), when the crown is handed over from Richard to Bolingbroke and is held between their hands, Richard commenting on this scenic picture with memorable lines. In this symbolic scene the crown becomes the pledge of continuity in history. It comes from the past and goes into the future. It has to carry the burden of the past, but it also contains the promise of the future. The whole abdication scene is, of course, rich in confrontations of past and future. But Shakespeare's dramatic art, appealing to the eye as well as to the ear, is most evident in those episodes which condense the essence of a whole play or the gist of a central theme into a visible act in which word and gesture combine to create a symbolic impact that will linger on in the memory of the audience.

The audience will surely remember this moment when watching the scene (IV, v) between the dying King and the Prince in 2 Henry IV. For here again the crown is the visible symbol for the transition from past to future. We may, however, observe the difference in method. In the concluding speech which the King addresses to his son the fundamental principle for the relationship between the past rule of the dying King and the ensuing reign of Prince Henry is clearly formulated:

> God knows, my son,
> By what by-paths and indirect crook'd ways
> I met this crown; and I myself know well
> How troublesome it sat upon my head:
> To thee it shall descend with better quiet,
> Better opinion, better confirmation;
> For all the soil of the achievement goes
> With me into the earth.
>
> (IV, v, 182)

But this final truth is arrived at only after a long series of misunderstandings and dramatic encounters in the course of which past and future are viewed under varying subjective perspectives and are even completely misinterpreted. The King's final speech resolves his own misconceptions about the Prince, misconceptions which have been a dominant motif throughout both parts of the play and which are even enunciated at the beginning of this very scene. The whole scene in fact looks back to III, ii of Part One, where we also find father and son in 'private conference' together, the sorrowful King recalling his predecessor's faults in the past, and taking them as a warning for his and his son's own future. This scene in turn looks back to II, iv where Prince Henry and Falstaff stage the famous mock admonition between father and son. Here again a symbolic scenic situation (the King on his throne and the Prince before him) impresses itself on our memory and ironically foreshadows subsequent colloquies between Henry IV and Prince Harry; it likewise obliquely hints at Falstaff's later fortunes. If we look at the subject-matter of this dialogue we find that past and future are the two chief points of reference.

But these are only two links which connect this death scene with earlier episodes in which past and future are joined. At the risk of simplification we could say that Part One looks ahead to Part Two, which in turn looks back to Part One. But this simple overall scheme is modified and twisted into many variations which are determined by individual situations and characters. The misconstrued, falsely rendered past and accordingly the misapprehended future as opposed to the objective past and future, play an important part within the intricate dramatic web of right and wrong expectation, defeated hope, misleading surmise, and true but hidden purpose. The beginning of Part Two with 'Rumour' misrepresenting the past by false report and consequently leading on to wrong expectations and wrong planning of the future in the next scene is only one case in point.

If we take another look at the scene in which the King dies and particularly at his concluding speech, we realize that it assumes the significance of final clarification, and of a reconciliation between past and future after many conflicting and contradictory developments. For this final solution Shakespeare has chosen a situation that is at once complex and of an elementary simplicity. For in this scene between the dying King and the Prince father and son are confronted with one another, the old and the new generation, the one taking leave of his rule and the other assuming his father's heritage. Past and future thus meet on several levels, though in the same characters.

Before leaving the histories we ought to mention that besides such crucial scenes, of which we have chosen a few striking examples, past and future are also combined (or opposed to each other) on many minor occasions. Indeed, a systematic and detailed survey would be needed to record all the recurring situations and typical ways in which past and future are juxtaposed. For brevity's sake I shall only enumerate the following cases to give an idea of their variety: the summarizing passages occurring mostly at the beginning of the scene and sometimes at the end, recapitulating the past and announcing impending plans and events; the summons to courageous action in the future recalling the memory of a glorious past;[1] the situations of 'challenge' and accusation in which the enumeration of past crimes is linked to the promise to bring to light the guilt denied by the adversary;[2] the 'dying speeches' in which the character may act as a prophet and a warner, speaking, as it were, as the mouthpiece of his whole country and surveying past and future from a distance;[3] the raising of a claim which is based on a right, due in the past, and which calls for execution in the future;[4] the curses, warnings, and prophecies, recalling the past, which will be remembered in the future when they find their fulfilment;[5] the indictments, laments, and arraignments which very often look backwards and forwards; the scenes of leave-taking combining woeful retrospect with hopes and fears for the future;[6] the concluding speeches, prayers, or orations at the very end of the plays which invariably combine retrospect with a look forwards into the future.[7]

The list could be continued. But it is enough to show in how many different ways references to past and future are brought in. We also see from this enumeration to what extent Shakespeare makes use of man's natural feelings and attitudes, thus consciously or unconsciously establishing a relation to past and to future. Hope, fear, and anxiety, expectation, warning and threatening, cursing and praying – all these refer

---

[1] e.g. the first scenes of *1 Henry VI*, *2 Henry VI*, *Henry V*.
[2] e.g. *Richard II*, I, i.
[3] e.g. *Richard II*, II, i.
[4] e.g. *2 Henry VI*, II, ii.
[5] e.g. *Richard II*, v, i; *2 Henry IV*, III, i.
[6] e.g. *Richard II*, II, ii.
[7] e.g. *Richard III*, v, v.

to the future. The past is implied in other recurring attitudes, such as repentance, guilt, and the feeling of obligation. However, all these references and attitudes become structural links, vehicles of dramatic technique. They help to organize, co-ordinate, and relate the wealth of historical detail, of single motifs and disparate events spread throughout the histories; they establish parallels and thematic connexions; they are a constant stimulant for our recording memory and our registering imagination. What in a single passage may appear as an insignificant detail nevertheless contributes to the overall impact: by its correspondence with similar references it makes us aware of the larger structure. It is this cumulative effect which matters, comparable to the role of the single metaphor within a chain of related imagery. I venture to submit that the comprehensive pattern of past and future in the histories as it has been pointed out by Tillyard, Reese, Leech, and others would not emerge so clearly before our eyes if it were not rooted in and supported by this mosaic of many minor passages which link past and future in some way or other.

Passing from the histories to the tragedies we come upon plays that stand by themselves and are not organized into a cyclical sequence. Moreover, the tragedies are not concerned with the national past with which the audience was to some extent familiar. This alone accounts for important differences in the treatment of past and future. Moreover, in the tragedies, although several of them are based on historical events, the sense of history is overruled by the sense of personal fate. As in the case of Hamlet, Macbeth, and Lear, the hero's relationship towards past and future is at the core of his personal destiny, revealing to us his essential mode of experience. Shakespeare's use of past and future in the tragedies, therefore, discloses many new features: it is adjusted to the concept of tragedy, but also to the peculiar time-structure of each tragedy, to its theme and atmosphere, so that in each instance we are faced with new problems.

Of all the tragedies, however, *Hamlet* shows the most striking confrontation of past and future, and I shall therefore limit myself to this play. At the beginning of this essay I included *Hamlet* among the three plays which are preceded by an important past which to some extent determines the future course of action. It is therefore pertinent to ask how Shakespeare brings this past into the play and how he joins it with the future. Technically speaking the Ghost's narrative is a piece of the exposition, informing us about the past. But this narrative is turned into a dramatic present of the utmost intensity that can even 'harrow up' the souls of those who watch this scene in the theatre. We witness the immediate effect of the Ghost's disclosure on Hamlet, for whom it becomes the turning-point of his whole life and the motivating cause of all his future doings, wiping away from the table of his memory 'All saws of books, all forms, all pressures past' to implant a new past unforgettably in his mind. Besides, this past is more than a reported event, for it has embodied itself in the figure of the Ghost who as a messenger from the world beyond is also a witness of the past that is thus perpetuated. The past, as it were, has stepped into the play to act as an incentive towards the future. The Ghost has therefore been taken by some critics as the most influential character in this play, the figure who secretly directs the further course of the action though remaining himself in the background.

However, the past revealed by the Ghost raises questions, doubts, and uncertainties not only for Hamlet but also for the audience. We can see how a past that is not fully revealed, or of which the truth remains uncertain, may have a stronger effect on the dramatic expectation, on the future in the play, than the undisputed and confirmed fact.[1] Questions that remain open act as a constant reminder of the past and again and again pose new problems for the future. The Ghost is a supreme example of the way in which past and future may be joined in a dramatic figure.

It goes without saying that Hamlet, too, has a peculiar relationship towards past and future. His keen memory recalls, with graphic precision, scenes and pictures of past times which have a bearing on his situation: the burial, his mother, his father's figure, etc. The Ghost's 'Remember me' is always at the back of Hamlet's mind although he accuses himself of 'bestial oblivion'. But the Ghost did not only say 'Remember me' but also 'Avenge me'.[2] The tension between 'remember me', pointing towards the past, and 'avenge me' pointing towards the future, is one of the sources of Hamlet's tragic conflict, and may indeed be a possible cause of his delay and procrastination. The past appears to hold Hamlet back from attaining the future. A recent critic, Mr Berry, even detects in this tension between past and future

[1] Cf. Harry Levin, *The Question of Hamlet*, New York, 1959.
[2] The line actually reads: 'Revenge his foul and most unnatural murder' (I, v, 25).

something like the structural principle of the whole play, putting it this way: 'So the whole of the presented action (up to the killing of Claudius near the end of act v) is perplexed or shadowed by a completed deed at a definite point in the past which demands a retributive deed at an indefinite future. Held taut between these two points in time, the play consequently refers to that past murder and that future. . . .'[1]

None of the tragedies so constantly broods over the past. The past creeping in by report and reference, by narrative and oblique representation, seems to hold up the movement of the play which is characterized by digressions, by 'indirections', and oblique turns. But the play can afford this discursive, slow pace, this wealth of retrospective passages because from the very beginning the future has been indicated by the Ghost's demand for revenge. However, the more the play advances, the more this future becomes indistinct, the more it is called in question and surrounded by disbelief and hesitation. Eventually we realize (as indeed does Hamlet) that in this case there is no future that could ever repair the past.

But our business is to look out for those moments which link past and future not only verbally but also visually. The grave-digger's scene naturally comes first to our mind. Hamlet's contemplation of Yorick's skull not only awakens memories of his own childhood, but also unavoidably directs his thoughts (as does in fact the whole episode) towards his own death, towards our common human destiny. In the bedchamber scene Hamlet, by displaying his father's portrait, evokes the past and turns it into a burning present that impresses itself on his mother's yielding mind.[2] The Ghost, at this moment the incarnate past and future, appears again in order to whet Hamlet's 'almost blunted purpose'. The scene thus links past and future on several levels. Hamlet, by shattering his mother's conscience and by evoking the past wants to pave the way towards a new future: 'Repent what's past; avoid what is to come' (III, iv, 150).

But there are two other scenes in this play which in a more oblique manner point towards the future though dealing with the past. The First Player's Speech (II, ii, 472), seemingly removed to a far distance from the actuality of the scene by its archaic, declamatory style and by its subject-matter, contains a number of subtle but very pertinent refer-

[1] Francis Berry, *The Shakespeare Inset*, London, 1965, p. 117.
[2] Cf. E. Th. Sehrt in *Shakespeare-Jahrbuch (West)*, 1966, pp. 63 ff.

ences to Hamlet's present and future situation and to the central theme ('So, as a painted tyrant, Pyrrhus stood/And like a neutral to his will and matter,/Did nothing. . . . A roused vengeance sets him new a-work . . .'). Besides, it serves as a cue and as a prologue to Hamlet's ensuing soliloquy. The 'Murder of Gonzago' play (III, ii), on the other hand, deliberately planned by Hamlet at the end of this very soliloquy ('The play's the thing wherein I'll catch the conscience of the King') is a reconstruction of the murder of Hamlet's father under the guise of a murder that happened long before in Vienna ('This play is the image of a murder done in Vienna', says Hamlet). Thus the past that precedes the beginning of the play and is disclosed in the first act by the Ghost, is here incorporated 'tropically' within the play, at its centre and turning-point. Again, this 'double' past, the one in Vienna and the other in Denmark, serves to bring about a decision in the present which must alter the future course of the action.

Our discussion of *Hamlet* began with the linking of past and future in the figure of the Ghost; and it is to the Ghost that we now return for our conclusion. Before the Ghost appears for the second time in the first scene Horatio links up the Ghost's appearance with the historic past of 'our last King', recalling the combat with Fortinbras of Norway and the enterprise of young Fortinbras. But then his recollections range backwards even further. For, taking Bernardo's reference to 'this portentous figure' as a cue, he recalls the forebodings recorded 'in the most high and palmy state of Rome a little ere the mightiest Julius fell'. Once again a 'double past' foreshadowing the future is here established. In three consecutive phrases the similarity between the forebodings in ancient Rome and the present situation is expressed:

> And even the like precurse of fear'd events,
> As harbingers preceding still the fates
> And prologue to the omen coming on,
> Have heaven and earth together demonstrated
> Unto our climatures and countrymen.

> (I, i, 121)

But this passage is 'prologue' in yet another sense, for the Ghost enters at the very same moment. What is the dramatic effect of this repeated digression into the past? For all the while the audience as well as the three figures on the stage have been secretly awaiting the Ghost's reappearance. The memory of a near and a far past may divert our attention from what is imminent. But in fact this deviation also serves as indirect preparation, for our sense of anticipation has been suspended, thus heightening the tension.

The passage under consideration, in which a remote past is called up for the sake of indirect foreboding, may serve as an example of Shakespeare's insertion of retrospective passages that have a preparatory effect or function as a foreshadowing. But while we can fit this last passage into the general pattern of past and future which is characteristic of *Hamlet*, we cannot do so with a great many other retrospective passages which occur on various occasions in the comedies and the tragedies. These 'insets', as Mr Berry has called them in his stimulating book,[1] are devices by which Shakespeare transports us for a moment from the dramatic present into a remote past or a remote future, building up, as it were, a second plane of reference, an imaginative background behind the foreground of the play on the stage. Sometimes, as in our last *Hamlet* passage, both past and future are involved. Of this usage I shall give three different examples, only to indicate a frequently recurring dramatic technique which nevertheless may take on very different forms.

My first example is from *A Midsummer Night's Dream*. In the second act Oberon orders Puck to fetch him the magic herb 'love-in-idleness'. This request, however, is clad in an imaginative recollection of that day when Cupid 'flying between the cold moon and the earth' missed with his fiery shaft 'a fair Vestal', hitting instead 'a little western flower; before milk-white, now purple'. Thus the herb is introduced which, as a supernatural agent, is to cause so much confusion in the following scenes. But not only the past transformation of this natural herb into a supernatural one is disclosed to us; we are also given a glimpse of that whole fairy world of myth and wonder that becomes alive in the fairies' songs and the many references to their nature. For an Elizabethan audience, however, the 'fair Vestal' unmistakably pointed towards Queen Elizabeth, so that here Shakespeare again, as he often does in the histories, makes the past suggest the actuality of his contemporary world.

The second example comes from *Julius Caesar*. Antony speaks to the

[1] Francis Berry, *The Shakespeare Inset*, 1965. Of the three examples given here, the passage from *Twelfth Night* has been discussed at length by Mr Berry.

crowd by the corpse of Caesar. He displays Caesar's mantle pierced by
the murderers' daggers and connects this visible object with the
memories of Caesar's victorious days in the past:

> You all do know this mantle. I remember
> The first time ever Caesar put it on;
> 'Twas on a summer's evening, in his tent ...
>
> (III, ii, 170)

But Antony makes these recollections cunningly serve his own future
purpose. And indeed the first signs of this future development, the
whole intention of his speech, appear in the crowd's raging cries: 'We'll
mutiny'/'We'll burn the house of Brutus'....

My third example is the beautiful and unforgettable passage spoken
by Viola in the guise of Cesario to Orsino about her father's daughter,
who

> never told her love,
> But let concealment, like a worm i' the bud,
> Feed on her damask cheek. She pin'd in thought;
> And with a green and yellow melancholy
> She sat like Patience on a monument,
> Smiling at grief.
>
> (*Twelfth Night*, II, iv, 109)

This is perhaps the most subtle and imaginative use of past and future
to be found within a short passage in the comedies. For Viola invents
this history of her sister's unrequited love to express her own past and
present sufferings as well as her apprehensions for her own future. Past
and future in these lines are both fictive *and* true or possible. The
visionary image of 'Patience on a monument' is a mirror of Viola's own
situation, and she contemplates this picture as from a distance but
nevertheless deeply involved with its implications. The effect of this
passage is thus a double one. Through the apparent remoteness of this
strange history of Cesario's sister the poignant actuality of Viola's
plight is most movingly expressed, though only the audience will
recognize this.

The three passages – and there are many more – give us three different examples of the way in which Shakespeare evokes some occurrence or some recollection from the past in order to link it with the

future. In *A Midsummer Night's Dream* the herb 'love-in-idleness' is introduced and given its appropriate imaginative background through Oberon's account; in *Julius Caesar* the pathetic sight of Caesar's blood-stained mantle is made more poignant by the recollection of his former glorious days and thus stirs the emotions of the gazing crowd and urges them towards a new future. In *Twelfth Night* Cesario's (Viola's) invented story indirectly and figuratively describes her own past and her own possible future. The three passages have this in common: the forward movement of the action is slowed down and comes almost to a halt while a window is thrust open admitting a glimpse of a remote past or of a sphere removed from the actuality of what we have just been witnessing on the stage. But Shakespeare's secret is that this past of which we are given an imaginative vision is itself actuality; it is intimately related to the present moment; it intensifies its significance, and, what is more, it anticipates and prepares the future.

But from such single passages which combine retrospect with forecast we could not infer any general principles on the use of past and future in the play concerned as we tried to do in the histories and in *Hamlet*. This, however, is possible again in the romances, of which I have chosen *The Tempest* for more detailed consideration. I have selected this drama, since 'more than any other play by Shakespeare *The Tempest* makes us conscious of both past and future', as Clifford Leech has put it.[1] As a matter of fact *The Tempest* and *The Comedy of Errors* are the only plays which strictly observe the unities. This has an effect on the bearing of past and future on the action of the play. In *The Tempest* the action takes place within the span of an afternoon between two and six o'clock, but a past that happened twelve years before and another past only a short while before precede this afternoon and impress themselves on the inner and the outward action, which, in its turn, points towards a new future which stretches beyond this day into a near and a very far distance. The condensation of the action into a very short period of time intensifies the pressure of the past on the present and fills this present with the expectancy of the future. The events on the island are like a brief passage between two worlds, a passage, however, that lends itself to amazing transformation as a result of the co-operation of several determining factors. Moreover,

[1] C. Leech, 'Shakespeare and the Idea of the Future', *University of Toronto Quarterly*, XXXV, 1966.

The Tempest begins, as it were, in the last act and is itself a last act, a final phase in which retribution and reconciliation, restoration and redemption are shown, all, however, in relation to a past that happened long ago. This past is by various means integrated into the play: it is not only mirrored; in certain respects it is even repeated, revived, continued during the progress of the action. The past indeed is ever present and it continually directs our attention towards the future.

This double aspect is evident by the second scene, the most conspicuous example of Shakespeare's art of exposition through a connected long narrative. For comparison we may look back at Egeon's equally long account of past events in the first scene of *The Comedy of Errors*. Egeon's story, for all its fullness of circumstance and economy, remains flat and without variation; it is not, as in *The Tempest*, shared by two partners who are both looking into the past (though each with a different perspective); it is not re-experienced again in the present nor does it, as in *The Tempest*, live on in the memories of the characters during the following scenes. It gives us, to be sure, the key to the understanding of the complicated business between the two pairs of twins and it may also arouse some expectations as to Egeon's future fate. But as Egeon completely disappears from the play to come back only in the last act, our remembrance of the past also goes, as it were, underground. It forms a background which withdraws a certain distance away, to be revived at the play's very end, but it does not form a constituent element of the play's structure.

For this is what we do find in *The Tempest*. Prospero's story does not come until the second scene, after the violent spectacle of the shipwreck, of which the fresh memory still lingers on in Miranda's mind, so that the remembrance of the events immediately preceding gives way to the reminiscence of a remote past which, however, is also in fact brought close to us by the shipwreck that we have just been watching. When Prospero tells his story we have already seen its characters on the stage, so that the remote past is linked up with the instantaneous present. These characters represent the burden, the guilt, the suffering in the past, but this past is now laid into Prospero's hands so that he may turn it into a new future. The narrator of the past becomes the secret ruler of the fates of all the characters involved. Not only is the shipwreck at the play's beginning (an ironic repetition of what his enemies had intended for him sixteen years ago) all his doing, but from now on he directs the movements of everyone, friend and enemy alike, with Ariel acting as his supernatural agent. But what are Prospero's plans for the future? We heard of his 'prescience' (180), but we can only guess what his future purpose is. His peremptory words to Miranda 'Here cease more questions' silence us as well as Miranda. Thus the future, although in some way predetermined by Prospero and in his hands, remains open, which contributes a great deal to the dramatic effectiveness of this first act. The fact that Prospero changes his mind (although this is not stated explicitly), that he turns out to be not only a prescient sage, a detached theurgic mystic but a suffering man who can become enraged and impatient, irritated and troubled, is an important counterpoise to the conception of destiny and predetermination as embodied in Prospero. Shakespeare uses subtle devices to dramatize Prospero's long account of the past, to relate it to the present situation, to reveal and at the same time to conceal what is the purport of the narrative. We are made to feel that Prospero's disclosure comes at exactly the right moment, for Miranda, who up to now has been denied the full story ('You have often begun to tell me what I am, but stopp'd . . .'), is now told by her father "Tis time I should inform thee farther . . . The hour's now come'. Moreover, we are given the illusion that the past is not something ready and definite, available at any time, but that it needs to be recovered by a deliberate act of remembrance which from casual recollections ('Had I not four or five women? . . .') may advance to a fuller vision. Although Prospero, of course, knows all about the past, he tries to revive a glimpse of it in his daughter's memory ('in the dark backward and abysm of time') before he relates it in full. Thus Miranda appears as a participant in what has happened 'far off'; she is to live through this past again re-enacting her former sufferings ('I, not rememb'ring how I cried out then, will cry it o'er again'). What she meant to her father then ('a cherubin thou wast that did preserve me . . .') mirrors and foreshadows the present relationship between father and daughter, while other parts of Prospero's story raise in Miranda a definite wish which anticipates the future ('Would I might but ever see that man'). Remembrance of the past is linked with suggestions for the future in the remainder of the scene too, and this is a recurring pattern in Prospero's exchanges with Ariel and Caliban later in the play. The word 'remember' (or some form of it) occurs eight times, the word 'forget' four times in this scene.[1] But although the past is recalled in almost every passage of this scene it is balanced by an equally strong sense of the present. We feel and we are shown by many minor hints that everything is happening 'now' and 'here', that it is the 'present business' (I, ii, 136) which matters. Observing this particular emphasis on the present, which can be traced throughout the whole play, a recent critic, Mr Ernest Gohn, has aptly called this present 'a crucial nexus uniting the past to the future: the past is relevant only as it affects the present, the future only as it grows out of the present'.[2] *The Tempest*, in fact, appears to be the play in which the past has been most closely integrated into the present.

In the later scenes with the courtiers we see how their past is put on trial, how their former qualities revive and are tested. Each situation, as it were, elicits from them impulses and reactions which are related to their past role in Prospero's former life. Gonzalo proves loyal, Alonso shows some remorse, Antonio and Sebastian contrive new crimes, Trinculo joins with Caliban. Thus when Ariel, as a 'minister of fate', calls them up for judgment, he reminds them not only of their former guilt but also of its continuation or repetition during their short stay on the island. Ariel's speech, which has been called 'the keystone upon which the structure of the play rests',[3] shows the 'tripartite division of time' into past, present, and future which has been detected in other scenes and speeches as well.[4] The past is submitted to a process of transformation, for with some characters it can be redeemed and forgiven, while with others it remains unchanged. In Ferdinand it will be overcome and forgotten, so that he can enter into the grace of his new life. The union of Ferdinand and Miranda, who will establish a new future as rulers of Naples, can take place only after the reconciliation of their parents has been achieved. And reconciliation in the romances always means that the past is clarified, redeemed, and transformed so that the path towards a new future is open. It is only then that the pressure of the past can be lifted. 'Let us not burden our remembrances with a heaviness that's gone' says Prospero when the union of Miranda and Ferdinand has been perfected (v, i, 199).

[1] T. F. Driver, 'The Shakespearian Clock', *Shakespeare Quarterly*, xv (1964).
[2] Ernest Gohn, 'The Tempest: Theme and Structure', *English Studies*, 1964.
[3] D. Traversi, *Shakespeare: The Last Phase*, London, 1954.
[4] T. F. Driver, *op. cit.*

But is the future towards which we are looking at the end of the play really the forthcoming reign of Ferdinand and Miranda at Naples and Prospero's return to Milan? Prospero, to be sure, after having taken leave of his own past as a magician, is attired by Ariel in his ducal robes and solemnly addresses Alonso: 'Behold, Sir King, the wronged Duke of Milan, Prospero.' But this revived image of his own past powerful state is not his whole and true self, nor are his thoughts for the future bent on rule and earthly business, for in Milan 'every third thought shall be my grave'. The future that we apprehend in the last act of the play is a future of a higher and a different order, of which we may divine something in Prospero's great visionary speech about the world's final dissolution (IV, i, 146). To take this speech as 'the view of an old and tired brain'[1] and as a sign of Prospero's disillusionment with the world does not do it justice. For Prospero gives expression here to a metaphysical vision of sublime and mysterious significance: he looks towards a world beyond, towards another life to come. Thus we could say that through this vision Prospero appears to transcend the categories of past and future, and that he stands aloof from the immediate action, of which he had so cunningly woven and manipulated the threads running from the past towards the future.

In concluding we might ask whether we find in the other romances a similar pattern of past and future, which would suggest that Shakespeare in these last plays seeks to give expression to a new vision of things that would bring past and future closer together. If we look at the last acts of these romances we note that past, present, and future are joined here in a striking and peculiar manner. In these scenes of reconciliation, restoration, and reunion a redeemed, a renewed, and even re-born past is transformed into the present, which can now initiate a new future. But in contrast to the situation in the tragedies this past is not irrevocable and irreparable, but a past that can be redeemed and regained. Persons who have been thought of as dead and lost can be brought back to life like Hermione, or found again like Imogen, Perdita, and Marina. Usually the future in these plays, as in *The Tempest*, is represented by a pair of young lovers who through their union mend what was amiss in the older generation of their parents. But their union can take place only when the unsolved past has been solved or

[1] D. R. C. Marsh, *The Recurring Miracle*, Pietermaritzburg, 1962, p. 187.

made up for. Forgiveness and penitence pave the way for this new future and though these acts of forgiving are sometimes effected rather improbably we may accept them 'as a manifestation of Shakespeare's symbolic technique transcending likelihood for higher purposes'.[1] There is always an element of strangeness about this new future which divorces it from reality and endows these last plays 'with a significance that extends beyond any last curtain or final Exeunt'.[2] We sense a mysterious vision of imponderable distances.

In the final acts the characters are confronted with their own past so that they repent or recover it. The late Una Ellis-Fermor, in a lecture given at Munich University some years ago,[3] pointed out to what degree this process of recognition and reconciliation leads to the characters' confrontation with and understanding of themselves. For they now understand their own past, they experience an inner rebirth and recover their own better selves. This is what Gonzalo, at the end of *The Tempest*, in fact expresses when he says that they all of them found themselves 'when no man was his own' (v, i, 212).

The process of regeneration and rebirth, shown in all the romances though with characteristic modifications, links both past and future in a mysterious manner that intimates the co-operation of supernatural powers. And in fact, there are supernatural agents or occurrences in each of the romances. We should cease to find fault with the improbability of it. For it suggests, to borrow a phrase from Kenneth Muir, 'Shakespeare's creation of a kind of myth which he could set up against the changes and chances of this mortal life'.[4] The supernatural in Shakespeare's romances suggests the rule of heavenly powers, full of grace, which can set everything right in the end. For only they can prevent the past from becoming irreparable; only they can transform a restored past into a new future.

I have come to the end of this study. I have considered the conflux of past and future within the context of history in *Richard III*, *Richard II*, and *Henry IV*; I have looked upon the tension between past and future as an expression of personal destiny and tragic dilemma in

[1] Stanley Wells, in *Shakespeare-Jahrbuch (West)*, 1966, p. 118.
[2] J. M. Nosworthy, Introd. to *Cymbeline*, New Arden ed. 1955.
[3] Una Ellis-Fermor, 'Die Spätwerke grosser Dramatiker', *Deutsche Vierteljahresschrift*, XXIV, 1950. The English original has not been published.
[4] K. Muir, *Shakespeare as Collaborator*, London, 1960.

Hamlet, and I have lastly observed the reconciliation of past and future in the romances. Thus to summarize these three stages in no way exhausts our subject, but it may suggest that Shakespeare's drama in the use it makes of past and future undergoes a significant development that certainly deserves further investigation.

4
Shakespeare's Soliloquies

The first thing that strikes us about Shakespeare's soliloquies,[1] if we compare them with those of any other dramatist, is their extraordinary variety. Looking at Euripides or Seneca, at Corneille or Racine, at Lessing or Schiller we find that each of these dramatists has developed his own specific but limited manner of composing and using a soliloquy. It is therefore possible to speak of the soliloquy typical of Corneille or Schiller. But what is the typical Shakespeare monologue? We cannot answer this question satisfactorily, for Shakespeare's soliloquies include not only Macbeth's 'If it were done' and Othello's 'It is the cause' but also Launce's comic performance of his family-scene with his dog and his shoes, Richard Gloucester's self-introduction, Malvolio's reading and commenting on Olivia's forged letter, Lear's harangues to the elements, the Porter's speech in *Macbeth*, Falstaff's speech on honour and the Bastard's railings on 'Commodity'. All these are typical of Shakespeare, but differ from each other widely in style, method and function. They are all soliloquies, but have little in common, serving different ends and producing different dramatic effects. We do not seem to gain much for our understanding by an attempt at classification and definition. For all these labels, such as 'soliloquy of reflection', 'of resolution', 'of passionate outburst', 'of comment' or 'of self-explanation', only partly fit. By these distinctions we grasp their superficial mark rather than their essence. Indeed, these categories apply with some accuracy only to those less remarkable monologues in Shakespeare's plays which are often given to minor characters but would not occur to us as instances of Shakespeare's 'great monologues'. For those which have become famous for their intensity and dramatic force transcend the pattern and the type. Our approach must therefore not be through classification.

[1] The most comprehensive treatment of Shakespeare's soliloquies, discussing their various functions, still is M. L. Arnold, *The Soliloquies of Shakespeare. A Study in Technic*, New York, 1911. Cf. Kenneth Muir, 'Shakespeare's Soliloquies' in *Ocidente*, vol. 67 (1967), Lisbon.

For in this field, too, the complexity of Shakespeare's art eschews such systematic treatment. Although these soliloquies contain recurring features and typical conventions it is not to them that their uniqueness is due. The conventions are not more than ingredients out of which Shakespeare builds up something new.

I have used the term convention and must say a few words on this aspect of Shakespeare's soliloquies.[1] For the convention of the monologue with its lack of psychological probability and its artificiality has often been a stumbling block to critics. There have been prejudices about the use of dramatic conventions. The progress of Shakespeare's dramatic art has largely been measured by its advance towards naturalism, towards a realistic presentation of characters and events. The soliloquy in which a character gives vent to his innermost feelings is far removed from being true to life. Long before the development of the naturalistic drama theorists pointed out the improbability of this convention. Dr Johnson's contemporary in Germany, Gottsched, drily remarked that 'clever people do not speak aloud when they are alone'.[2]

Producers have found it hard to give dramaturgic and psychological credibility to Shakespeare's soliloquies. They have tried to overcome the difficulty of a solitary monologue by adding stage business, movement and other effects. Thus the opinion expressed by the *Encyclopaedia Britannica* in its short article on the monologue, that 'it has always been liable to ridicule' may still be shared by many. Although our age has seen the revival of poetic drama and the turning away from naturalism in the theatre, our apologetic attitude about the convention of the soliloquy, which we feel we ought to defend, betrays the fact that we are still secretly in the grips of naturalism.

Moreover, it was found that not only in pre-Shakespearian drama, but also in Shakespeare's plays the monologue serves a number of

---

[1] For a discussion of the convention of the soliloquy in Shakespearian and Elizabethan drama see among others: H. Granville-Barker, *Prefaces to Shakespeare*, London, 1958, vol. 1, pp. 16 f.; M. C. Bradbrook, *Themes and Conventions of Elizabethan Tragedy*, Cambridge, 1935, pp. 124 ff.; A. C. Sprague, *Shakespeare and the Audience*, Camb. Mass., 1935, pp. 62 ff.; B. L. Joseph, *Elizabethan Acting*, Oxford, 1951, pp. 117 ff.; Arthur Sewell, *Character and Society in Shakespeare*, Oxford, 1951, p. 22; E. F. C. Ludowyk, *Understanding Shakespeare*, Cambridge, 1962, p. 35.

[2] 'Kluge Leute aber pflegen nicht laut zu reden, wenn sie allein sind', Gottsched, *Versuch einer kritischen Dichtkunst*, 4. Auflage, Leipzig, 1751, p. 648.

purposes which have little or nothing to do with 'self-expression'. For the monologue is used as a means of informing the audience, of identifying characters and explaining their double role, of linking scenes and bridging the gap between them, it is used as a device of exposition and narration, as prologue, commentary and chorus. And all this is still further removed from the self-revelation of a character and has provoked manifold criticism.

However, the stress laid on the conventional features in Shakespeare's soliloquies has given undue importance to what is only *one* aspect among others. The total effect of a soliloquy does not depend on the existence of certain conventions. It derives rather from the whole context in which various factors combine to produce a convincing effect. And then, the conventional element will also convince us. For any convention can be used with a greater or smaller degree of appropriateness. Not that convention in itself is a bad thing but only its indiscriminate, its too obtrusive, its 'unmotivated' use. But this 'motivation' need not necessarily be psychological and has little to do with the soliloquy's adjustment to realistic requirements.

Besides, we must remember that the soliloquy in Shakespeare is only one convention among others. The play in itself is a convention, and Shakespeare constantly uses conventions on several levels. The telescoping of time, the selective method of presentation, the bold imagery and the poetic language – all these are virtually 'conventions' which belong to the tacit agreement that exists between playwright and audience. The test is not the rational and psychological analysis to which scholars may submit the soliloquy afterwards, but the test must be the credibility of the soliloquy within its proper framework. We feel that characters such as Shakespeare creates them, endowing them with a peculiar kind of poetic speech and self-expression, must soliloquize at certain moments of tension, heightened awareness or inner conflict. And we feel, too, that poetic drama, such as Shakespeare shapes it – with its rhythmic sequence of movement and halting suspense, of outer and inner drama – must give space to the monologue. The illusion of character will not be broken by the soliloquy if it has been built up beforehand by similar means, among them again some 'conventions'. This, with some modifications, even applies to our present-day stagecraft and dramaturgy, although it was so much easier in the Elizabethan theatre to use conventions. In particular, the protruding

Elizabethan platform stage, creating a closer intimacy between audience and actor, was a better basis for the convention of the soliloquy than our modern stage of scenic illusion. This platform stage placing the actor in the middle of the audience indeed called for the 'direct address' which was often identical with the monologue in its early stages.

However, Shakespeare's art is only partly conventional, it consists rather in a continual transition between conventionalism and naturalism.[1] There is no clear line of division between these two modes of dramatic presentation. We do not even find a conscious and consistent use of convention in Elizabethan drama, as T. S. Eliot has pointed out.[2] Shakespeare's is 'a mixed mode' of dramatic art, he blends realistic and conventional elements and so often and so subtly shifts from the one to the other that we do not know where we are. The criterion must therefore not be the amount of conventionalism or of naturalism which we can trace within a monologue, but its total impact. Shakespeare avails himself both of realism and of conventionalism, but he also transcends both, creating a new and characteristic mode of presentation by which the poetic drama of the Elizabethans became Shakespearian drama. Far from discarding the conventions which he found in the drama before him, Shakespeare exploited the possibilities yielded by these conventions to an even greater extent than his contemporaries. This applies in particular to the soliloquy. Shakespeare constantly discovers new possibilities inherent in the soliloquy, he reveals an extraordinary ingenuity in finding new ways of integrating the soliloquy into the play's organism, adjusting it to the speaker and to the situation as well as to the atmosphere, theme and movement of the play, linking it up with important developments and charging it with dramatic significance and effect.

This, then, should be our approach: to ask what Shakespeare can do with a soliloquy and what the soliloquy can do for his play, how he turns the soliloquy into a necessary part of the dramatic structure.

Irritation at the 'unnaturalness' or the 'primitive technique' of the convention of the soliloquy had indeed obscured our recognition of its great positive values. Shakespeare teaches us with his soliloquies not

[1] Cf. S. L. Bethell, *Shakespeare and the Popular Dramatic Tradition*, London, 1944, Ch. I.
[2] T. S. Eliot, *Selected Essays*, London, 1932, p. 115.

only that a convention – once it has been accepted – can carry conviction if dramatically handled, but also that it can release effects and reveal levels of existence and of inner development which could not otherwise and certainly not by a naturalistic technique be shown to us. I should like to quote two sentences from Una Ellis-Fermor's *The Frontiers of Drama*: 'But at its finest, as at the height of the Elizabethan period, the soliloquy, by its rapid and profound revelation of thought and passion, serves the very ends of drama. It reveals what we could not otherwise divine of the depths of the speaker's mind, compressing into some twenty lines of vivid illumination what might else have taken the better part of an act to convey.'[1]

As the phrasing of this passage implies, this perfection of the soliloquy is to be found only at the height of the whole period, that is to say in Shakespeare's great tragedies. But even there we find some instances of soliloquies which – far from being revelations of inner states of mind – are a mere means of informing the audience. Shakespeare's development, on this sector too, is not a consistent one. Throughout his work we find between his monologues great differences regarding the degree of dramatization, of complexity, of integration. With these modifications in mind we may trace various stages in Shakespeare's art of the soliloquy, even within the limited range of a small and necessarily arbitrary selection of about a dozen monologues which I have chosen from more than two hundred.

Richard Gloucester's self-introduction at the beginning of *Richard III* is an example of a soliloquy that serves as an exposition and as an opening to the whole play.[2] This soliloquy has not been prepared for and therefore cannot grow out of the dramatic structure. It is difficult to begin a play in this way and Shakespeare has never attempted to do it again. But in spite of the obviousness and informative function of this self-introduction it strongly impresses Richard's personality on us. Shakespeare here combines within relatively few lines several types of the traditional soliloquy which in the drama before him occurred separately: the expository prologue which reviews the situation, the self-introduction and the planning-monologue which discloses the hero's future aim. The soliloquy is thus made to serve several purposes

---

[1] Una Ellis-Fermor, *The Frontiers of Drama*, London, 1945, p. 105.
[2] For a detailed interpretation of this soliloquy see my *Commentary on Richard III*, London, 1968.

at a time, a tendency which we can trace in many of Shakespeare's monologues. But the three functions are divided up into three distinct paragraphs. There is no mention of Gloucester's own person during the first thirteen lines beginning:

> Now is the winter of our discontent
> Made glorious summer by this sun of York;
>
> (I, i, 1)

but even these lines, reading like an impersonal epic description rather than a dramatic opening, are tinged by Richard's irony and reveal his spiteful mockery of the warrior's effeminate demeanour who 'instead of mounting barbed steeds' 'capers nimbly in a lady's chamber'.

The following self-portrayal ends with the famous lines

> I am determined to prove a villain
> And hate the idle pleasures of these days.
>
> (I, i, 30)

This crude self-explanation and motivation of his future career as a villain is in keeping with the vice-tradition of the Moralities and has often been quoted as an instance of the primitive expository technique to be found in Shakespeare's early soliloquies. Indeed Richard describes himself as an outside observer, detached and as it were objectively. But even in this passage we seem to hear Richard's own voice when he speaks with scornful awareness of his own deformity, impatiently piling up the phrases:

> I – that am curtail'd of this fair proportion,
> Cheated of feature by dissembling nature,
> Deform'd, unfinish'd, sent before my time
> Into this breathing world, scarce half made up.
>
> (I, i, 18)

The final announcement of his villainous plans directed against Clarence is an overt 'informing of the audience', though the phrasing betrays Richard's gleeful sarcasm, with which he applauds his own plotting. However, the plan thus laid open before us is a ready-made one, we are not present – as in later soliloquies – while it is hatched. The whole soliloquy is like a well-planned and orderly speech which is given *after* the process of thinking, planning and self-analysis has come to an end; we are told the results but are not drawn into the process itself.

Comparing this soliloquy with possible models in Senecan drama, including its imitations in England, we note how Shakespeare is much more concrete and graphic, integrating many significant details into his soliloquy. Instead of the abstract emotional outbursts or general reflections which we find in Senecan monologues Gloucester's soliloquy contains a wealth of pertinent matter and thus links up with the coming scenes.

The detached attitude in which a character describes himself as if he were an outside observer still applies to the long soliloquy which we hear from Richard II before he is murdered at Pomfret Castle (v, v, 1–66). But the self-characterization we find in this soliloquy is more complex and more subtle than in Richard Gloucester's self-introduction and its dramatic function more convincing. After the short conversation between Exton and a Servant (v, iv), which precedes this soliloquy, the audience will expect the murder of the King. This premonition lends a particular tension to Richard's monologue in his prison cell. The loneliness of captivity, the closeness of death, the contrast between a royal past and a miserable present, all this gives a special justification and motivation to Richard's soliloquy. There is no need of exposition or of informing the audience now, so that the soliloquy can concentrate on a full expression of Richard's character and situation. We see Richard here not merely 'explaining' but *doing* something in his soliloquy, though this activity takes place only in his mind. He imagines a little scene that develops out of his initial comparison

> how I may compare
> This prison where I live unto the world.
>
> (v, v, 1)

It is characteristic of the king's imaginative aspiration that this comparison is too far-fetched to be carried out without difficulty:

> I cannot do it. Yet I'll hammer it out.
> My brain I'll prove the female to my soul,
> My soul the father; and these two beget
> A generation of still-breeding thoughts,
> And these same thoughts people this little world,
> In humours like the people of this world,
> For no thought is contented. . . .
>
> (v, v, 5)

These thoughts are then even given a voice and enter into dialogue with one another: 'Come, little ones' one group says to the other. The audience, anticipating the king's impending murder, will follow these sophisticated speculations with feelings of suspense, of apprehension and concern. This soliloquy, while once more arousing our sympathies for the king, gives us a last portrait of him and epitomizes several features of his character: his imaginative nature and his self-deception, his ability to mirror and to pity himself. It also shows his faculty of not only observing himself with extraordinary awareness of his own situation but also of giving poetic expression to this his own role and state of mind, indulging in symbolic ceremony and imagery, acting his part with conscious royal dignity and exploiting the theatrical possibilities of even his utmost misery. That this heightened capacity for self-expression should eventually find its outlet in a long soliloquy is dramatically convincing. But this self-expression is by no means spontaneous, it is given with that explicitness and elaborateness typical of the whole play. If we hear a statement like

> Thus play I in one person many people,
> And none contented
>
> (v, v, 31)

we shall accept it as being in keeping with this whole style, although it is a logical deduction and a well-considered self-interpretation rather than an unpremeditated monologic utterance. For even in his soliloquy the king still keeps an eye on the spectators. He *demonstrates* what he is instead of just being what he is by means of his language and his behaviour, leaving the implications to the audience. He is not only his own actor but also his own interpreter and commentator.

But let us not overlook the new features in the handling of this soliloquy: the scene of this soliloquy, the prison, is transformed into a metaphor of inner experience, spoken dialogue (between the various kinds of thoughts) is introduced, the imagination itself is shown at work and the irrevocable and futile passing of time enters the king's inner consciousness by that fine comparison of himself with a 'numb'r-ing clock'. Indeed the emphasis in this soliloquy is no longer, as in Gloucester's self-introduction, on outward experience, on plans and political circumstances, but on inner experience.

But an introverted self-awareness is only one of the conditions which may lend credibility and inner motivation to a soliloquy. The Bastard in *King John* is an example of the way in which a character of a very different cast of mind may also use the soliloquy with dramatic cogency. When, at the end of the second act (II, i, 561), he remains alone on the stage to rail on 'Commodity', he is ostensibly set apart from the rest; his isolation, his being so different from the others, his cynical reaction to what has just happened and his sharp observation of the ways of the world, all these find expression in that famous soliloquy. It is a critical comment on what has just happened, as well as a manifestation of the Bastard's own attitude and his odd character. Indeed, this soliloquy, placed as a mirror at the end of that long scene, makes us look at the preceding dispute with critical awareness so that by this retrospective function we gain a somewhat changed outlook. We see what has happened with the Bastard's eyes, without, however, identifying our-selves wholly with his view. For this very soliloquy in which the Bastard attacks 'Commodity, the bias of the world' reveals that this character's strong individuality is itself not quite without a bias. Of the five soliloquies occurring in *King John* the Bastard is given three, which emphasizes the peculiar position he holds in this play. It is through his soliloquies that the Bastard becomes so alive for us, and it is here that he gives us the best instance of the individual vivid speech with which Shakespeare endowed him. We can also note how the soliloquy is gradually becoming 'acted monologue' which in itself contains the indications for gesture, mien and movement as well as a dramatization through spoken dialogue. We may take the following lines from the Bastard's first soliloquy:

> Why then I suck my teeth and catechize
> My picked man of countries: 'My dear sir,'
> Thus leaning on my elbow, I begin,
> 'I shall beseech you' – that is question now;
> And then comes answer like an Absey book:
> 'O sir,' says answer, 'at your best command,
> At your employment: at your service, sir!'
>
> (I, i, 192)

This is one way of dramatizing a soliloquy. But Shakespeare has tried many other methods of dramatization. In the fourth act of *Romeo and Juliet* we find the scene in which Juliet drinks the 'distilled liquor' given her by Friar Lawrence (IV, iii). There are thirteen lines of an introductory talk between Juliet, the Nurse and Lady Capulet, but then for the rest of the scene (for forty-five lines) Juliet is left alone and her long soliloquy is an accompanying text for the action, in the course of which she drinks the vial, deposes a dagger at her bedside and eventually throws herself down on her bed. The soliloquy thus creates and interprets the action, but we still find the self-awareness and 'self-dramatization' so characteristic of Shakespeare,[1] for Juliet introduces her performance by the words: 'My dismal scene I needs must act alone.' The lines that follow are an example of the way in which Shakespeare contrives to combine quite different things in a soliloquy, so that the concept of 'self-reflection' or 'introspection' does not suffice. Doubts about the efficacy of the potion, apprehensions of what might happen if she should wake up before Romeo's arrival, a suggestive pictorial anticipation[2] of the

> vault
> To whose foul mouth no healthsome air breathes in,

a grim illusory scene of 'mangled' Tybalt's resurrection, a parting address to Romeo – all this is made vivid and articulate in Juliet's soliloquy. Even the most rhetorical and stylized of all the monologues we find in this play – Juliet's apostrophes:

> Gallop apace you fiery-footed steeds
> Towards Phoebus' lodging; . . .

> (III, ii, 1)

lines which give us a fine relish of gorgeous Elizabethan poetry – are closely linked up with the surrounding atmosphere of the night and the concrete situation. The night and Romeo are interchangeable partners to this monologue and the impatience with which Romeo is expected lends it dramatic immediacy.

Shakespeare has been most ingenious in finding imagined partners for his soliloquizing characters. For the monologue, lacking the real partner on the stage, calls for such fictitious partnership. The monologue in Greek and Roman tragedy had developed the apostrophe as a

[1] Cf. T. S. Eliot, 'Shakespeare and the Stoicism of Seneca', *Selected Essays*, London, 1932, p. 129.
[2] Cf. Chapter 1, p. 43.

sort of substitute for this lacking partnership. The apostrophe could be addressed either to the speaker himself, to his heart, his thoughts, his eyes and other physical attributes or to an absent person, or to heaven, hell and the elements, or to some personification. Shakespeare, in his soliloquies, links up with almost all of these traditions. But the partnership which he introduces in his soliloquies is – as a rule – more closely tied up with the situation and more concrete than it had been in Senecan drama.

Thus King Henry IV addressing 'sleep, Nature's soft nurse' during a sleepless night in Westminster Palace (*2 Henry IV*, III, i, 5–31) forms an unforgettable scene which illustrates for us the tragedy of this king 'so wan with care'. And of equal symbolic import, again expressing a whole and complicated case both through soliloquy *and* scenic representation, is Prince Hal's address to the golden crown, the 'polish'd perturbation! golden care!' which he, still speaking in soliloquy, seizes and carries out of the room in which the king will instantly wake up to find himself bereft of his royal emblem (*2 Henry IV*, IV, v). Even addresses to abstract personifications can achieve an immediate dramatic impact when used within the appropriate context. In *Julius Caesar*, in the scene of Brutus' nocturnal conference with the conspirators in his house (II, i), Brutus is given five short monologues before the party of Cassius, Casca and the others actually enters. The last of these soliloquies consists of a repeated address to 'Conspiracy':

> O conspiracy,
> Sham'st thou to show thy dang'rous brow by night,
> When evils are most free? ...
>
> (II, i, 77)

But this personification has not only been prepared for by Brutus' preceding meditations, it is, together with its imagery, born out of the whole situation, for the conspirators are waiting before the door and will enter at once, coming out of the dark night with their faces 'buried in their cloaks' (74). Of even greater closeness to the concrete situation is Othello's address in his last soliloquy:

> Put out the light, and then put out the light;
>
> (v, ii, 6)

for the candle which burns before Desdemona's bed also stands for the light of Desdemona's life and the soliloquy thus condenses the essence of this decisive moment into a symbolic image which could not be more simple, more cogent, more appropriate.

The most forceful example, however, for the emergence of a symbolic partner in a soliloquy is Macbeth's dialogue with the phantom-dagger (II, i, 33). Here 'the heat-oppressed brain' (39) has created by the power of imagination its symbolic counterpart. The dagger is more than a mere recipient of a speech, it has become a fearful partner in a process of struggle, hesitation and final resolution which is transposed into this compelling and terrible picture of the receding, bleeding dagger which, though not palpable and indeed a 'false creation' (38), is nevertheless more real than any real object could be.

Macbeth appears from the very beginning predestined for monologic speech. His asides during the first encounter with the witches are no longer in the tradition of information for the audience but are called forth as spontaneous utterances prompted by his disposition for sudden absorption which his partner Banquo early observes in him (I, iii, 57; 143). There is an imperceptible transition from these asides to longer asides which are indeed short soliloquies. And when Macbeth in the seventh scene enters for his first long soliloquy, 'If it were done when 'tis done', we have learned to know him as a character from whom we might expect this kind of lonely labouring self-reflection which combines visionary imagination and suffering obsession with a lucid awareness of his criminal purpose. But 'reflection' is no adequate term to cover the depth and range of Macbeth's soliloquies. For these soliloquies not only show us his mind at work, so that we enter into a process of thought and believe ourselves present while these thoughts are being formed, these soliloquies by virtue of Macbeth's imagination also carry the inner drama to a higher plane of metaphysical vision, they expand as it were the whole tragedy's scope so that we get a glimpse of things which may happen in another world. In Macbeth's and Lady Macbeth's soliloquies the powers of evil and the powers of good assume shape, they become realities and appear before our mind's eye.

Shakespeare's supreme art of illustrating an inner process, of expressing feelings, thoughts and moods not by abstract terms but by concrete images and precise symbols, has reached its climax in these soliloquies by Macbeth. The dramatization of the soliloquy, too, is particularly forceful here, as we not only watch with eager tension the way in which an inner conflict is made articulate through poetic vision, but we also see a development taking place each time so that the point reached at the end of the soliloquy is different from the attitude at its outset. Macbeth is no longer describing – as if from outside – what passes in himself; we are in fact drawn into the process of his inner experience which fuses thinking, feeling, imaginative vision into one complex mood. When Brutus, during the scene we have just mentioned, says in his fourth short soliloquy

> Between the acting of a dreadful thing
> And the first motion, all the interim is
> Like a phantasma or a hideous dream,
>
> (II, i, 63)

he still describes and states what in Macbeth's soliloquy has taken the form of a direct expression of something that happens within himself at just this moment.

We would have to go to great lengths to do full justice to Shakespeare's art of the soliloquy as it emerges in *Hamlet*, *Macbeth* and *Lear*. But it is clear that we would miss half the play and fail to understand these characters if we had not their soliloquies. In these soliloquies Shakespeare has not only developed a new mode of character revelation, he has also simultaneously worked out a new form of drama which by putting the emphasis on the inner drama and on a complex dramatic representation which proceeds on several levels calls for the soliloquy as an indispensable and subtle instrument. Each soliloquy comes at a significant moment and it carries on developments and reveals inner moods which can be made articulate in an appropriate manner only through monologic speech.[1]

This is not to say that all soliloquies in these plays consist of revelations of inner experience. Let us look for one moment at Hamlet's first soliloquy after King Claudius, with the Queen and the courtiers, has left the stage. During this scene Hamlet – though appearing for the first time in this play – has been unwilling to speak though our attention has been focused on his person all the time. When he remains alone on the stage we know that he will now open his mouth and speak without the restraint he has forced upon himself in the presence of others. But

[1] For a fuller treatment of Shakespeare's soliloquies see my study *Shakespeares Monologe*, Göttingen, 1964.

what we get in his soliloquy 'O that this too too solid flesh would melt' is not a train of thought nor a consistent process of feeling but a turmoil of emotion, recollection, and violent accusation breaking out into disrupted outcries, exclamations and sudden recognitions. The agonizing scene through which he has just passed transforms itself into vivid images and concrete symbols which flash before his mind to express not only his disgust at the world as it now presents itself to him, but also his clear remembrance and his love of his father, and his poignant realization of the 'hasty marriage'. We too, the audience, may live again through this past scene for which the soliloquy gives us the right background so that retrospectively this scene assumes a new significance for us. The soliloquy thus carries the tragedy to a different plane of reality and we are given new eyes, Hamlet's eyes, to look back at what has happened and to guess at what is still hidden in the future. In Hamlet's soliloquies Shakespeare has created a new kind of dramatic speech which by its rapid transitions, its dissolution of syntax, its extraordinary economy and its fusion of several emotions and ideas can follow the quickly changing reactions of a sensitive mind better than speech in dialogue ever could.

But what about 'To be or not to be'? (III, i). It is a superb example of the way in which Shakespeare turns into monologic speech an intricate chain of thought which is, as it were, connected subterraneously so that only parts of it reach the surface of the spoken text leaving it to us to supplement the missing links. But this most celebrated soliloquy, I venture to say, is one of the less typical of Shakespeare's monologues. For it is one of the very few soliloquies entirely given to 'reflection'. Shakespeare's soliloquizing characters, as a rule, not only think but feel and see, they look at themselves and at others, they remember and anticipate, they have their visions and presentiments, they address absent partners, they plan and make up their minds. But here a man only thinks and though the thought is transformed into unforgettable images it does not anywhere link up with the inner or outward action. And this sheer detached meditation, although most characteristic of Hamlet's present mood, is indeed rare in Shakespeare.

In Lear's monologic speeches to an even greater extent than in Hamlet's, Shakespeare has discovered the freedom given by the soliloquy to express in concentrated language the medley of images, visions and thoughts before they have been filtered, adjusted and arranged in orderly sequence for communicative speech as it is used in dialogue. This, to be sure, does not apply to all soliloquies and not even to all passages in those soliloquies which could here be quoted for the use of such 'monologic language'. Shakespeare has not pursued this path to its end, he has given us merely inklings of what might pass through a character's mind if he were endowed with the faculty to speak out when left alone.

It is necessary to recognize these modifications in order to understand the curious mixture of poetic licence, convention and quite unconventional expression which we find in these monologic speeches. For it appears that Shakespeare, exploiting the convention of the soliloquy, has nowhere moved farther away from 'conventional language' than in his soliloquies. Of the monologues spoken by Richard III, Richard II, the Bastard, Henry IV, Romeo and Juliet it could be said that their diction and structure do not differ much from speech as used in Shakespeare's dialogue-scenes in those same plays. In Hamlet's, Lear's, Macbeth's soliloquies, however, something new emerges; their crucial passages are built up and worded in such a manner that they would not fit into dialogic speech.

But, as I said before, this holds true only with modifications. For even in Hamlet's passionate outbursts we find relics of the old conventions, the announcement of future plans and the explanation of his own behaviour (obviously meant for the audience), features which have little to do with 'monologic self-expression'. The last eighteen lines of Hamlet's long soliloquy spoken after the Hecuba speech of the First Player in which Hamlet puts forth his plan of the mouse-trap play

> the play's the thing
> Wherein I'll catch the conscience of the king
>
> (II, ii)

are only one instance of the way these conventions live on. Nor should we forget that *King Lear*, which has some of the most remarkable monologic speeches (spoken by the king himself), also contains some of the most primitive self-explanations in the short monologues spoken by Edgar, Kent and Edmund who declare what they are and why they behave as they do. Shakespeare did not care whether he applied these primitive devices in his soliloquies[1] which, in the same play, he could transform into a medium of extraordinary intensity and boldness. And his late Romances[2] afford many instances of the survival of these primitive techniques in the soliloquies. Shakespeare made use of these conventions wherever he needed them and he would have smiled at our critical distinctions. His greatness lies not in the consistency but in the inconsistency, or let us better say freedom, with which he availed himself of all possible resources of dramatic tradition and stagecraft to create plays the mystery of which we shall not and should not exhaust.

[1] Many instances of Shakespeare's use of primitive devices in his soliloquies are pointed out by L. L. Schücking in *Character Problems in Shakespeare's Plays*, London, 1922.

[2] On the 'frankly informative' quality of the soliloquies in *Cymbeline* cf. H. Granville-Barker, *Prefaces to Shakespeare*, Second Series, London, 1946, pp. 240 f.

5

Appearance and Reality in Shakespeare's Plays

We are all familiar with the so-called casket-scene in *The Merchant of Venice*. This is where Portia puts her three suitors to the test and makes her own choice dependent on whether one of them can choose the right casket with her portrait in it. The two wealthy suitors, the Prince of Morocco and the Prince of Arragon, choose the golden or silver casket and are rejected, for they have made the wrong choice; they have allowed themselves to be deceived by outward appearance. Bassanio on the other hand selects the lead casket and so wins Portia's hand.

> You that choose not by the view,
> Change as fair and choose as true!
>
> (III, ii, 131)

are the words he finds on the note inside, whereas the Prince of Morocco learns from the note in the golden casket that:

> All that glisters is not gold,
> Often have you heard that told;
> Many a man his life hath sold,
> But my outside to behold.
> Gilded tombs do worms infold.
>
> (II, vii, 65)

Shakespeare himself did not invent the motif of the caskets. It had already been used in the Middle Ages. Indeed it belongs to a series of related motifs that appear in the most diverse places in world literature. One might think that a motif which is not of Shakespeare's own invention and a proverb that expresses a truism ('all that glitters is not gold') would not necessarily bring us to the discussion of an important theme in Shakespeare's works. However, we often find that in spite of self-evident and trivial beginnings Shakespeare finishes with some profound and hidden truth. In the choice of the caskets in *The Merchant of Venice*, Shakespeare has simply given expression, in a very striking way,

to the contrast between outward appearance and inner value. Nevertheless even this scene might make us be on the alert when we hear the
words Bassanio utters on the contrast between appearance and reality,
as he stands pensively before the caskets. He speaks of the way in
which, throughout the universe, appearance hides from us by falsifica-
tion and deception the real heart of things; in law, in religion and in the
behaviour of men whose vices are disguised as virtues:

> So may the outward shows be least themselves;
> The world is still deceiv'd with ornament.
> In law, what plea so tainted and corrupt
> But, being season'd with a gracious voice,
> Obscures the show of evil? In religion,
> What damned error but some sober brow
> Will bless it, and approve it with a text,
> Hiding the grossness with fair ornament?
> There is no vice so simple but assumes
> Some mark of virtue on his outward parts.
> . . .
> Thus ornament is but the guiled shore
> To a most dangerous sea; the beauteous scarf
> Veiling an Indian beauty; in a word,
> The seeming truth which cunning times put on
> To entrap the wisest. . . .
>
> (III, ii, 73)

If we examine the vocabulary of this passage and look at words like
'outward show', 'ornament', 'seeming truth', 'veiling' etc. we hit upon
associations that can be traced throughout all Shakespeare's works.[1]

[1] Shakespeare has far more words to denote 'appearance' than he has to express
'reality'. 'Show', 'falsehood', 'shadow', 'semblance', 'seeming', 'painted', 'illusion',
'counterfeit', 'visage', 'colour', 'cover', 'mockery', 'devision', 'deceit' and other
terms are used in connexion with 'appearance', which word, however, is itself
very rarely used in this sense, signifying 'semblance' (e.g. *2 Henry IV*, I, i, 128),
whereas 'reality' is not used by Shakespeare at all. He gives preference to 'truth'
and 'substance' in order to express 'reality' in our context. There are many revealing passages in which 'show' is used to denote 'appearance'. Cf. *Richard III*, III,
i, 9; *Henry V*, I, ii, 69; *Macbeth*, I, vii, 81; *Othello*, I, i, 49; II, iii, 339; *Cymbeline*, V, v,
52; *Pericles*, I, iv, 75; IV, iv, 23; *Romeo and Juliet*, III, ii, 76; *Lucrece*, 1513; *Comedy
of Errors*, III, ii, 8; *Much Ado About Nothing*, IV, i, 31. For further examples see the
full notes added to the German original of this essay (see p. viii) which may
also supplement the footnotes on the following pages.

We notice that the contrast between the outward and the inward,[1] between what man pretends to be and what he really is, between what he says in the presence of others and what he thinks alone – that this contrast pervades Shakespearian drama in a multiplicity of different forms. Again and again we find in Shakespeare's language turns of phrase and juxtapositions which represent exactly this. We perceive the contrast between the physiognomy of man and his essential being,[2] between the beautiful husk on the outside and the mouldy kernel on the inside, between the deceptive appearance and the hidden purpose. We find the notion of the devil in the form of an angel or of vice lurking under the disguise of virtue. These contrasts appear in a great variety of comparisons and images; we could arrange them in different groups and we could trace in them *topoi* from classical and medieval literature.[3] The theme of appearance and reality has always been one of the major themes of literature. We find it in Greek and Roman tragedy, in the comedies of Plautus and Terence, in medieval allegorical literature and in Dante. What distinguishes Shakespeare from all these and justifies a special examination of this contrast between appearance and reality in his plays is the comprehensive diversity with which he treats this theme. He lets it flicker up in the most diverse of contexts and the most varied of dramatic situations. He presents us with psychological situations in which it is just this contrast that finds expression, and he uses the resources of his dramatic art to transpose this contrast into plot and character.[4]

In drama as in real life the characters themselves are to a large extent responsible for the way in which appearance and reality diverge from each other. Dissimulation, hypocrisy and deception, and indeed the use

[1] For this contrast between 'outward' and 'inward' cf. *Merchant*, I, iii, 97; *Measure*, III, ii, 253; *Tempest*, I, ii, 104; *Sonnet*, 16.

[2] To describe this contrast Shakespeare often uses the opposition between 'heart' and 'tongue', or 'face' and 'heart'. Cf. *Macbeth*, III, ii, 34. See John L. Harrison in *Shakespeare Quarterly*, v, 1954. For the opposition between 'shadow' and 'substance' see Maria Wickert, *Anglia* 71 (1953).

[3] Thus Gregor's *vitia virtutes mentiuntur* was a *topos* in medieval and Renaissance literature. For illustrations in connexion with Shakespeare see Bertram Joseph, *Conscience and the King*, London, 1953, Ch. I.

[4] Within the limited space of this essay a number of plays which are of particular importance for the theme of appearance and reality could not be discussed here. For *Troilus and Cressida*, see L. C. Knights, 'The Theme of Appearance and Reality in *Troilus and Cressida*' in *Some Shakespearian Themes*, London, 1959.

of disguises and masks, are but a few of the devices that make this clear to us. The most frequent case is that of one character consciously producing a false appearance, to which another unconsciously falls victim. Sometimes, however, this unconscious deception by outward appearance can occur in drama without the deliberate intervention of a second person. This happens most frequently in the form of delusion, and self-deception. Situations, facts and circumstances, just as much as personal agents, can deceive by false appearances. Man is unable to see through the outward appearance of his surroundings or even of his own character – a situation that is particularly characteristic of the tragedies, but equally true of the comedies.

Let us begin with the deliberately arranged divergence of appearance and reality as we find it in the age-old motifs of disguise and mistaken identity, and as it confronts us particularly in the comedies of Shakespeare. Here, as in the plays of Aristophanes and Plautus and in the Italian comedy of the sixteenth century, disguise is used to bring about complications, comic surprises, unexpected disclosures and confrontations. Disguise, in Italian comedy, serves to produce comic situations rather than subtle characterization. One case of disguise and mistaken identity is added to another in order to increase the confusion and surprise to the point at which the audience is completely bewildered.[1] Here the situations and the artistic manipulation of the plot are dominant, for the characters are mere pawns in a puzzling game.

Now when we come to Shakespeare we see immediately how differently, how much more subtly and profoundly, he uses this motif and how in his hands it becomes a vehicle for a multiplicity of relationships in this very contrast between reality and appearance. The thing he usually does first is to reduce the number of disguised characters in each play so that our attention is entirely directed towards one person, who is usually the heroine in the disguise of a page. Furthermore Shakespeare avoids the overwhelming recurrence of complications and surprising situations, which would be only too easy to arrange in connexion with disguised roles of this kind, and instead he places all the emphasis on the characterization of this one disguised person.

Shakespeare's women disguised as pages (Julia in the *Two Gentlemen of Verona*, Rosalind in *As You Like It* and Viola in *Twelfth Night*) as

[1] Cf. V. O. Freeburg, *Disguise Plots in Elizabethan Drama. A Study in Stage Tradition*, New York, 1915.

a result of their very disguise find themselves in situations in which the fate of their own love is deeply involved and rendered more complicated. In the disguise of a page they stand unrecognized before their lovers and become even more painfully aware of their own destiny. In the page's cloak they speak to their unfaithful lovers about themselves, they confess their own love in such a way that their partners know neither who is meant nor, of course, who is speaking. Thus the words and gestures of Julia, Rosalind and Viola all bear a double meaning appreciated by the audience. These perpetual contrasts and confrontations of characters belong to the very essence of drama. Shakespeare not only uses them when individual characters are placed beside or opposite each other, but sometimes he also confronts a character with two opposing personalities in the same role. Julia, Rosalind and Viola act the part of a page and at the same time they act their own parts; indeed they are forced to act as themselves, for in all those scenes where they stand facing their own lovers in disguise and often in a precarious role, it is their own fate which is at stake. For the audience, who have been let into the secret of the disguise, this constant duplication of personalities is fraught with particular dramatic tension. They can, of course, recognize what is reality and what is appearance in the game that is being played on the stage, and they may follow with the greatest of pleasure the way in which the pages constantly keep up as much false semblance as is necessary for the expression of their own real personality, unrecognized under the disguise.

In the *Two Gentlemen of Verona* these effects are mainly achieved in an artificial manner with a wealth of puns, pointed remarks and antitheses. In *As You Like It* and *Twelfth Night*, however, we find this juxtaposition of appearance and reality in a more complex and subtle form. For the strange thing is that here, under the mask of the page, the real personality of the woman in love is able to reveal itself far more completely and with much greater originality and tenderness. In *As You Like It* Rosalind as the page Ganymede rehearses with her lover Orlando a feigned love-scene between him and Rosalind. Thus in the guise of a page she can not only be herself but also what she would like to be in her successful relationship with Orlando. In this disguise she can be more open, more loving and more tender than she could ever be as her real self. Quite aware of what she is doing, she takes full advantage of every opportunity of expressing in this artificial situation what she really is and thinks. Thus the second mask removes the first, and appearance becomes self-revelation, anticipation and expression of the character's real self.

In *Twelfth Night* Viola in the guise of Cesario has to become the bearer of messages of love from the Duke whom she herself loves, whereas Olivia instead of returning the Duke's passion, loses her heart to Cesario, whom she can never win. We have here then two situations of false appearance. In Italian comedy, too, there were paradoxes of this kind where the fates of characters became inextricably entangled with each other and roles could be exchanged and positions reversed. Shakespeare, however, does not treat these situations merely as scenes of comedy and farce. These juxtapositions, to be sure, may provoke our laughter, but below the surface there is a new and sublime consciousness of the characters' own feelings, and of their own capabilities. In her role as messenger between the Duke whom she loves and the woman whom he is courting, but who rejects him, Viola is the spectator of a situation that concerns her profoundly and in which she takes part as a willing and unwilling participant. As if in a mirror, she recognizes her own woman's destiny as well as her present position. And thus in her disguise she realizes far better than she would have done without it that Olivia, too, has created around herself an unreal situation and in fact is wearing a mask – though one of which she herself is unconscious. We can gather this from the following piece of dialogue:

> *Olivia.*   I prithee tell me what thou think'st of me.
> *Viola.*   That you do think you are not what you are.
> *Olivia.*   If I think so, I think the same of you.
> *Viola.*   Then think you right: I am not what I am.
>
> (III, i, 135)

As early as their first meeting Olivia had with some foreboding enquired of Cesario as he entered: 'Are you a comedian?' (I, v, 171), to which the latter replied: 'No my profound heart; and yet, by the very fangs of malice I swear, I am not that I play.' (I, v, 172 f.)

However, like an actor who grows more and more into the role he is playing and discovers capabilities of which he was unaware, Viola also finds that in this game a part of her own nature is rediscovered. Out of deliberate appearance has grown reality that was not intentional, just as for other characters a new fate has developed.

But are not all of us actors who act a part in which we are never quite our real selves? Shakespeare put this very question in *As You Like It*, where Jacques compares the world to a stage on which each man plays his role. He was making new use of a very ancient metaphor, which E. R. Curtius has traced through the whole range of world literature.[1] However, this comparison meant more to Shakespeare than to others. It was not just a metaphor that came easily to the mind of Shakespeare the playwright and actor, who had continually to think in roles, to write them and to act them. Behind it lay one of the fundamental elements in his view of the world and of life: man as an actor, the world as a stage,[2] our behaviour as ostensible behaviour, not indicative of our real selves. The drama is thus a reflection of man's actions in actual life, and the deceptive appearance of the action on the stage is by no means so far removed from the deceptive appearance of our own play-acting in real life. We can see how this contrast between reality and appearance reveals itself in more far-reaching and fundamental relationships. For the task of the playwright, as indeed of any creative artist, is to enthral us by the illusion of the play so that at least for the duration of the performance we accept it as a kind of reality. All art requires illusion so as to demonstrate reality to the spectator.

And is not disguise within a stage role really a double disguise? For every actor who portrays a person in the drama (and the word 'persona' in antiquity meant 'mask') is really someone in disguise. We said that in the disguised role of Rosalind the second mask removes the first. As far as the Elizabethan audience and the Shakespearian stage are concerned, this is in a particular sense true of all the female characters who disguise themselves as pages or as youths. For on the Elizabethan stage female parts were always taken by youths, with the result that when Rosalind, Viola or Julia appeared as pages they had for Shakespeare's audience reassumed their natural sex. This situation of appearance versus reality in the inner working of the play is thus ironically reversed. Many of the veiled remarks uttered by female characters disguised as pages and furthermore many a dramatic moment

[1] E. R. Curtius, *European Literature and the Latin Middle Ages*, transl. W. R. Task, London, 1953. The inscription on the Globe Theatre *Totus Mundus agit histrionem* derives from John of Salisbury's *Policraticus*, as Curtius has shown.

[2] Of the many passages illustrating this the following may be quoted: *Merchant*, I, i, 78; *2 Henry IV*, I, i, 155; *Macbeth*, V, v, 25; *Lear*, IV, vi, 1, 83; *Sonnet* 15. See Anne Righter, *Shakespeare and the Idea of the Play*, London, 1962.

in the plot play upon this ambiguity. Thus many of their subtle and comic effects are lost upon the audience of to-day.

Let us now return to *Twelfth Night*. The appearance of Viola disguised as a page not only deceives Olivia but in the end gives rise to such confusion that no one knows quite what is happening nor what is illusion and what reality. This chaotic situation, which can often be found at the end of other comedies, is produced in *Twelfth Night* by the arrival of Sebastian, Viola's twin brother, who himself is now taken to be Cesario. The device of mistaken identity, so successfully employed in the *Comedy of Errors* is now added to the device of disguise. And so in the end everybody is fooled by appearance. 'A natural perspective, that is and is not' (v, i, 209) as the Duke remarks. It is in fact the eye that is deceived. 'I am ready to distrust mine eyes/and wrangle with my reason. . . .' (IV, iii, 13) says Sebastian after his first unexpected and inexplicable meeting with Olivia. What the characters themselves believe they have unmistakably perceived becomes confused and inexplicable, indeed contradicts and refutes itself. Sebastian just cannot understand what is going on and declares:

> Or I am mad, or else this is a dream.
> Let fancy still my sense in Lethe steep;
> If it be thus to dream, still let me sleep!
>
> (IV, i, 60)

Puzzled remarks of this kind are often made by Shakespeare's characters in similar situations.[1] Time and again in the comedies the characters find themselves in this position towards the end of the play. They are confronted by facts which are incomprehensible, for visual evidence is matched by conflicting visual evidence, and often enough material proofs are also available that are above all suspicion of being false. At the end of *All's Well That Ends Well* Bertram and the King are completely helpless when confronted by the physical evidence of the rings, which they are unable to reconcile with the facts as they know them. In *Much Ado About Nothing* Claudio is convinced of the faithlessness of Hero for the simple reason that he saw another man talking at her window after midnight.

Shakespeare's plays abound in examples of this kind. Time and again

---

[1] Cf. *Comedy of Errors*, II, ii, 181; *Two Gentlemen*, v, iv, 26; *Merry Wives*, III, v, 123; *Much Ado*, IV, i, 65 etc.

characters are fooled by appearances, deceived by pieces of apparent evidence, and time and again it is their own senses, their eyes and their ears that deceive them.[1] It is not until the end that an explanation (in most cases a very simple one) is found for all the mysteries; the deft hand of the dramatist unravels the knots, and what was incredible can now be believed. The scales fall from the characters' eyes when they become aware of their deception. However, not one of them escapes it, for deception penetrates into the life of all these people in a great variety of forms: misleading events, lies, calumny, misunderstandings, mistaken identity, news wrongly interpreted, unfortunate chains, of coincidences, hypocrisy, dissimulation, disguise, hallucinations, all of which are forever causing man to take appearances for reality.

And yet in Shakespeare the final and most decisive source of deception is to be found in self-deception. The character is so open to deception from outside because he deceives himself, because his vanity, his fear, his pride, his arrogance, his grievances or his cravings deceive him and prevent him from seeing reality and true proportions in his environment.[2] This invisible mask that man unknowingly wears and that we noticed earlier in connexion with Olivia in *Twelfth Night* is a sign that he does not know himself, that he is not what, according to his essence, he ought to be. 'O, that once more you knew but what you are!' (Ind. ii, 76) are the words we find in the *Taming of the Shrew*, and again in the thirteenth sonnet, 'Oh that you were yourself'.[3] Thus in Shakespearian drama self-deception is most intimately connected with deception in general. This delusive appearance, to which man falls easy prey, penetrates into his very being, into his knowledge of himself.

However, the confusion and chaos that arise in these comedies because people are deceived by outward appearance are never final or completely tragic. They lead us only as far as the threshold of tragedy. Where Shakespeare's comedy grows serious it is mere illusion: the threatening catastrophe is discovered to be appearance and not reality, or else it is averted. In *Othello* the apparent evidence of Desdemona's

---

[1] e.g. *Cymbeline* IV, ii, 302.
[2] This process could be illustrated from many passages, e.g. Bertram's account of his self-deception with regard to Helena *All's Well*, v, iii, 44.
[3] Cf. Arthur's words to Hubert in *King John*, IV, i, 126.

> O now you look like Hubert! All this while
> You were disguised.

handkerchief finally seals the catastrophe and in *Romeo and Juliet* the apparent death of Juliet is not recognized in time by Romeo for what it is. In the comedies, however, what appear to be tragic complications are not irreparable. Helena in *All's Well That Ends Well* is not dead, but merely appears to be. The alliance between Hero and Claudio in *Much Ado About Nothing* is not irretrievably broken, Viola in *Twelfth Night* will not be the rejected lover for ever and Claudio in *Measure for Measure* is not executed despite the sentence of death passed upon him.

Of course with the comedies much more than with the tragedies, the audience is expected from the very beginning to take the play as a play and to look at the whole comedy in this perspective of appearance and reality. From the very beginning we are waiting for the dramatist to wave his magic wand and so dispel the illusion. And since comedy is a game, the playwright can make much freer and more masterful use of his magic wand. That is why – from the point of view of the audience – appearance in the comedies in the form of disguises, mistaken identities, deceptions and other devices is much less convincing than in the trage- dies. In the comedies we are conscious of the hand of the dramatist directing the play; we are conscious of his magic wand. Indeed in one or two comedies we encounter real magic where appearance and deception cease to be the work of man. In *A Midsummer Night's Dream* as well as in the Romances we find ourselves in a world where meta- morphosis and spells, fairies, elves and airy spirits create this appear- ance which presents its deceptive self to the eyes of men, which misleads him and indeed may often lead him. In this sphere appearance and reality merge imperceptibly with one another so that we really believe ourselves to be in an unreal world of dreams. And we, the spectators, are expected to look on it as a dream we have dreamt ourselves. As Puck says in the epilogue to *A Midsummer Night's Dream*

> If we shadows have offended,
> Think but this, and all is mended,
> That you have but slumb'red here
> While these visions did appear.
> And this weak and idle theme,
> No more yielding but a dream.
>
> (v, i, 412)

But even in this world of appearance and deception that we find in *A*

Midsummer Night's Dream[1] the symbolical significance of the play for our own human existence remains the same: we are all deceived mortals; we are deluded by others and by ourselves. Deception and error are the inescapable destiny of man. In all his plays Shakespeare admits this quite candidly and is in this respect much more tolerant than many of his contemporaries who brand error as a sin.[2] For as Helena says of God and mortals in *All's Well That Ends Well*:

> It is not so with Him that all things knows,
> As 'tis with us that square our guess by shows.
>
> (II, i, 148)

However, falling prey to appearance is not only the common lot of man, but also a necessity if he is to reach himself. For wherever there is appearance there is also the removal of appearance, and where there is a mask, the lifting of the mask; and this not in the sense of some superficial happy ending but rather in the sense of an elucidation, a clarification. People, things and relationships are examined down to their real core, what is unreal and deceptive in them is uncovered, and truth and reality are brought to light.[3] In Shakespeare's plays the relationships between the characters have first to pass through a welter of misunderstandings and erroneous evaluations before they are allowed to appear in their true colours. It is seldom the case that a true relationship is established from the very beginning. Those who are wearing masks or who do not know themselves (both can sometimes apply) must first be transposed into certain situations where they find themselves without a mask.

However, for a person's mask to be recognized and his deceptive appearance to be exposed, he must above all be placed in some excep-

---

[1] Cf. my introduction to *A Midsummer Night's Dream* in The Signet Classic Shakespeare, New York, 1963.

[2] Thus in the *Faerie Queene* error is looked upon with much greater severity. The official Puritan attitude is even more intolerant. Cf. W. H. Frere and C. E. Douglas, *Puritan Manifestoes*, London, 1907.

[3] In *Measure for Measure* Isabella admonishes the Duke

> but let your reason serve
> To make the truth appear where it seems hid,
> And hide the false seems true.
>
> (v, i, 65)

This applies to many other plays, too.

tional situation. If the Duke in *Measure for Measure* had not appointed Angelo as his representative with complete and unlimited authority, Angelo would never have revealed himself in his true colours. It is the attraction of power, the intensity of temptation, the elevation of rank and position, and the unusual nature of the situation that put the person to the test and bring out the real nature that is hidden inside him. The Duke hints at this in the first act when he says of the high position that Angelo has now been given:

> Hence shall we see,
> If power change purpose, what our seemers be.
>
> (I, iii, 53)

Of course, Angelo himself is also aware that hidden in this new position of power lies the danger of 'false appearance', and in his important monologue in the second act before his second meeting with Isabella he tells us:

> O place, O form,
> How often dost thou with thy case, thy habit,
> Wrench awe from fools, and tie the wiser souls
> To thy false seeming!
>
> (II, iv, 12)

Appearance of this kind is soon recognized in Angelo and exposed. 'Seeming, seeming!/I will proclaim thee, Angelo, look for't.' (II, iv, 150) is the threat Isabella uses to her extortioner in the same scene and shortly afterwards she informs her brother what 'this outward sainted deputy' (III, i, 90) really is. In the next scene the Duke has also realized that there is something quite different hidden behind Angelo's respectable and unimpeachable exterior:

> O, what may man within him hide,
> Though angel on the outward side!
> How may likeness, made in crimes,
> Make a practice on the times,
> To draw with idle spiders' strings
> Most ponderous and substantial things!
>
> (III, ii, 253)

And yet we do not do full justice to Angelo by applying to his case this contrast between reality and appearance. Angelo has not deliberately worn a mask before; he does not belong to those of Shakespeare's villains like Richard III or Iago who consciously dissemble and play the hypocrite. In their case it is quite easy to draw a clear, sharp line between reality and appearance in all their actions and words. Angelo, on the other hand, wears no conscious disguise. He feels very seriously about his responsibility to use severity and to enforce the law. Angelo's qualifications for the exalted office of Regent cannot be dismissed as deceptive appearance. His qualities as a ruler are just as much a part of his being as the temptation of his blood, which until then had been completely unknown to him and which now shatters his whole personality.

We have reached the point at which we can see some of the problematical issues of our subject. For in the plays of his middle and late period Shakespeare often leaves open the question of what is indeed appearance and what reality in a character's actions and words. In several cases the characters themselves tell us quite clearly what is to be considered as reality and what as appearance in their character, as, for example, when Desdemona in her apparently merry and light-hearted conversation with Iago states:

> I am not merry; but I do beguile
> The thing I am by seeming otherwise.
>
> (II, i, 122)

However, in Shakespeare's tragedies appearance and reality often merge into each other. The madness of Hamlet, as he himself tells us, is a mask, a kind of self-protection. But under the surface of this feigned insanity may there not lie hidden something of a genuine disturbance of his mental equilibrium?[1] And how are we to interpret the behaviour and words of his uncle, King Claudius, at the very beginning of the play in the great banquet scene – as pure hypocrisy, as a stratagem, as a manœuvre to deceive the world? Should we not rather understand the manner of his speech as an expression of court ceremonial, as a demonstration of regal responsibility and position? Of course, we are taken aback and warned when we hear Hamlet himself speaking for the first time at some length in the same scene. His mother had asked him 'Why

[1] Cf. Harry Levin, 'The Antic Disposition' in *The Question of Hamlet*, Oxford, 1959.

seems it so particular with thee?', referring to her words that it is common to die, to which Hamlet replies:

> Seems, madam! Nay, it is; I know not seems.
> 'Tis not alone my inky cloak, good mother,
> Nor customary suits of solemn black,
> Nor windy suspiration of forc'd breath,
> No, nor the fruitful river in the eye,
> Nor the dejected haviour of the visage,
> Together with all forms, moods, shapes of grief,
> That can denote me truly. These, indeed, seem;
> For they are actions that a man might play;
> But I have that within which passes show —
> These but the trappings and the suits of woe.
>
> (I, ii, 76)

So here we have the question about appearance and reality asked explicitly by one of the most reflective characters that Shakespeare ever created, and one of the most honest with himself. And indeed in the whole of Shakespearian tragedy Hamlet is the character who sees through appearance most sharply, and himself almost entirely avoids being deluded by it. It is not just by chance that Shakespeare chose to put this same Hamlet into a situation where more than in any other the deceptiveness of our human existence is unforgettably expressed: the grave-diggers' scene. Yet Hamlet, who abhors appearance more than any other Shakespearian character, resorts to it himself in order to survive. He needs the mask so that he can unmask others with it.[1] For much of what Hamlet says to Rosencrantz and Guildenstern, to Polonius and Claudius and even to Ophelia can be understood as the unmasking and exposure of appearance. Yet, on the other hand, Hamlet, in a sinister and almost unfathomable manner, is capable of blending mask and reality, disguise and exposure. He says the truth, yet does not

---

[1] Several critics have dwelt on this aspect. J. Dover Wilson calls the whole second act a 'comedy of masks' and says of Hamlet that he 'Touchstone-like uses his madness like a stalking-horse and under the presentation of that he shoots his wit' (*What Happens in Hamlet*, 1935, p. 95). The mask as a means for unmasking others is a recurring motif in Shakespeare. Cf. Max Lüthi, *Shakespeares Dramen*, Berlin, 1957. With regard to *Hamlet* cf. R. A. Foakes in *Shakespeare Survey* 9 (1956), B. Joseph, *Conscience and the King*, 1953 and J. Paterson in *Shakespeare Quarterly*, II (1951).

disclose his secret; he allows a glimpse to be caught of his real self only to draw a mask over it again at the very same moment. Thus in Hamlet we are called upon in a particularly obvious manner to distinguish between appearance and reality, and yet we discover how difficult this is and how complicated all the questions connected with it are. We should add, however, that it must be complicated because in our own lives, too, this interaction of reality and appearance, and the true recognition of them, are among the most complicated facts of our existence. For in real life we do not meet a Viola disguised as a page, knowing that he is not one; we are dealing the whole time with characters in disguise, and with them we do not know, and often never find out, where disguise ends and reality begins. Indeed we are often in disguise ourselves!

Now in tragedy this vacillation between appearance and reality is more frequent, the interaction and fusion with one another more subtle; the deception, however, is more complete and thus the self-deception more tragic and more terrifying. The play with appearance which we found in the comedies has become a harrowing and painful experience. As spectators we are not let into the secret to the same degree as in the comedies, where the disguise is a striking indication of the juxtaposition of reality and appearance. The dividing lines are by no means always as clear as in *Othello*, where on the one hand we have Iago who appears honest, but is really diabolical (and this he is for ever telling us himself), and on the other hand we have the Moor who lays himself open to deception from the very beginning because of his guileless and upright character and his ignorance of human nature. If, however, we think of *Macbeth*, of the intricate relationship between deception and truth, between reality and appearance in the prophecies of the witches and their fulfilment, and above all if we think of appearance and reality in the person of the hero himself, in his experiences, his bearing and his conduct, we realize how complicated and all-embracing our original question has become in the case of tragedy. The discussion of it must necessarily in a tragedy like *Macbeth* lead us to the very heart of the drama.

It is thus quite impossible within the space of a single lecture to take each of the tragedies and to examine in them the juxtaposition of reality and appearance. All we can do at this point is to limit ourselves to one tragedy, namely *King Lear* and to indicate how the different aspects of this contrast are intricately woven into the fabric of the play. For all the motifs which we have so far considered are to be met with in this tragedy: disguise, dissimulation, deception of others and of oneself, dependence on appearance, and the ability to see through it. And they all serve to unfold a comprehensive view of life, that suggests more universal issues beyond the confines of the plot.

In the very first scene we see how a character's misunderstanding of himself and of others causes him to be deceived by false appearance. Although he invited them himself, Lear takes Goneril's and Regan's hypocritical protestations of love for him as genuine and sees only lack of affection in Cordelia's silence and refusal to declare her love in a multitude of words. Cordelia seems to be wanting in affection, but is in fact the only daughter who really loves her father.[1] Goneril and Regan, on the other hand, appear to love their father deeply but in reality have hearts of stone. In both cases the false appearance is quite easy for the informed spectator to see through. Thus, because of the psychological improbability of the situation, Goethe considered Lear's behaviour in this scene as *absurd*.[2] Yet the old man's extraordinary misunderstanding of the reactions of his daughters, provoked as they were by his own wrong-headed questioning, is nothing more than an expression of the false situation in which Lear finds himself, an indication of his captivity in a world of privileges and royal isolation, where flattery, obedience and absence of any kind of contradiction are at home. An Elizabethan audience was perfectly well aware of this and could appreciate how difficult it was for a king to distinguish between reality and appearance in those who stood before him. However, for the rather grotesque form of misunderstanding that we see in the first scene Lear needed a particular frame of mind: obstinate, irascible, petulant and egocentric. But even this would not have been decisive, if Lear had only understood himself. For in the final analysis Lear's misunderstanding of the situation results from his misunderstanding of himself. This is made quite clear in the very first scene in the apt commentary of the two sisters Goneril and Regan:

> *Goneril.* He always lov'd our sister most; and with what poor
> judgment he hath now cast her off appears too grossly.

---

[1] Cordelia's role in the first scene has, however, also found adverse criticism. See Ivor Morris, 'Cordelia and Lear', *Shakespeare Quarterly*, VIII (1957).
[2] Goethe, *Shakespeare und kein Ende*, III (1813–16).

Regan.   'Tis the infirmity of his age; yet he hath ever but slenderly
            known himself.

(I, i, 289)

Misunderstanding of others is thus very closely connected with misunderstanding of himself. Lear could only fall prey to the false appearance of the situation in the first scene because with one part of his
existence he belongs to this illusion himself. His misunderstanding of
the situation is not just limited to the answers of his three daughters.
His abdication and the division of the kingdom, whereby he relinquishes all the power and yet wishes to retain his royal prerogatives,
are also a failure to recognize the actual situation. This misunderstanding also includes Kent, who by contradicting his master and intervening on behalf of Cordelia endeavours to make the king see through
appearances and recognize the truth ('See better, Lear . . . ', I, i, 156).
He has to pay for this service with banishment. Thus Lear starts out at
the beginning of the play as one blinded to reality and does not fall into
blindness only in the course of the action, as do Othello and Macbeth.
In such a situation his eyes cannot be opened; the way must be barred
to Lear for the time being.

This is one meaning, though not the only one, of the path of suffering that Lear has to tread in the next few scenes and acts. In his wret-
chedness, his expulsion and finally in his madness, the king gradually
perceives what is illusion in the world and what until the present has
been illusion in his own life. And we are shown step by step how Lear
overcomes this world of false appearances. Paradoxically, this is
achieved through people and situations making use of false appearances
themselves. In the guise of a simple servant, Kent offers the king his
services, and behind this mask, can now do for the king what he was
prevented from doing before. Here the disguise is not an escape from
his own self, but rather an aid to the realization of those intentions of his
own which at the court were doomed to failure. Thus there is profound
meaning in the words with which Kent answers the king's question:
'What dost thou profess?' He says:

> I do profess to be no less than I seem, to serve
> him truly that will put me in trust, to love him
> that is honest. . . .

(I, iv, 13)

Kent is acting a part and yet able to be himself, indeed more himself than he could be before. He renounces only his person and not his nature. In fact he now can give even freer rein to his real self and even more unreserved expression to it than at any time in the past. This is true not only of his dealings with Lear, to whom he can now say the truth with much less reticence, but also of his dealings with a courtier like Oswald, whose false character is immediately shown up by the sterling qualities of Kent.

Besides Kent, Lear is accompanied throughout the whole of these scenes by the fool, whose very profession it is to appear other than he really is. This fool, the wisest and the most sympathetic that Shakespeare has created, sees more clearly than all the other people in the play and recognizes more astutely the pretences and appearances in which Lear still believes, and he knows more exactly than any other the laws of reality. It is the fool who opens Lear's eyes. His jokes, his merry songs and proverbs reveal his insight into the ways of the world, but in spite of being formulated as general maxims they always fit the case of Lear himself. Thus even here, on the level of linguistic expression, we also see the counterplay of reality and appearance. For in the form of apparently non-committal proverbs and statements of general wisdom the fool can bring home to Lear truths which the king would have refused to listen to in a more direct form. But even in his own personality the fool seems to be different from what he is. Beneath the frolicsome high spirits that he displays to the outside world lies a painful need to share the griefs of others; under his fool's clothes this apparently mocking jester conceals a tender and sensitive heart.

In the heart-rending scene on the heath the rejected king with his two companions, Kent and the fool, is joined by a third man in disguise. This is Edgar, who under the pretence of being a wretched idiot appears on the heath as poor Tom. His mask is self-protection and refuge. Maligned and hunted by his brother, Edgar has given up his own identity in order merely to be able to remain alive:

> I will preserve myself; and am bethought
> To take the basest and most poorest shape
> That every penury in contempt of man
> Brought near to beast.
>
> (II, iii, 6)

In the juxtaposition of Edmund and Edgar we see the same kind of reversal of reality as in the case of Goneril, Regan and Cordelia. For Edgar, who is accused by his brother of patricide and villainy, appears to be what Edmund now actually is.

What is the significance, however, of this contrasting picture of poor Tom, the Bedlam beggar, who pursued by the foul fiend, with mud-stained face, naked, wretched and abject, now appears before Lear? Here we have a character simulating madness confronting another who is himself to become mad. This feigned madness mirrors the genuine madness and shows up the reality of it in an even more hideous light. Tom's voluntarily assumed appearance of an unprotected, wretched and naked figure makes even more obvious the homelessness and in-security of the king. On the other hand at the sight of poor Tom's wretched nakedness Lear at last perceives what man really is: man with-out clothes and finery, without pomp and title, without the artificiality of 'lendings' as Lear himself calls them.

> Is man no more than this? Consider him well. Thou ow'st the worm no silk, the beast no hide, the sheep no wool, the cat no perfume. Ha! here's three on's are sophisticated! Thou art the thing itself; unaccommodated man is no more but such a poor, bare, forked animal as thou art. Off, off, you lendings!
>
> (III, iv, 103)

And with a symbolic gesture of self-dispossession and in imitation of the figure standing before him, Lear tears these 'lendings', his clothes, from his body. The image of clothes that conceal and envelop, that are so often deceptive and show only what is external and 'borrowed' in man, finds frequent and significant use in the language of the drama.[1] In fact it has become a *topos* in English literature, which has also been used by other authors, for example Swift and Carlyle, as the symbolic expression of the contrast between reality and appearance.

In the passage that we have just quoted Lear seeks to sound the real nature of man and in doing so penetrates again and again through the hypocrisy and dissimulation on the surface. Here he conjures

---

[1] Cf. Th. Greenfield, 'The Clothing Motif in King Lear', *Shakespeare Quarterly*, v (1954); R. B. Heilman, *This Great Stage. Image and Structure in King Lear*, 1948, Ch. III; the clothing-metaphor is used by Shakespeare in other plays, too, to denote appearance. See the German notes.

up a vision of the most varied kinds of people and situations. And everywhere he discovers sham, deceptive appearance and dissimulation:

> Thou perjur'd, and thou simular man of virtue
> That art incestuous; caitiff, to pieces shake,
> That under covert and convenient seeming
> Hast practis'd on man's life.
>
> (III, ii, 54)

> The usurer hangs the cozener.
> Through tatter'd clothes small vices do appear;
> Robes and furr'd gowns hide all.
>
> (IV, vi, 163)

This contrast between appearance and reality reaches its highest dramatic expression in the mock trial of his daughters which the mad king holds in the wretched hovel on the heath. This is play-acting within the play, in which the three men in disguise, Kent, Edgar and the fool, take part. Lear assigns to them the roles of the learned judge and his assessors, while Goneril is represented by a stool. Thus this weird trial develops as much from the imagination of the demented Lear as from the co-operation of the King's three loyal followers, who suffer under their own disguises and are here at one and the same time both assistants and spectators. Their 'asides', such as Edgar's words:

> My tears begin to take his part so much
> They mar my counterfeiting.
>
> (III, vi, 59)

make this tension between appearance and reality more and more perceptible to the audience.

These are, however, by no means all the forms of the contrast between reality and appearance that we meet in this drama. The Gloster plot which in many respects repeats and mirrors that of Lear, begins in the same way with a father mistaking his children and allowing himself to be deceived by false appearance. Further obvious variations of this reality and appearance theme are Edgar as a peasant standing at the side of his blinded father and making him believe that he is about to leap into the void from the summit of the high cliff at Dover, and also Edgar in the guise of a jousting knight in the last scene of the drama. In many of these cases a curious inversion of this motif of disguising and unmasking is to be seen. For we may notice the ambiguity inherent in this theme as we find it in Shakespeare's great tragedies. The false appearance and deception that originate from Edmund are devilish deceit, whereas in Edgar's case they have a very positive value; they heal and restore. Edgar too, deceives his father but in so doing guards and protects him.

It seems as if Shakespeare in *King Lear* wanted to show us how much deception, disguise and false appearance are not only an inevitable but also a necessary part of our human existence so that, in particular situations, they can even be a permissible way of intervening and of helping.[1]

> Only, in this disguise, I think't no sin
> To cozen him that would unjustly win.
>
> (IV, ii, 75)

This is what Diana says to justify her conscious use of disguise in *All's Well That Ends Well*. Edgar and Kent assume humble roles and appear in a disguise that allows them to seem far below their real rank. However, by this very device they are enabled to render a service to their fellow men which would have been quite impossible in their original roles.

So far we have observed the juxtaposition of reality and appearance in the contrast between mask and genuine character, in man's readiness to deceive and his addiction to false appearances, and in the sham and deceptive nature of particular situations. More often than not, in Shakespeare's last dramas, in his Romances, *The Tempest*, *Cymbeline*, and *The Winter's Tale*, we have the impression that reality itself is looked upon as illusion. A dream-world, in which fantasy and magic hold sway, begins to drive out reality, which in comparison appears inconstant, merely relative and unreal, whereas the dream-world itself signifies genuine reality. Prospero's famous words:

---

[1] Although the opposite function of disguise and deception is more frequent in Shakespeare, and would correspond to Viola's lines in *Twelfth Night* II, ii, 25.
> Disguise, I see thou art a wickedness
> Wherein the pregnant enemy does much.
Cf. *TN*, v, i, 234 and *Love's Labour's Lost*, IV, iii, 253.

> We are such stuff
> As dreams are made on; and our little life
> Is rounded with a sleep.
>
> (IV, i, 156)

express this idea more closely than any other passage in the Romances. However, it would be too much of a simplification to try to fit all these facts into the one formula of 'the world as a world of appearances'. Even Prospero, important as he is, is only one voice out of many. He stands before us as a sage with a magic wand, perhaps a secret portrait of the dramatist himself taking his leave. In the same speech Prospero allows his eyes to survey the whole of this world, and at this moment it appears to him as illusion, as an 'insubstantial pageant':

> And, like the baseless fabric of this vision,
> The cloud-capp'd towers, the gorgeous palaces,
> The solemn temples, the great globe itself,
> Yes, all which it inherit, shall dissolve,
> And, like this insubstantial pageant faded,
> Leave not a rack behind.
>
> (IV, i, 151)

Parallels have been drawn between passages such as these and the Spanish Baroque drama of Calderon and Lope de Vega. For it is under this aspect that in their plays the antithesis between appearance and reality is treated.[1] But what in Shakespeare constitutes only one aspect of a complex phenomenon, becomes in these baroque plays the predominant point of view which is even suggested by the titles of some plays by Calderon such as *La Vida es Sueño* (*Life is a Dream*).

However, a warning must be pronounced against extending the concept of Baroque to cover the significant and manifold role played by the antithesis of appearance and reality in the literature and culture of the sixteenth century. But it could form the subject of a fascinating study to trace the occurrence of this antithesis not only in Elizabethan prose and poetry[2] but also in the cultural and intellectual life of the period, and to enquire into the various reasons which came together to make of

---

[1] Cf. Hugo Friedrich, *Der fremde Calderon*, Freiburg i. Br., 1955.
[2] Cf. the dissertation by Edgar Faas, '*Schein und Sein*' *in der früh-elisabethanischen Lyrik und Prasa* (1550–1590), Diss. München, 1965.

this perspective an all-pervading view point and conception. Nevertheless Shakespeare gives us the most complex representation of appearance and reality to be found in any author of the sixteenth and
seventeenth centuries. The way in which he does it may make us forget,
by its timeless appeal and its sheer humanity, that his depiction of appearance and reality had also been determined by important changes in
psychology and contemporary influences. For behind Shakespeare's
dramatization of the appearance and reality theme lies a new conception
of man which emerges in some European writers of the period. An
examination of the interpretations of human nature current in the
decades at the turn of the century would show that the notion that man
is different from what he appears to be closely corresponds to the other
concept that man is altogether a contradictory creature with many
layers to his character. The neat and simple conception that man consisted of a few clearly perceptible traits, had now been replaced by a new
conception that recognized his complexity, that admitted his inner paradoxes and contradictions and repeatedly testified to his inscrutability.
Montaigne, whose name I mention here as the most important in this
connexion, observes in his *Essais* (I, I) which in John Florio's translation[1] were widely read in England, 'Surely, man is a wonderfull,
vaine, divers, and wavering subject: it is very hard to ground any
directly-constant and uniforme judgment upon him.' In fact between
Montaigne's interpretation of mankind and Shakespeare's representation there are striking similarities that have apparently not yet been
adequately exploited by research.[2]

Almost all the fundamental problems of man's life which we noted
in Shakespeare in connexion with our topic can also be found in the
writings of Montaigne; and in his *Essais* they form a very similar pattern of thought within which the antithesis of reality and appearance
can be observed as a recurrent main theme. For Montaigne, too, is fully
aware of the contrast between man's external appearance and his real
nature; he well knows the gulf that lies between outward behaviour and

---

[1] *Montaigne, Essais* transl. by John Florio, ed. L. C. Harmer, Everyman Library,
London, 1910/1965.
[2] The emphasis of comparative studies has so far been on parallels and similarities
of phrase and motif. Cf. Elizabeth R. Hooker i. *PMLA* 17 (1902); J. Churton
Collins, 'Shakespeare and Montaigne' in *Studies in Shakespeare*, Westminster,
1904; G. C. Taylor, *Shakespeare's Debt to Montaigne*, Cambridge, Mass., 1925,
New York, 1968; Susanne Türck, *Shakespeare and Montaigne*, Berlin, 1930.

inner character, between deeds and their motive, between what someone says and what he really means.

> For certainly, howbeit the greatest number of our actions bee but
> masked and painted over with dissimulation and that it may some-
> times be true,'

> Haeredis fletus sub persona risus est. (Anl. Gell.)

> The weeping of an heire is laughing under a visard or disguise.
> Yet must a man consider by judging of his accidents, how our
> mindes are often agitated by divers passions.[1]

(I, 37)

And like Shakespeare Montaigne is constantly discussing man's suc-
cumbing to appearance and his self-deception[2], which can be furthered
by passions and prejudices and even more so by flattering surroundings,
success, fame and high position. Montaigne is frequently concerned
with man's capacity to assume a mask and even to convince himself that
his character should be interpreted otherwise. Both Shakespeare and
Montaigne mistrust the evidence of the senses, acknowledge the uncer-

---

[1] The quotations are taken from John Florio's translation (1603).
[2] These notions could be illustrated from many passages in Montaigne. The
following quotations are intended only to give an idea of the kind of relationship
which a close study would reveal.

> But that our minde beholds the thing with another eie, and under another
> shape it presents it selfe unto us. For every thing hath divers faces, sundry
> byases, and severall lustres.
> And therefore, intending to continue one body of all this pursuit, we deceive
> ourselves.
>   (I, 37)

> All the world doth practise stage-playing. Wee must play our parts duly, but
> as the part of a borrowed personage. Of a visard and appearance, wee should
> not make a real essence, nor proper of that which is another. Wee cannot dis-
> tinguish the skinne from the shirt. It is sufficient to disguise the face, without
> deforming the breast.
> We onely seeke to save appearances, and there whilst betray and disavow our
> true intentions.
>   (II, 10)
> See how all those judgements, that men make of outward appearances, are won-
> derfully uncertaine and doubtfull, and there is no man so sure a testimony, as
> every man is to himselfe. . . .
>   (II, 16)

tainty of human judgment and the ambiguous complexity of persons and of things. They both show how many factors contribute to the deception of mankind and cause our statements to be faltering and subjective.

This accounts for the curious method of unmasking and of careful observation that both authors employ in their portraits of mankind. They place man in situations where the mask is forced to fall. By allowing his veil, his disguise and his masks to become visible, they seek to plumb the depths of his character. They strive to penetrate through appearance into reality, by allowing appearance as such to become manifest.

This is, however, only the first step. Montaigne himself has to admit that this nucleus of true character which he is anxious to lay bare is by no means so straightforward. In the case of man we cannot simply conclude from the outside what is inside, because either consciously or unconsciously he would put on a mask; but on the inside it is just as difficult, because he is controlled by changing contradictory traits of character. Montaigne avows: 'We are all framed of flaps and patches and of so shapelesse and diverse a contexture, that every peece and every moment playeth his part. And there is as much difference found between us and our selves, as there is between our selves and others' (II, I). Man is in himself an inconsistent, enigmatic, variegated being 'but a botching and party-coloured worke' as Montaigne avows. When we have penetrated through the deceptive exterior of appearance and imagine we have come to the real man, a new uncertainty arises. For what is the real man?

Both Montaigne and Shakespeare recognize how immeasurably difficult it is for a human observer to grasp the true nature of man.[1] For man is contradictory and unstable. He can scarcely understand himself! How very much more difficult it must therefore be for his observers, his fellow creatures, to look inside him and to pierce through the layers of his personality to its very core. Thus we see finally that the examination of the contrast between exterior and interior, between appearance and reality, develops and expands into just this recognition of the ambiguity, the diversity and the problematic character of human nature.

---

[1] Montaigne's new conception of man is very aptly set forth in Hugo Friedrich, *Montaigne*, 1949.

Viola's gay words 'I am not what I am', spoken in the security of her disguise in *Twelfth Night*, take on in the tragedies a different and more disturbing meaning. Brutus, Hamlet and Macbeth stand looking at themselves, questioning and puzzled, bewildered at the dichotomy in their own natures, and themselves uncertain what they are or what they would like to be. The way to reality hidden under the veil of appearance is now not so easy as in the choice of the caskets in the *Merchant of Venice*. Bassanio really was able to find 'reality' in the lead casket once he had it open. But in the tragedies Shakespeare's tragic heroes ask with Lear and we begin to ask with them:

> Who is it that can tell me who I am?
>
> (I, iv, 229)

6

Shakespeare and the Modern World

Today it would be a commonplace to say that the greatest poets may be read and understood anew by each age and each generation, that new aspects of their work are continually being discovered and that they appeal to each generation in a new and different manner. This statement, however, provokes the question whether the understanding and interpretation of Shakespeare in each new generation is a reflection of the preoccupations and contemporary problems of that generation or whether it represents a genuine advance of scholarly insight – a better, because fuller and more objective comprehension. The truth may perhaps lie between these two alternatives: for our present knowledge and appreciation of Shakespeare, besides incorporating some of our own concerns and predilections, is also cumulative; much of what was discovered in Shakespeare during the eighteenth century, the Romantic period and the later nineteenth century has been taken over by present-day criticism and has been included in and integrated into our reading of his plays. Thus an analysis of Shakespeare's impact on the modern world would have to point out the connexion existing between new and characteristic responses on the part of a modern audience to Shakespeare's plays and the chief trend of modern Shakespeare criticism, both seen in relation to the typical problems and preoccupations of our own generation.

There appear to be three main questions at issue when we follow up this enquiry. The first is to discover how far the aspects of Shakespeare, which contemporary critics have singled out for particular attention, have been dictated to them by the kind of problems which they find themselves faced with in the modern world. Would they have noted or emphasized these aspects unless they had been already powerfully present in their minds? The second question concerns the new critical methods or approaches applied to Shakespeare. How far may they be understood as a result of our changed sensibility, reflecting a new stage of consciousness and awareness? Thirdly, we would have to ask ourselves which elements in the plays may today be seen in an altogether different light. Often these three questions will be interrelated.

A good example is the understanding of character in Shakespearian drama. Even if we grant that a character in a play is by no means the same as a living person and must not therefore be subjected to the procedures of psychology, the interpretation of dramatic characters is nevertheless bound to depend, to a large extent, on the views or theories which are held by each generation about the nature of human character. The nineteenth century aimed at a clear-cut picture of character which was thought to consist of certain unmistakable qualities, qualities which would reveal themselves in a man's actions and would change little during his life. This rationalized concept of a fixed character composed of definable qualities, from which a man's actions could be logically derived, appears to underlie the approach to Shakespeare's characters in the nineteenth century and later, though allowance must be made for the oversimplified formula used here to indicate a more complicated issue. But a perusal of nineteenth-century Shakespeare criticism discloses that the critic's business was often to establish a consistent picture of the hero's qualities. The critics appear to have been employed in supplying the characters with coherent motives for all their actions, rationalizing their conduct and supplying any logical links which seemed to them to be missing from the structure of the plays. They tried to bridge the gap between what appeared to be the psychological core of the character and his behaviour. This rationalizing and psychologizing analysis of Shakespeare's characters necessarily led to the discovery of inconsistencies in his portrayals of character and called forth complaints about insufficient motivation. Any discrepancy between the hero's character and his deeds was detected and stamped as 'unpsychological'. And if the critics, by their standards, were unable to find sufficient motivation for a character's actions, they were apt to blame the primitive stage conventions which Shakespeare was using. What, however, the critics often did not take into account was the fact that these so-called 'inconsistencies' and incompatibilities in Shakespeare's portrayals of character entirely escape the unbiased playgoer in the theatre and are noticed only through the spectacles of scholars who scrutinize the play line by line. In the two decades after Bradley's *Shakespearean Tragedy* it was more and more recognized that the criteria of psychology and of realism could not be applied to Shakespeare's characters and that characters in a play moved in a sphere different from that of reality. But this did not stop the search for motivation and the effort at character-analysis went on. Certain features in Shakespeare's characters were still therefore either misunderstood or not grasped at all.

However, the situation has changed greatly within the last thirty years, for in our own days much more complex ideas of human character have been developed. These make it possible for us to accept those very features in Shakespeare's characters which were formerly either misunderstood or rejected. Moreover, certain traits of Shakespeare's characters and problems connected with them which thus have become intelligible can appeal to us today more strongly because they are the very problems which modern experience has brought home to us. We now believe that there is no such thing as a fixed and thoroughly consistent character, and we also know that man is full of surprises and contradictions, full of paradox and unpredictableness, inscrutable and elusive. Consequently, we not only sympathize with Shakespeare's presentation of these very features but we feel that we are watching a phenomenon which we recognize around us daily. And we invariably discover even in ourselves such potentialities.

A few of those character problems may be tentatively mentioned here which in this sense appeal to us as being akin to our modern consciousness of man. Recent critics have observed that many of Shakespeare's main characters display a clash of opposites and reveal contrarieties. They do this not only in the moral sense that 'the web of our life is of a mingled yarn, good and ill together' (*All's Well*, IV, iii, 81–2), but also in the more complex sense of contradictory attitudes, qualities and states of mind. It also looks as if the situation of frustration, of disillusionment, and of inner dilemma, so often occurring in Shakespeare's plays, is not only more acutely noted and analysed by present-day critics, but also meets with a more intense response on the part of modern readers and audiences. We are strongly impressed by the fact that Shakespeare's characters look at themselves as at something strange and unknown, wondering what they themselves actually are, searching for causes or motives and not finding any, or failing to find the right ones – a situation well known from Hamlet, Macbeth and Angelo. We are willing to accept these persons as they are, we are willing to accept the mystery, the uncertainty of human character; and we are accordingly ready to give up the vain effort to supply logical causes or missing links in the chain. The changed attitude in the criticism of Hamlet's character is a case in point: 'Shakespeare's triumph is to make the hero fail to understand himself. Hamlet gives us reasons enough for delay, causes none; for the cause remains unknown to him, and to us.' Thus we read in Lawlor's recent book *The Tragic Sense in Shakespeare*.[1] A similar warning is expressed by L. C. Knights: 'Hamlet's state of mind, the Hamlet consciousness, is revealed not only at the level of formulable motive, but in its obscure depths; and it is revealed through the poetry.'[2]

Thus the modern reader and student is ready to elicit the meaning of a character and of a whole play not from explicitly formulated utterances and passages only; he seeks to apprehend it also through other media which need not be enumerated here. This readiness, towards which we have been trained by modern poetry and modern criticism, has considerably helped us to get closer to the truth. And it is ultimately not only an 'advance of scholarship', or more refined and complex methods of interpretation, but the changed consciousness of modern man which has produced this change in critical attitude. There also appears to be more readiness to see the interrelation, indeed the fusion, of thinking and feeling, of abstract thought and emotion in Shakespeare's characters. We no longer so easily separate reflection from emotion, for we know that this division of man's faculties into reasoning, abstracting, concluding, feeling, perceiving, and so on is artificial. Coleridge's warning 'to keep alive the heart in the head'[3] has been fully accepted by our own generation, even without reference to the findings of modern psychoanalysis.

The situation is similar with regard to the modern reader's attitude towards Shakespeare's dramatic method of presenting fundamental problems, of raising and answering questions in his plays. Not infrequently critics of the nineteenth century tried to find out what Shakespeare himself may have thought about the theme or the problem which he appears to make the central issue of a particular play. The effort has been made to define Shakespeare's *Weltanschauung* and to deduce

[1] John Lawlor, *The Tragic Sense in Shakespeare*, London, 1960, p. 67.
[2] L. C. Knights, *An Approach to Hamlet*, London, 1960, p. 50.
[3] Quoted by Dorothy Emmet in her paper *Coleridge — on the Growth of the Mind*, Bulletin of the John Rylands Library, XXIV, 2, 1952: see Knights *op. cit.* p. 69.

what we may call Shakespeare's 'beliefs and attitudes' from certain passages in his plays. The fallacy of such an undertaking was discovered in due course; for the passages quoted to illustrate Shakespeare's beliefs proved – when looked at more closely and within their context – to be utterances made by certain dramatic characters at certain moments in the course of the action. Often enough these utterances were prompted by private intentions of these characters and could therefore not be taken as revealing their inner convictions. Thus the endeavour to get at the core of Shakespeare's beliefs, to establish his scale of 'values', has again and again eluded critics and scholars. This desire to discover Shakespeare's own 'philosophy of life' will probably never die out, but there appears to be, in our present world, more readiness to accept the impenetrability of Shakespeare's own *Weltanschauung*. In fact we even see a mark of greatness in the dramatist's ability to hide himself behind the multifarious world of his characters and to give shape and dramatic reality to their views and principles rather than to his own unknown convictions. Shakespeare's capacity to enter the minds of his characters, to identify himself wholly with their attitudes and opinions and to present even a villain's set of beliefs with extraordinary objectivity and impartiality has long been recognized as one of his greatest achievements. But only in our century has it been fully realized that this 'negative capability' precludes to some extent the dramatic presentation of a consistent and definable 'philosophy of life' which could with some assurance be described as Shakespeare's own. This is not to say that there are not, within the total volume of Shakespeare's plays, recurrent features, ideas and principles which strike us as unmistakably Shakespearian and which may – with due reserve and caution – serve as pointers and clues to what we may call Shakespeare's world picture. But the ultimate mystery of what Shakespeare himself may have believed will remain and is indeed more readily admitted by the modern reader than by the one of the nineteenth century. We have come to realize that this mystery is intimately bound up with Shakespeare's growing impact on our present-day generation.

Almost the same holds true if we consider, not Shakespeare's *Weltanschauung* in general, but the *Weltanschauung* of a single play. Earlier critics were more optimistic and self-assured in defining not only the problem put by a play, but also the answer given to it, as it was expressed by the whole action and by scattered pronouncements of the leading characters. It has indeed been one of the major concerns of Shakespeare criticism to elucidate and analyse the main themes, issues and problems of the individual plays, especially the tragedies. But the more work was done in this field, the clearer it became that even this limited critical endeavour to find out the *Weltanschauung* of a single play has its fallacies.

A case in point is *King Lear*. Here, again and again, the problem of the justice of the gods is put before us and we are led to enquire into the 'ultimate power' that moves this world and directs the actions of men. These questions emerge not only from the total effect of the play and from the course of the action; the characters themselves ponder over it. However, the answer they give to this fundamental question and the references they make to it contradict each other to a considerable degree.[1] It appears then that these statements are conditioned by the temperament of the individual character, by the moment at which he speaks and by the hidden intention he may have in mind. Again, it would be misleading to take any one of these single passages as revealing the tragedy's underlying idea. But the effect of these pronouncements on the audience is nevertheless great, for they stir up the same questions in the spectator's or reader's mind: they produce that mood of inner restlessness, of questioning perturbation which is, on the part of the audience, a major factor of the whole play's profound impression. Generations of theatregoers may have felt this in the eighteenth and nineteenth centuries, too. But critics, in search of a definable answer to the problems posed by the play, were unwilling to recognize this peculiar effect as belonging to Shakespeare's greatness as a dramatist. It appears, however, that this art of Shakespeare's of raising questions but not answering them, of making us think intensely about a problem of which the solution may elude us or be grasped only with difficulty, finds a better response in the modern reader and theatregoer and is more readily accepted and in fact admired than in the nineteenth century. Shakespeare's way of leaving it to the audience to draw its conclusions and to form its views both presupposes and demands a more active co-operation on the part of his readers and spectators. It strikes us as being in some measure akin to what modern poetry or modern art do with their readers or spectators. The open question, the unsolved

[1] This was first pointed out by A. C. Bradley in *Shakespearean Tragedy*, London, 1905, p. 271.

problem, the unanswered issue and the never wholly disclosed and unveiled idea are powerful incentives and elements in the wide realm of modern art.

King Lear yields another example of Shakespeare's dramatic presentation of fundamental issues which may be said to appeal strongly to a modern audience, for in *Lear* Shakespeare does not take over any of the traditional moral or religious tenets which could serve, either positively or negatively, as underlying principles for the action and for what the characters say. On the contrary, he calls all these habitual values in question; during the great scenes on the heath we feel that the foundations of our human existence are shattered and that the very essence of man's nature is weighed and exposed. Nevertheless, the play moves forward towards positives which dimly emerge on the horizon when we come to the fourth and fifth acts. But these positives, taken by L. C. Knights as 'fundamentally Christian values', are reached, as Knights aptly says, 'by an act of profound individual exploration: the play does not take them for granted; it takes nothing for granted but Nature and natural energies and passions'.[1] Our own generation will share the doubts raised by *King Lear* about traditional values, and the 'act of profound individual exploration' will appeal to this generation as a more convincing, and better, way of reaching a new assurance or of acquiring belief. And even the immense suffering and the painful breakdown of past creeds and illusions which in *Lear* are necessarily connected with this ultimate goal may, for a modern audience, be more meaningful than for past generations. We are apt to acknowledge the validity of only those values which, in the crucible of hard and painful experience and of utter exposure, have gone through the test that can show what is to survive and what is to perish.

The problems of life, the aspects of man's nature and the vicissitudes to which he is subject in the world as presented in Shakespeare's plays are numerous and cover a very wide field of human experience. Most of these aspects are moreover the eternal themes of life, which in each generation will evoke response. But it looks as if, even with these everlasting themes, some appeal to our present generation more strongly than to the nineteenth century. Thus the attention recently bestowed by critics on the theme of appearance and reality in Shakespeare's plays appears to reflect our own growing awareness of this

[1] L. C. Knights, *Some Shakespearean Themes*, London, 1959, p. 91.

discrepancy in our modern world. This is not to claim that our generation has been the first to discover that man deceives himself and is constantly deceived, that our world consists of illusions and fallacies and
that we all of us wear a mask. But modern psychology and the ruthless
searching eye of modern novelists may have sharpened our perception
of the manifold and hidden contrasts between outward behaviour and
inner intention, between the spoken word and the actual motive. And
although our civilization is poisoned by false slogans and pretensions,
having developed a whole system of deception and misleading presentation of 'appearances' instead of 'realities', those who care for art and
literature today and belong to our 'sceptical generation', may be better
trained to look 'below the surface', to seek for the naked and undis-
guised truth, to shun romantic illusion and find out reality. The gullibility of man, the extreme difficulty of recognizing and seeing things as
they actually are, the readiness of the individual as well as of mankind
to be deceived by appearances or even to be satisfied by them, all this
constitutes one of the great problems for everyone who tries to find his
way 'among the thorns and dangers of this world'. Thus Shakespeare's
multifarious presentation of this clash between appearance and reality,
leading up to many dramatic situations and subtle effects, but underlying, too, his shaping of characters and his manipulation of plot and
story, will be followed up and understood with an intense sympathy by
an intelligent modern audience.

In this connexion the modern concern for irony and ambiguity in
Shakespeare's plays should also be noted. For these effects, too, pre-
suppose the existence of an obvious or 'outward' meaning contrasted
with an inner hidden meaning, or an opposition between conscious and
unconscious utterance. Ambiguity and irony are closely related to the
universal and comprehensive theme of appearance and reality and
should therefore be studied with a view to this wider frame of reference.
But the detection of ironies and ambiguities in Shakespeare's dramas
may also offer an example of how Shakespeare's 'modernity' in this
respect is likely to be overrated. For although the modern reader's
faculty for understanding a text 'on several levels' and his ability to
look at words and phrases with a sharpened eye for their multiple meaning has undoubtedly led to the discovery of many subtle effects which
so far had been hidden, helping us for example to understand many of
Shakespeare's puns, the search for irony and ambiguity in Shakespeare's

texts seems frequently to have been overdone. And it may well be that after two or three generations this preoccupation of modern critics with irony and ambiguity in Shakespeare's language, justified though it be when applied to contemporary poetry, will be taken as an exaggeration and an idiosyncrasy of our own generation.

On the other hand, the emphasis on irony and ambiguity is related to the new appreciation of the poetic texture of Shakespeare's plays, including his imagery. The renewal of poetic drama in our time by T. S. Eliot, Christopher Fry and the dramatists of the 'Irish Revival' was accompanied and stimulated by the re-discovery of the dramatic impact of the poetry in Elizabethan plays, in fact by a recognition that poetic drama possess *dramatic* effects which may reach further and exert a more profound influence than the language and devices used by prose drama. The false notions about the superiority of prose drama over verse drama (as being less 'artificial', more 'natural' and therefore more 'acceptable') were re-examined and eventually replaced by a new evaluation of poetic drama and consequently by a new understanding of its specific elements. The recognition that 'The human soul, in intense emotion, strives to express itself in verse' and that 'if we want to get at the permanent and universal we tend to express ourselves in verse' (T. S. Eliot), strange and revolutionary though it may have sounded in 1928, has meanwhile become an inherent factor in the surprising and intense response of modern audiences to the poetry in Shakespeare's plays. The more aesthetic appreciation of this poetry as shown by the Romantic age has in our times been superseded by a new feeling for the dramatic qualities, the unsurpassed 'modern' expressiveness and force of Shakespeare's poetic language and his imagery. Thus Shakespeare's impact on the modern world includes among other elements this new spell exerted by the poetry and imagery in his plays on even an average audience. The ascendancy of poetic drama in our age has unsealed a new organ in the modern reader and theatregoer for perceiving these essential elements of Shakespearian drama; it has moreover opened up a new field of reciprocal influences and encounters between modern and Elizabethan drama and theatrical practice.

7

Characteristic Features of
Shakespearian Drama

What is the unique form, the individual quality of Shakespearian drama? Critics have often tried to answer this question by defining it as 'great drama' in an absolute sense – as a synthesis of everything which they consider to be dramatic. But if we look closer we can see that Shakespeare is exceptional and unique in the history of European drama. For this reason all the attempts which have been made to derive the basic rules and norms of drama from his work have proved to be so difficult and usually so fruitless.

In this essay I should like to define the individual and unique quality of Shakespearian drama by selecting, from the numerous possible points of view, what is perhaps most prominent in our minds. We shall commence by asking ourselves what it is that primarily occurs to us when we think of Shakespeare's plays. First of all there is a vast crowd of human figures: kings and great barons, fools and tradesmen, princesses and peasant girls, eccentrics and outcasts of society, soldiers, actors, witches and magicians, mythological figures and fairies, cardinals and pagan deities; a whole *theatrum mundi*, in fact, which appears to play in the remote past and in the immediate present as well. If we now go on to ask ourselves in what visual context this world of figures impresses itself upon us, then we see again the most varied and contrasting scenes: ceremonies of state alongside tavern drinking-bouts and rough brawls, tender love-scenes alongside court festivities, marching armies and solemn coronations, masquerades and village fêtes, assassination and pensive soliloquies, merry dances and dumb shows, songs and the melancholy music of the lute. There is similar variety in the language, for we hear stylized speeches as well as rapid prose dialogue, rich and formal Elizabethan verse alongside coarse jokes, witty repartee of high comedy and the slang of everyday speech, melodramatic rhetoric in the scenes of grand passion, and simple, terse utterances in moments of distress.

These are merely casual impressions and associations, such as may occur to all of us. Here they are only intended to indicate a starting-point from which we easily reach the first two distinctive marks which may help us to characterize the individual quality of Shakespeare's work. For Shakespeare's drama appears to be a free and open form of drama, continually changing and not subject to prescribed rules, and also a form of drama in which the most varied and mutually opposed elements combine to form a new unity.

The first of these two characteristics provides the conditions necessary for the second. So I shall begin with this first characteristic: a free form of drama. This means both that Shakespeare does not feel himself limited by any rules, any three unities or superimposed sense of decorum, and also that exceptional possibilities are provided for bold inventiveness and experiment, possibilities of which Shakespeare takes equally exceptional advantage.

This free, unrestricted form gives rise to the receptiveness of his drama for many features and suggestions from the non-dramatic literature of the time. For not only dancing and music, but also lyric and epic elements exercise their influence and are readily adopted by the poet. This is an inclusive, not an exclusive form of drama, for it has an extraordinary power of assimilation, and is consequently able to include many things which according to later standards would have been left outside the drama. Thus Shakespeare's work becomes a melting-pot for many elements of form and expression which we find in Elizabethan prose and poetry, but which Shakespeare subordinates critically and consciously to his dramatic intentions.

This receptivity for new and different material was due to the fact that the form of Shakespeare's drama was not strictly fixed or laid down. When he began to write he found that there was no predominant dramatic tradition, but on the contrary a great diversity of types of drama of various origins. There was on the one hand the neo-classical rhetorical drama in the Senecan tradition, and on the other the crude popular play. There were Lyly's courtly comedies with their refined wit and polished dialogue, there were pastoral plays, masques employing allegory and pantomime, and Marlowe's powerful tragedies; the mystery-plays and moralities were still being performed, and Shakespeare may well have seen them in his youth in one of the neighbouring towns.

Probably no other period in the history of the European theatre has offered at one time such a great variety of different dramatic styles and possibilities; and these were not clearly separated, but capable of being combined and fused with one another in many different ways. Both the interest in drama and the participation in its creation and production were common to all classes of society; drama came into existence in the most diverse places and from a multiplicity of causes.

This varied abundance proved to be exactly the right soil, in which Shakespeare's dramatic art was able to take root and flourish. The very fact that no single clear and authoritative conception of drama could come into existence was a necessary condition for the development of the free and open form of which I have spoken. Shakespeare was not obliged to commit himself to a fixed type, and he never did; on the contrary, he continually changed his manner, from one play to the next. This lack of commitment to a particular form has given us the most flexible and adaptable type of drama in the history of the European theatre.

Let us consider for a moment the extraordinary differences between plays which follow one another. *Richard II*, with its lyrical and reflective richness and its comparative lack of sensational stage action, follows the utterly different history of *Richard III*. And what an astonishing difference there is between *The Merchant of Venice* and *A Midsummer Night's Dream*, though both are called comedies! In *The Merchant of Venice* we have what is virtually a serious play with a happy ending, and even the beginning of a tragedy of character, if we look at the figure of Shylock.

How different is *A Midsummer Night's Dream* with its inter-weaving of the world of the fairies, the mechanicals' sub-plot, and the entanglements of the Athenian lovers! Here none of the characters are at all 'true to life', with the exception of Bottom. But in spite of this *A Midsummer Night's Dream* is one of the greatest plays in the whole of literature, and if we examine its dramatic form we see that it represents a bold advance along new paths.

A comparison of the tragedies also reveals more differences than points in common, and any attempt to ascertain a kind of basic structure of Shakespearian tragedy would be fruitless unless we were to be content with a few external similarities. Following upon the tragedy of *Othello*, with the closely woven, uninterrupted progress of its plot and the clear logic of its architecture, comes *King Lear*, which rests upon an utterly different principle of composition, in which expansion and breadth dominate, so that the plot often comes to a halt to permit a fuller portrayal of a character's state of mind.

Shakespeare had shown in *Othello* how much he was a man of the theatre and in full command of all the possibilities of the stage, but in *King Lear* it is apparent that he has attempted something quite different. For here we are faced with the great design of a new dramatic form, which in some respect even transcends the conventional framework of the theatre.

And is there anything in the whole field of satiric drama which can be compared with *Troilus and Cressida* – the strangest, boldest, most provoking and therefore the most difficult comedy Shakespeare ever wrote? This is another unique case, it is nothing less than the invention of a new dramatic form!

And finally Shakespeare's last works: the romances *Cymbeline*, *The Winter's Tale*, and *The Tempest*. Here, as in *King Lear*, Shakespeare has turned to a new manner of dramatic composition which seems at first to ignore the obvious dramatic effect, but which then grips the spectator in a new way. These three plays are three different solutions which emerged in the course of the search for a new dramatic form.

We are perhaps not yet sufficiently aware of Shakespeare's remarkable inventiveness, to which his development of new dramatic forms, methods of composition and combinations all bear witness. In the course of many years we have become so familiar with all these plays, most of which we have seen on the stage, that we are no longer surprised at the great differences which exist between them. We are accustomed to thinking of Shakespeare in terms of abundance and variety. So why should this not also be evident in the development of the most varied types of drama?

But a glance at Calderon, Racine, Lessing, Schiller or Ibsen can show us that such a diversity is by no means self-evident, and that in fact no other dramatist has ever been endowed with a comparable versatility in the construction and development of new dramatic forms.

Freedom from rules, the absence of over-powerful literary models, receptiveness for every impulse from outside, and the lack of a fixed dramatic form, – these were the conditions which made possible the development of an inventive creativeness able to prove, again and again, that our conventional views of what drama is are much too narrow.

But in Shakespeare's case creative invention does not mean the ability to create something new and original out of nothing, but rather the adaptation and transformation of material already present, and above all it means the combination of diverse elements to form a new whole. In the course of time the diligence of scholars has enabled us to pursue back to some definite source a great many motifs and even forms and figures of speech, proverbs and maxims. It is well known that Shakespeare did not, as a rule, invent the plots of his plays, but borrowed most of his subject-matter from others. Much less well known is the degree to which single details in his plays, including some of the best-known lines, are taken from some source. We believe we are hearing Hamlet's own voice and mood when he says 'There's nothing good or bad but thinking makes it so' or 'The readiness is all' or when he dwells upon the nature of man in his speech: 'What a piece of work is man!' However, each of these sayings derives from a source in medieval or Renaissance literature. And so Shakespeare's contemporary, the dramatist Greene, was not so wrong when, in his embitterment at the success of his new rival, he accused him of being 'an upstart Crow, beautified with our feathers'. It is true that, living in an age in which our concept of originality was still unknown, Shakespeare must be considered a great plagiarist. But he was not only a plagiarist, he was an 'amalgamator' as well, by which we mean that he was an adaptor of genius, and understood the art of employing everything that fell into his hands for his dramatic purposes, often by means of very slight alterations and transpositions.

This unhampered and masterly skill in borrowing from the most diverse fields, however, could only bear fruit in a form of drama which was itself unrestricted and prepared to take its basic elements from any available source.

This gift of assimilation is most evident when Shakespeare combines opposite and diverse material in order to form a new unity. For this constitutes the second feature which is especially characteristic of Shakespearian drama. It is true that the pre-Elizabethan and early Elizabethan theatre had already known the clash of contrasting features. But not until Shakespeare does this combination of diverse elements attain a level of significance and mutual relevance. Only in his plays does it result in a greater unity which can contain and resolve opposites. Let us return to *A Midsummer Night's Dream*. The world of the fairies, the night full of dreams and enchantments for the Athenian lovers, and the theatrical activities of the mechanicals – all these seem at first to have very little to do with each other. But quite apart from the various encounters in the course of the action they are interwoven with each other by means of many cross-references and subtle contrasts, and as a result we receive the impression of a thoroughly homogeneous and unified play, although it is constructed out of such different elements.

Shakespeare developed the use of contrast as an artistic device to a greater degree than other dramatists. The effect and significance of something is heightened again and again by the juxtaposition of its opposite. This use of contrast can take place on many levels: in the language, in the interplay of character, in the combination of individual motifs and in the juxtaposition of scenes and moods. Sometimes the whole plot of a play is contrasted to a parallel sub-plot; Shakespeare found examples of this in the sub-plots of pre-Shakespearian comedy, but he developed the technique further to enable the plots to reflect and complement each other, and for one to enrich the meaning of the other. The most famous example is to be found in *Henry IV*, where the Falstaff plot is enacted in the prose scenes on a lower floor of the play, as it were, in Mistress Quickley's inn and elsewhere. However, it is much more than a contrast of language or atmosphere. For the action of the main plot is not only parodied and reflected here, but also anticipated, echoed and commented upon with incomparable skill, so that although the two plots touch each other only at a few points, they necessarily belong to each other like the two complementary halves of a single whole.

The contrast between the world of Falstaff and the world of the king is among other things a contrast of comedy and tragedy. For most of us Shakespeare's artistry in the uniting of opposites is to be seen most clearly in this combination of the serious and the light. And can we think of any other play in the literature of the world in which the blend of comedy and tragedy has been achieved more successfully? Again we may say that here, too, the unrestricted form of Shakespeare's drama was a necessary condition, for the poet never kept to the strict boundaries of tragedy and comedy.

As Dr Johnson observed,

'Shakespeare's plays are not in the rigorous and critical sense either tragedies or comedies, but compositions of a distinct kind; exhibiting the real state of sublunary nature, which partakes of good and evil, joy and sorrow, mingled with endless variety of proportion and in-numerable modes of combination; and expressing the course of the world, in which the loss of one is the gain of another; in which, at the same time, the reveller is hasting to his wine, and the mourner burying his friend; in which the malignity of one is sometimes defeated by the frolic of another; and many mischiefs and many benefits are done and hindered without design.'

In these apt sentences Dr Johnson has indicated that the linking of the serious and the comic, which can be found in such rich variation in Shakespeare's work, is by no means to be regarded only as an effective dramatic device, but reflects a view of the world which keeps the two poles of human existence constantly in view, and regards them as com-plementary. These two spheres are often combined in one and the same person, and even in the same moment. We feel that the Fool in *King Lear* is not only a jester, but a tragic figure who shares in the suffering, whose jokes incorporate the sphere of the absurd into the tragedy, and who makes us aware of the close relationship between the grotesque and the tragic. The gravediggers' scene in *Hamlet* and the porter's scene in *Macbeth* are interludes of light relief in a superficial sense only. In fact their grim humour serves to make us even more aware of the sombre mood of death surrounding them. And even Falstaff is far from being only a comic figure, for the effect of his words and actions is to appeal to our sense of tragedy as well as to our sense of comedy. And the same holds true of the comedies. Portia in *The Merchant of Venice*, Rosalind in *As You Like It*, Viola in *Twelfth Night*, and even Beatrice in *Much Ado About Nothing* – they are not typical figures of comedy, but women whose audacity and gaiety never allow them to forget the seriousness which underlies these qualities, and for all of them merri-ment and melancholy are seldom far apart.

Laughter through tears, despair masquerading behind a witty remark, cheerfulness overshadowed by melancholy – these are blends of mood, to which nobody has given better dramatic expression than Shakespeare.

This capacity to correlate opposites can be demonstrated in a great many other ways. In his essay on Shakespeare written in 1773 the German writer Herder said that Shakespeare had 'created a miraculous unity out of the most heterogeneous materials by virtue of his creative spirit'. He will have had in mind above all the way in which incongruous motifs and characters are fused to form a unity which convinces us by its imaginative power and truth to life. In this way Shakespeare's drama continually contrives to make the improbable seem probable and convincing. In *The Merchant of Venice*, for example, we have the old fairy-tale motif of the choice between caskets of gold, silver, and lead establishing the right suitor for Portia, and in addition to this the motif of the bond that carries a forfeit of a pound of flesh. Both these motifs are highly improbable and quite unrealistic, but the course of events in this comedy is completely dependent upon them. And the basic content of the play, its truth to life, its inner unity and immediate effectiveness are not lessened by this in the least. This is also true of the many similarly absurd or incongruous motifs which can be found, for instance, in *Cymbeline*, *The Winter's Tale*, *All's Well That Ends Well*, in *Measure for Measure* or in *The Comedy of Errors*. And it holds true for many cases of motivation and for many details of the subject matter in the tragedies as well. But we can go further than this and say that it also holds true for the artistic devices which Shakespeare employs. In the depiction of character we find primitive conventions of self-dramatization alongside the most subtle psychology, some of the plays contain long narrative episodes, and sometimes there are scenes which appear to be totally undramatic. Unrealistic conventions can be found side by side with naturalistic methods of depiction. So critics have always been able to find much that is contradictory and to discover all kinds of inconsistencies in Shakespeare's work. They have been right, but at the same time they have been wrong. For the real test in Shakespeare's case can never be the rational analysis after the event; it must be the degree to which the illusion of the theatrical performance is capable of convincing, and sometimes of overpowering, the spectator.

So we can perhaps say that there are two different forces, two basic tendencies, active in Shakespeare's work simultaneously. On the one hand there is the expansive force, which is always exploring new paths and forming new combinations, and which seems intent on breaking out of the limitations of the theatre, and on the other hand there is the binding-force, which moulds all these parts into a complete unity and correlates all the different aspects of the play. At the height of his art Shakespeare is even able to give each play an organic harmony of its own. For each of his greater plays has its individual atmosphere and mood, its characteristic imagery and dramatic technique, and above all an individual poetic idiom which pervades the whole work. And it is Shakespeare's mastery of language that enables him to achieve this inner cohesion.

This brings me to the third characteristic feature of his work. Shakespeare combined a practical sense of the theatre with poetic genius, and in the same way his work reveals the unity of a supreme stage artistry and a matchless artistry of language. In this unity each half permeates and enriches the other. The language is an end in itself only in the early plays, if at all, and in Shakespeare's hands it soon develops into the direct vehicle of dramatic representation; it becomes the medium for what has to be shown, both through the action on the stage and through the behaviour of the actors. Shakespeare's spoken text actually contains both the actor's tone of voice, movements and gestures. In fact the poet must have borne the actor in mind speaking and moving with every line he wrote. Hamlet's advice in his speech to the players – to suit the action to the word, the word to the action – was followed by Shakespeare himself in the composition of every play. The result is the uniquely fortunate case of poetic language which is of great complexity and expressiveness, but which always gives us the impression that we are listening to the speaking voice of the actor. This is another combination which has never again been achieved so successfully.

Shakespeare has to rely on the language alone to evoke all those things like the scene of action, landscape, local colour, atmosphere, and time of day, which the drama of later centuries could include in the stage directions and put into effect with the technical devices of the modern stage, such as scenery and lighting. Shakespeare has none of the technical resources of later periods at his command, but he makes a virtue of necessity, and conjures up all these things for us by the evocative power of his language. In doing so he compels our own imagination to help in this process. A great deal of action takes place on the stage in every Shakespeare play, but still more is suggested by the language, and takes place before the mind's eye, so that the spectator is called upon to take part in the creative process and to contribute himself towards the total effect of the performance of a play.

Shakespeare refers several times to the fact that his stagecraft is dependent upon the imaginative co-operation of his spectators, for example in the Prologue to *Henry V*, where the Chorus says to the audience: 'Let us . . ./On your imaginary forces work/ . . . ./Piece out our imperfections with your thoughts!' Thus the poetic language appeals to our 'imaginary forces'. In doing this it achieves two aims. In the first place all those aspects which can only vaguely be described by terms such as local colour and atmosphere can transcend the limitations of physical reality, they can take over important functions and assume a wider, indeed a symbolic significance.

And secondly they can be adapted to the individual idiom of a particular character, and thus be integrated into his experience. As a result the statement which helps to conjure up an atmosphere for us can at the same time reveal character. Let us take one of many possible examples: Othello has just landed in Cyprus, and embraces Desdemona with the words:

> O my soul's joy!
> If after every tempest come such calms,
> May the winds blow till they have waken'd death,
> And let the labouring bark climb hills of seas
> Olympus-high, and duck again as low
> As hell's from heaven.
>
> (II, i, 182)

In these words Othello gives us an idea of the wide rough sea across which he has just sailed; his lines contribute to the sea-atmosphere in the play. But in these lines he also gives expression to his own dynamic character, and, although not conscious of it himself, he anticipates the way he is to go, from Heaven down to Hell. In this manner the evocative power of Shakespeare's poetic language replaces the illusion of reality otherwise provided by stage scenery and other devices. This means that the scene of action in the drama is now wider instead of narrower. For now, free of the material limitations imposed by any stage apparatus, however perfect it may be, the play can take place upon a stage which represents the whole world. This stage can present what is close at hand and what is far away at the same time, and can even disregard the limits of this world in order to provide a setting of cosmic dimensions. In Shakespeare's plays we often have the impression that more is at stake than merely a series of events involving several people; other forces seem to be involved, and beyond the world of human beings there is the world of nature, of the elements and cosmic powers, which appear to be taking part in the action. When Lear invokes the elements – the storm, the thunder and lightning – in the great scene on the heath, he is giving expression to the hurricane in his own soul, but at the same time he is calling upon the forces of nature to intervene in the course of events, as indeed they do in many different ways in this play.

Alongside this evocative power of the poetic language we may set its ability to anticipate what is coming, to make us conscious of earlier and later developments, and to enrich the single present moment with an awareness which includes the past and the future as well.[1] And in this way the poetic language becomes an instrument with which the listener may be influenced secretly. It makes him aware of much more than the concern of the moment. It arouses expectations and tensions, reminds the hearer of what he has already been told, and makes him conscious of the way in which time slowly trickles away or hurries quickly on. And all these various effects are the specifically dramatic results of the working of the poetic language.

No other poet has ever exploited the dramatic possibilities of poetic language in such divergent ways as Shakespeare has. The idiom of verse drama, as he uses it, proves to be a flexible instrument, capable of fulfilling many different purposes and of conveying several meanings at one and the same time. And this is what I should like to define as the fourth basic feature of Shakespeare's drama: the presence of several different levels of significance and of effect. So Shakespeare's drama can be considered multi-levelled in two different ways; for it not only contains on the plane of action one or two sub-plots which vary and comment upon the theme of the main plot, but it also combines several layers of meaning. Under the surface of the external action it is possible to trace a complex network of images and concepts. These express and vary the themes of the play in a manner comparable to musical counterpoint. Similarly reminiscent of music is the way in which the *Leitmotiv* technique is applied in order to appeal to our subconscious. From the point of view of the twentieth century, it seems that here a great genius has anticipated much more recent processes of poetic com-

[1] See Chapter 3.

position, such as have only been examined more closely by literary criticism in the course of the last thirty years. For on this deeper level of significance we can now find the same subtle parallels and double meanings, the same indirect echoes and references, and the same forms of irony and paradox that are characteristic of modern poetry. It is true that critics have sometimes exaggerated Shakespeare's use of these techniques. But even if we make sufficient allowance for the various exaggerations of this branch of modern criticism, we must still continue to be astonished at the abundance of inner relationships, hidden allusions, and additional meanings in Shakespeare's texts.

It is difficult for us to estimate now how many of all these double meanings and ambiguities were understood by Shakespeare's own audience. However, it is very probable that the Elizabethans had a better memory for words, a more acute sense of language, and a more lively verbal imagination than we have to-day. Puns and ambiguous figures of speech were not confined to literature, but were among the colloquial habits of speech of educated people. And could we account for the large number of allusions and references to the stylistic models of the day, unless they were noticed, at least by the well-informed? This observation leads me to a further important point which I wish to suggest as the fifth characteristic feature of Shakespeare's dramatic work. These plays were written for an extremely mixed audience in which all classes of society and degrees of education were represented, and they were capable of meeting the varied expectations and demands of this mixed audience. So the various levels of significance in the plays correspond to the different levels present in the audience. Perhaps it is characteristic of all great art that it should be able to appeal to the uneducated spectator and to the cultivated sensitive person as well, and to satisfy both. But Shakespeare's range of appeal is so great that he achieves a synthesis of crude and refined effects, of simple and subtle devices. This particular balance was never regained by later dramatists, for either they were coarser and more limited, without Shakespeare's breadth and subtlety, or they were altogether more literary, and wrote without Shakespeare's uninhibited vitality for a primarily middle-class audience. 'Good plays must be straightforward in appeal' ('Gute Dramen müssen drastisch sein') stipulated Friedrich Schlegel[1] two

---

[1] Friedrich Schlegel, *Athenäums-Fragmente* in *Kritische Schriften*, ed. W. Rasch, Munich, 1957, p. 28.

hundred years after Shakespeare. Shakespeare followed this principle in all of his plays, for there are certainly enough bloody murders and other sensational, heart-rending episodes and gripping scenes to delight the heart of the most unsophisticated theatregoer, from his own time till the present.

And is it not typical that Shakespeare's plays should have such a strong effect on young people! The main reason for this is the magnificent simplicity and vividness of action and situation, which possess such expressive power in themselves that we can grasp their meaning even without a specific comprehension or intellectual analysis of the text. These moments of great theatrical power are what remain in our minds when we think of performances we have seen. Brutus and Antony speaking over Caesar's body, Hamlet and the ghost on the platform, Hamlet meditating over Yorick's skull, Lear with his three daughters and the map of his kingdom, Lear with Cordelia dead in his arms, Lady Macbeth walking in her sleep with a lighted candle, Othello at Desdemona's deathbed, Timon with his guests at the last banquet. Or in the histories: the abdication scene in *Richard II*, where the golden crown is held between the hands of the two rival kings, or the scene in *Henry IV* in which the prince puts on the crown and takes it away from the bed of his dying father. All of these tableaux, interpreted in each case by the text, compress the essence of a figure, and sometimes of a whole play, into a single visual image. These symbolic moments on the stage are often more eloquent than many speeches because of their simplicity, for they can make the meaning vivid to every spectator. So young and old, novices and experts, can all be moved by Shakespeare's work. And similarly we can observe the way in which it affects our own faculties of perception on many different levels. These plays appeal to the eye as well as to the ear, to our emotions as well as to our moral judgment, and occupy our intellect in addition to our imagination. They may be compared to the richest orchestral scores which have ever been written.

But they are of course not only obvious and *drastisch* (straightforward); they do not consist solely of colourful events, for each play forms a finely woven texture of skilfully graduated and varied effects, which range from the melodious cadence of a line to the moments of great theatrical power about which we have just spoken.

The interweaving of the most diverse kinds of figures, effects, and dramatic devices – devices which are often simple and often refined, sometimes artificial and sometimes direct, often improbable but always convincing – this fact has at all times been considered an almost incomprehensible miracle. Shakespeare has always defied theories about what is possible and permissible in the theatre, and anyone who has tried to establish the derivation of his art from certain basic principles and rules has soon got into difficulties. For his plays not only overpower us with the dramatic illusion, they also give us the impression of being incomparably true to life, which makes us feel even today that he is 'holding a mirror up to nature'. In the classical period of German literature in the late eighteenth century an attempt was made to define Shakespeare's instinctive feeling for what was both dramatically effective and true to life, in terms of a phenomenon of Nature, as the Spirit of the World expressing itself in poetry, and as a form of completely irrational and subconscious creativity. Today we are more inclined to recognize a conscious artistic intention in this interweaving of different effects – a highly refined art of composition which orders all its resources with perfect harmony.

But it certainly is an art which conceals its own rules and resources to such an extent that it gives the impression of being without art, and seems utterly and totally natural. In *The Winter's Tale* Shakespeare touches upon this secret of art transformed into nature, when he makes Polixenes speak to Perdita about gardening:

Polixenes.   You see sweet maid, we marry
A gentler scion to the wildest stock,
And make conceive a bark of baser kind
By bud of nobler race. This is an art
Which does mend nature – change it rather; but
The art itself is nature.
Perdita.   So it is.

(IV, iv, 92)

These last words of Polixenes certainly hold true for the whole of Shakespeare's drama.

Nevertheless we would like to ask in closing whether this true reflection of life which we have mentioned cannot be seen in relation to certain basic qualities in the construction of the plays and characters. And this now leads us to the sixth and last of our characteristic features: this is a drama of inner balance, and consequently displays the greatest possible objectivity of characterization.

Inner balance: this means, that every play contains both light and shade, both good and evil, even if these two halves are not always of exactly equal weight. None of these plays makes the attempt to lead us in one direction only, in none of them does one kind of human character dominate the stage alone, and there is no play that stays, as it were, in one key. Everywhere we find that one attitude is corrected by the other, the opposites serve to counterbalance and clarify each other. Should an extreme or exaggerated attitude assume dominance, then a moderating influence is bound to appear too, and we shall hear the commentary of a neutral observer or perhaps a parody, by means of which the balance is restored, and we are made doubly aware of the exaggeration. At Lear's side we find Kent, who makes the king's blindness and lack of moderation clear to us in the very first scene, just as Cordelia takes her place alongside Goneril and Regan, and Edgar alongside Edmund. Romeo's emotional enthusiasm is accompanied in the first part of the play by Mercutio's wit and mockery, and in *Henry IV* Hotspur's impetuousness is contrasted with the dispassionate judgment of Prince Hal. Even Hamlet has the neutral voice of Horatio at his side. We could pursue this technique of constant juxtaposition and contrast on many different levels. Besides intensifying the delineation of character it helps to produce what we have called the inner balance of the plays. But it has its roots in a concept of the totality of life which has here found an adequate form of artistic expression.

We are aware of the absence of any philosophical or religious bias in Shakespeare's plays, as opposed to the French, German, and Spanish drama of his age, and this enhances both the correspondence to real life and the equilibrium in his work. A royal decree of 1559 had forbidden the treatment of religious matters on the stage.[1] Whereas the theatre on the Continent became a platform for theological disputes, Elizabethan drama was on the whole able to steer clear of such polemics, which usually resulted in artistic sterility. The emphasis lay on the depiction of human relationships, and a secular type of drama developed, in which the religious element is only peripheral.

Shakespearian drama cannot be identified with any dogmatic beliefs, and even less with any kind of philosophical or ideological propaganda.

[1] Cf. E. K. Chambers, *The Elizabethan Stage*, Oxford, 1923/1951, Vol. IV, p. 263.

For although Shakespeare's depiction of character often appears to be based on Christian principles, these nearly always remain unspoken, and very rarely attain the level of clear expression.

But what Shakespeare himself really believed we do not know. And the fact that we do not know is part of the unique quality of his work, and this brings us to touch upon the personality of its creator. For the exceptional objectivity of the dramatic writing, which has always roused the admiration of critics and readers, has its roots in the fact that Shakespeare himself always remains in the background. Each of his creations has become a completely independent figure and exists in his own right. Villain and hero alike are treated with the same understanding and emerge as credible and living persons. Shakespeare does not take sides. So the world full of people which he has given us cannot be reduced to a few basic types, for the individual human beings which it displays in such astonishing abundance remain in our minds as fully rounded personalities, including in some cases even those who appear only in one single scene. For it is impossible to say that Shakespeare devoted less creative sympathy to Caliban than to Prospero, or that the treatment of Polonius reveals less loving care than the treatment of Laertes. It was this completeness of vision which Dryden must have had in mind when he described Shakespeare as 'the man who of all modern and perhaps ancient poets had the largest and most comprehensive soul'.[1]

But what was Shakespeare's own position? We cannot tell. And if we could tell, it would mean that the incomparable objectivity of this dramatic world would be less perfect than it is. The anonymity which surrounds Shakespeare's person in the eyes of posterity is hardly a matter of chance. It is merely another way of expressing the permanent and imperishable vitality of a dramatic work which completely overshadows the personality of its author. And as a person he is indeed not so important, for he lives on in all the characters he created.

[1] Dryden, *Essays*, ed. Ker, New York, 1961, 1, p. 79.

8

How to Read a Shakespeare Play

In order to read a Shakespeare play with pleasure and profit we do not need any specialized knowledge. Shakespeare himself sees to it that we soon learn what it is necessary for us to know about the plot; he ensures that not only the audience but also the reader is rapidly drawn into the magic circle of the play. But reading a play, like listening to a symphony or looking at a picture, is a process of observation and absorption which may be intensified and differentiated. We can increase our power of observation, and in so doing we gain a larger share in the wealth of the play. A reader with an eye trained to see what really matters will be aware of subtle relationships and correspondences, and will observe finer points of detail than will the unpractised reader, whose attention tends always in the same direction. The purpose of this chapter is to give just this kind of help; even a complete scholarly commentary cannot and should not do more than offer suggestions, which the reader may or may not make use of. There are no binding rules or regulations concerning the approach to works of art. Each reader will want to proceed in his own way, following different interests. Scholarship must remain in the background, offering help now and then, but never intruding with cumbersome apparatus between the reader and the play. For it is essential that a direct contact should be established between the reader and Shakespeare.

Shakespeare's plays were written for the stage, only in performance can their potentialities be fully realized. They are not primarily intended to be read. But this should not lead us to suppose that reading a play is only a meagre substitute for seeing it. On the contrary, there are several factors which commend reading a Shakespeare play as something in its own right, that opens up paths which might otherwise remain inaccessible.

Reading and seeing a play are complementary processes and each may increase the value of the other; they lead to different experiences. Only in a performance which is successful from every point of view does a Shakespeare play come to life fully. But such an ideal performance is very rare. A mediocre production, or a very subjective one, loses much that is evident to the careful reader who has the text before him. Moreover every performance presents us with a particular interpretation, it arbitrarily emphasizes certain aspects of the play, leaving others in the background. The reader, on the other hand, is free to choose his own interpretation; he can pause and consider various meanings, and various possible ways of staging a scene, before he decides in favour of one or the other. As he reads he will realize time and again that in all his plays Shakespeare allows for a variety of interpretations, of plot, of character, and of words. It will hardly ever be possible to arrive at an interpretation which can incontestably be described as 'the only right one'. If one reads a play again after seeing it in performance, one will almost always make new discoveries, supplementing or modifying the memory of what one saw on the stage. In reading one becomes more conscious of the complexity and wealth of meaning in the play. Thus a fruitful correlation may exist between seeing a Shakespeare play, and reading it before or after.

In fact, a real knowledge of a Shakespeare play is only possible when one has read it several times. For we may have to wait for years for the performance of a play, particularly of a less common one. Whoever has become acquainted with the plays beforehand, even though the performances may be rare, will be attuned to Shakespeare's language when he hears it in the theatre, and much will seem familiar to him. Shakespeare's language is so compact and full of meaning, so flexible and so expressive, that one often wants to linger, to read or hear a line again. Here the reader is at an advantage, for he may pause and consider, while the audience may at times be unable to appreciate the wealth of meaning, the sound, the rhythm, and the modulations of the verse (which nowadays is sometimes not spoken as verse at all). When one reads Shakespeare one is not only caught up in the progress of the play – one is also confronted with great literature, with a text which through its very complexity calls for literary analysis of a complex kind. The reader by looking at these texts may enter into the process by which the language of poetry is turned into dramatic speech.

If we take up a Shakespeare play which we did not know before, we usually look first at the *dramatis personae*, just as in the theatre, before

the curtain rises, we look at the cast list. Unlike most modern dramatists, Shakespeare gives us as a rule a cross-section of society, not taking
his characters exclusively from one social class, though the distribution
may be weighed in a particular direction. Also we see that in a Shakespeare play there are more characters than in the majority of modern
plays; instead of a few selected types we find in Shakespeare's plays an
abundance, a colourful throng which thrusts its way across the stage,
leaving us with the feeling that here we have to do with a whole world,
and that sometimes we are going to see even the darkest corner of it.
Heading the list we almost always find a man of royal or aristocratic
blood, a king, a prince, a duke, a statesman or a nobleman. Even in the
comedies this holds true, though the duke who so often heads the list
in the comedies is not usually the main character. But in him we see the
top of the hierarchy which forms the background of every Shakespeare
play.

From the king or duke the list descends to the milkmaids, rustics,
messengers, watchmen and servants. It will strike the reader that the
'lower classes', which for Shakespeare include not only the countrymen
and craftsmen, but also the townsfolk, are often designated anony-
mously, or in groups. The emphasis is on the aristocracy, from which
almost all the main characters are drawn.

Another striking feature which is evident from the list of characters
is the propensity towards ties of kinship: father and child, the father
with several sons or daughters, mother and children, brothers and
sisters, brothers-in-law, grand-children and nephews. Often such
relationships occur in double or contrasting form, so that a glance at the
dramatis personae may already suggest conflicting elements between
parents and children, between the older and the younger generation.

Finally the reader will be struck, particularly in the comedies, by the
tendency towards symmetrical correspondences, and this is even more
obvious in the early comedies than in the later ones. We find three
lords and three ladies, the English and the French kings with their
retinues, the heads of two hostile families with their household, two
pairs of twins, and time and again two lovers, two mistresses, two maids
of honour, two servants, two counsellors, two generals, two brothers,
two princes.

At the beginning of most scenes, and during the course of some of
them, the reader finds information about the place of the action, and

stage directions. Most of these explicit directions do not come from Shakespeare himself. Some were taken from early prompt books, some added by later editors, particularly during the eighteenth century. Why is it that most of these stage directions have been accepted by editors down to our own time, while only the indications of place have undergone modification? If one looks closely at the text of a particular scene, one often finds that the locality cannot be specified as closely as some early editors thought. But nevertheless the text provides much information about the atmosphere and feeling of a scene, about the way in which characters enter the stage and leave it, and about stage properties and costume. The text enables us to visualize gestures and looks, to see how people behave and how they speak, to see groups forming and reforming, and the stage directions utilize only a part of this information.[1]

If the reader looks closely he will find that in almost every speech there are lines which have some bearing of this kind, or – and this again is a veiled stage direction – he finds lines which evoke the atmosphere and mood that had to fill the empty Elizabethan stage. Without making use of those explicit stage directions which later dramatists considered indispensable, Shakespeare enables us to follow the progress of the events and actions on the stage, and even enables us to imagine storm and rain, a fanfare of trumpets, horses galloping, and many other sounds, by means of the text alone. The reader will observe that these directions and descriptions are usually given indirectly and unobtrusively, often in remarks which ostensibly say something quite different; they are 'smuggled in', concealed in a metaphor, a command, a question, or in arrangements for some future meeting.[2] Thus they never seem to be imposed from outside, but to be expressed quite naturally and involuntarily by the characters. They range from explicit description to veiled allusion. Again one finds passages offering definite directions, which cannot be disregarded, and some which have only a few implications, and others which are so undefined that Shakespeare clearly intends to leave everything to the producer.

As the reader by paying more attention to these implied stage directions becomes increasingly aware of the action, and visualizes the characters, their gestures, and the stage itself, Shakespeare makes him, in a

---

[1] This aspect has been explored by Rudolf Stamm in several articles. Cf. *The Shaping Powers at Work*, Heidelberg, 1967.
[2] See Chapter 1, 'Shakespeare's Art of Preparation'.

sense, a co-producer, and asks for his active co-operation in making the play come alive in his imagination. In the mind of the reader the characters, talking and moving, emerge out of the text and he may even see before him the locality, the scenery and the background.

For the reader, visualizing the action is the first step, but Shakespeare makes further demands, both on the reader and on the audience. For they must visualize the action in different places, and on different planes, far away or just off stage, past, present or future, real or imaginary; thus we are able to see events of proportions inappropriate for the stage, or events far removed in history or in legend, or in the realm of the imagination.

Behind the 'Here' and 'Now' of the action on the stage the reader will constantly be aware of reminiscences, visions, presentiments, associations, which appeal also to the imagination of the audience in the theatre. A double illusion is created, enabling us to see the action both on the stage and in the distance, reaching even into the sphere of supernatural and cosmic powers. Thus there results a whole network of relationships between these different levels, evoked by the text itself. Once the reader begins to observe this, he will see how the play is given an unusual dimension of height and depth, how the consciousness of the characters is extended beyond everyday reality into the realm of the imagination. The reader will become increasingly aware that the action on the stage, whether the scenes be long or short, forms only a part of the play.[1]

This double illusion, arising from the text of all Shakespeare's plays, though in varying degrees, should be viewed in connexion with the arrangement of the Elizabethan stage. The reader should recall a few facts which may help him towards a better appreciation of his text. The Elizabethan stage had no drop curtain and few properties. There was no curtain fall between the acts, the plays were performed without an interval. Shakespeare does not attach any great structural significance to the division between the acts. Sometimes this division was imposed later. In a play by Shakespeare a scene is (as a rule) over when all the characters have left the stage. There is a continuity between scenes and acts, in a diversity of ways the threads of the action are interwoven, sometimes contrasting with one another, and the dove-tailing of the scenes becomes an important element in the structure of the play. If

[1] Cf. Chapter 7.

218

the reader observes this remarkable interlocking between the scenes, conditioned by the continuity of the action, he will become aware of certain fundamental differences between Shakespeare's plays and the classical French and German drama of later periods.

The stage remained almost empty; only a few simple 'properties' could be brought on to the stage and taken away again, presumably by masked or liveried servants. In the background a curtain or perhaps a sign bearing the name of a place may have helped to ensure that the audience continued to exercise their imagination, and the reader must do the same. For the Elizabethans this stage challenged the imagination in a way unknown, for instance, in the early decades of this century, when splendid productions with realistic sets and ample properties more or less prevented the audience from taking an active part in creating the illusion. Thus in Elizabethan times the attention of the audience, who listened more closely than the audience today, was concentrated on the actor and the text, whereas the later elaborate staging and scenery distracted the attention. However, in the last thirty years Shakespeare productions have tended more and more towards the original style, centred round the words and bearing of the actor.

Most readers will know that the Elizabethan stage could be divided up into three parts: the wedge-shaped platform extending into the auditorium, the 'inner stage' i.e. the rear part of the stage which could be curtained off, and the 'upper stage', the balcony which was originally part of the gallery. Of these three stages the reader will be conscious in almost all the plays. The 'upper stage' will be used when characters appear on a balcony or at an upper window (*Romeo and Juliet*, ii, ii), on a parapet or tower (as in the histories); the 'inner stage' will be used for scenes in prison (*Richard II*, v, v), in a burial chamber (*Romeo and Juliet*, v, iii), in a bedroom (*Hamlet*, iii, iv), or for the hatching out of plans. 'Simultaneous' scenes, in which several events occurred at the same time (a technique which has reappeared in modern drama), become less difficult for the reader to imagine when he bears in mind the possibilities of the three-part stage.

The reader may also bear in mind that the protruding platform, with the audience on both sides as well as in front, created a much closer contact between actors and audience than is possible with our modern stage, which is separated from the auditorium by a ramp. It was quite natural on the Elizabethan stage for the actor to address the audience, ceremoniously or confidentially, or in quick asides. Soliloquies, asides, naïvely informative passages, introductory passages spoken by prologue or chorus (*Romeo and Juliet, Henry V, Henry IV*) lengthy messenger's reports, grave death-bed speeches, funeral orations, 'choric' speeches – these are only some of the many conventions which will come more alive for the reader when he relates them to what he knows about the Elizabethan stage. In using these conventions Shakespeare was not restricted by the striving towards realistic credibility which grew up in the centuries following. Nevertheless, the reader will find, if he compares Shakespeare's early plays with the later ones, that the use of the conventions changes according to the dramatic purpose; they are transformed in order to serve new ends. One of Macbeth's soliloquies, unveiling his inner conflict, will have a significance quite different from that of the villain's 'disclosure' in the early plays. Again in the early plays the aside imparts information to the audience, and is not integrated in the dialogue, but in the later plays the actor when speaking an aside appears to be 'talking to himself', while in listening to him the audience receives vital information.

In every Shakespeare play the reader will find a number of conventions typical of Elizabethan drama, but he will also find some which were common to European drama as a whole. He will find that the conventions are often accompanied by distinctive features in the language, by elevated rhetoric or by stylized declamation. A character, who just a few moments ago was talking to another in everyday prose, will suddenly discourse in solemn and ornate verse, as if he had climbed on to a platform. The champions of naturalist drama have criticized this discrepancy in level of style. But Shakespeare was well aware that the different levels of speech and action which the Elizabethan theatre put at his disposal could serve to portray his characters from different angles, close up and at a distance. The Claudius who opens the state council is not the same when he is alone with the queen. The Romeo whose lips declaim a highly polished sonnet when he first sees Juliet at the ball (I, v), or the Romeo whose euphonious verses greet Juliet at her window (II, ii), is quite different when he roams the streets with his companions, and jokes with Mercutio (I, iv). Even a character like Prince Hal in *Henry IV*, not at all inclined to pathos, speaks in grave and solemn verse when he stands before the king his father, and is called to account for his deeds.

One should refrain from regarding these different levels of style according to psychological or realistic aspects alone. It is more a question of variation in presentation, in distance and perspective, within which both stylized and realistic speech, directness and remoteness have a part. Once the reader opens his eyes to the range and complexity of the language, he will realize that in the plot too there is an alternation between symbolic and realistic action, between melodrama and subtlety, naïve over-emphasis and delicate intimation. The insertion of allegorical scenes, dumb shows, songs, dances and music, splendid processions and magical transformations – all this exemplifies to the reader the mixture of dramatic styles, but this mixture transcends such obvious differences, and penetrates the smallest details of composition. Most later dramatists committed themselves to one type of dramatic style, as the different styles became more distinct, but there is no such limitation in a Shakespeare play.

This wide range of styles in Shakespeare's drama will manifest itself to the reader more clearly if he reads a play several times, and then transfers his attention to other plays by way of comparison. Above all he will be more aware than the theatre-goer can be of the multiplicity of linguistic levels, of the different modes of speech and the varying forms of dramatic language. As he reads he will ask himself what it is that causes the changes in the language, and in what way they contribute to the characterization of the speaker, or help to express the dramatic significance of the situation, or the underlying theme of the play.

Poetic drama, in the differentiated form which Shakespeare gave it, offers greater possibilities than does realistic drama, in that basic ideas and themes can be made to sound through the spoken text, though they may remain beneath the surface. One and the same sentence can have several meanings and can be taken in different ways. This ambiguity, and the irony of many utterances, can be recognized more clearly by the reader than by the theatre-goer, who will have difficulty in catching these subtleties unless he has become attuned to them by previous reading.

But this is only one of the aspects of language which deserve the attention of the reader. He will soon realize that Shakespeare has many different means of achieving varied and heightened levels of language, contrasting with what could be (though only theoretically) understood as 'norm': similes and metaphors, rhetorical figures and mythological allusions, obscure and archaic words, new word-formations, puns and quibbles, unusual phrase and sentence structure, assonance and alliteration, sound and rhythm.[1] Here it is not very important that the reader should be able to classify and identify the many forms of linguistic modulation and variation, recognizing which rhetorical figure is being used at a particular point, as one would expect a scholar to do. It is much more important for him and for his profitable enjoyment of reading that he should develop an awareness of these features of the language, so that he is struck by more and more details of linguistic variation, and begins to ask why they are there. For there is always a certain significance when Shakespeare makes use of imagery or implicit statement, instead of expressing something directly, and when he inverts the word order, or has his characters speak in long-winded sentences, a clause within a clause, or adds one antithesis to another. If the reader looks closely into the function of such departures from the norm, he will usually find himself on the right path, even if he is not familiar with the linguistic distinctions. Shakespeare, when he used these devices, had in mind the reader, or rather the audience, and not the expert scholar. The devices were designed to achieve certain dramatic effects, and the lay reader can appreciate the effect intended if he considers the linguistic variation in the light of characters, situations and themes.

Another important field in which the reader should exercise his powers of linguistic observation is the variety in the verse structure. If he reads aloud, as he should from time to time, he will see to what an extent Shakespeare re-shaped the regular blank verse line, using an increasing proportion of irregular lines from one play to the next. A wide range of metrical alterations becomes apparent as one reads, and these changes, too, have their meaning and their function. The reader will see how, in the later plays, the lines are more and more frequently torn apart and curtailed, and how the interlocking of the half-lines, to be found particularly in rapid dialogue, helps to bind the comments of the speakers to one another, giving them coherence, and imparting to the whole dialogue a drive and texture which could not have been achieved by the use of regular blank verse lines.

The reader will see how the border-line between verse and prose

[1] An excellent and concise introduction to Shakespeare's language for the general reader is given by Alfred Harbage, *William Shakespeare. A Reader's Guide*, New York, 1963.

often becomes indistinct in the later plays, so that we find gradual transitions. If the reader pays attention to this alternation between verse and prose he will find that it not only serves to give each play an individual dramatic rhythm, but also contributes to characterization or to the heightening or relaxing of tension within the progress of the action. Again if he looks more closely at the many prose passages in Shakespeare's plays, he will find almost as great a variety of linguistic forms – in vocabulary, syntax, imagery and rhetorical figures – as in the verse passages. Only when he glances at a play for the very first time will he see the prose as prose.

When one reads a Shakespeare play for the first time, it is a good idea to read it through with as few interruptions as possible, perhaps even in one sitting. This enables the reader to experience some of the tension preceding the play's climax and catastrophe, to follow the over-all development of the plot, and to see the characters come alive within a limited span of time as Shakespeare intended them to. The progress of a play is usually connected with the gradual clarification of certain things which at the play's beginning had been mysterious or uncertain. From the very beginning both reader and audience receive impressions which point towards the future; expectations arise, and questions which demand an answer. Shakespeare's plays are constructed in such a way that seeds are sown in the first scenes and acts which come up later on.[1] A contact is established to be resumed only after several scenes have passed. Themes are hinted at, but their real significance does not become apparent until much later; little things happen but their full effect is felt only in the last act. Opinions and assumptions, likes and dislikes, are formed, and though they may seem unimportant at the time, after several scenes they become decisive. Thus we ought to be able to recall the opening scenes as we read the closing ones. This intricate network, working more on the subconscious than on the conscious mind of the reader, should not be torn apart by interrupted reading.

If the reader thus has attained a grasp of the drama as a whole he will profit more fully from the observation of detail. He will read certain scenes and passages again more slowly, and because he knows the whole play he will now see how many threads lead backwards and forwards, how much is touched upon now that is to be realized only later. Because he knows the whole play he will understand, too, why

[1] For a fuller treatment of this aspect see Chapter 1.

Shakespeare, with regard to future events, constructs a particular scene just the way he does and not differently. When he first reads the text the reader may sometimes ask 'What is Shakespeare actually saying here, what is the literal meaning of these lines?' but when he reads it through a second time more slowly he should ask 'Why does Shakespeare place this comment here, in these words, why does he add at this particular point that reminiscence, this description or that narrative, formulated in this way? Why does he introduce this new character now and not later on, and why does he bring at this point, when the action seemed about to reach a climax, a scene which delays everything and departs from the central theme? Why does Shakespeare have a character like Iago in *Othello* talk now in verse, now in prose? Why does he sometimes make a song or an eloquent silence take the place of words?'

With questions of this sort – and there are many of them – which are focused less on *what* than on *why* and *how*, the reader can gain access to Shakespeare's dramatic art without having to devote himself to systematic academic studies. The complex organism, the intricate structure of the play, will become clearer to him if he observes, for instance, how two threads of the action may continue side by side to begin with, in alternating scenes, to be entwined with one another in a single scene at a later stage. The handling of the plot, and of the characters (which involves the frequency and the length of the characters' appearances in different scenes), is a complicated matter for a dramatist who, like Shakespeare, sets out to write a play with many characters, several scenes of action and several plots and sub-plots; the complications are almost of a mathematical nature, and a reader who is interested in this kind of thing may even like to set up a graphic diagram. For what seems to develop on the stage as spontaneously as a fragment of life itself, so that each entry and exit seems a natural consequence of what went before, requires from the dramatist a series of exact calculations, if the right framework is to be created, within which scenes evolve and characters emerge, and a balance is struck between the straining and easing of the tension.

If the reader wishes to gain more insight into the organic structure of the play, he may take three further steps. He may examine the sequence of the scenes, and he will find that there is frequently a rhythmic contrast between scenes with many characters and scenes with few, in public and in private, now tense and now relaxed, now full of action, now devoted to reflection or to contemplation of things past. Major scenes, with crucial decisions and conflicts, in which something that might almost be called a self-contained drama may evolve, are preceded and followed by shorter scenes which serve chiefly to convey information, to allow orders to be given, or to arrange things which are to follow. If the reader looks again at the sequence of the scenes, he will feel something of the rhythm of continuity and contrast, particularly if he observes the difference in the structure of one scene and another. Reading through the play again he will see how the segments of the action overlap, and he may ask where the catastrophe and the climax of a tragedy are to be found, where the conflict actually begins and where it ends. Moreover, except in two plays, Shakespeare disregards the three unities, of time, place and action, and the structure of his plays is flexible and varied, not easy to define.

A comparable flexibility will strike the reader even more forcibly when he looks again at the sequence of the scenes and puts a second question: What does Shakespeare do with time? Even a first reading will have given him the impression that in some scenes time passes much more quickly than in others; in some it seems to stand still while in others it passes rapidly. If the reader enquires into actual details of time – time of day, of the week, of the month, of the year – which are given here and there in the plays, and if he asks what has happened between the scenes, so that one episode may be linked to the next, then he sees something of the masterly way in which Shakespeare abridges, overleaps and extends time. The actual duration of a performance or reading, the span of time in the play itself (which may be a few hours but also several years), the subjective feeling of time in the audience and reader, and also the characters' own consciousness of time, are different elements which combine to form a coherent whole within which the action takes place. The reader will see that the time element is vital to the great dramatist, and he will see how Shakespeare's art is keyed to illusions and impressions rather than to calculated probabilities.

After each reading and after each performance one is left with striking memories of certain scenes but also of individuals. Usually it is the central figures who impress themselves most forcibly on our minds, but sometimes it may be minor characters too. A way of renewing contact with such a character would be to follow his role throughout the play, and then perhaps, in order to adjust the perspective, to put oneself in the place of an antagonist, or the character playing opposite him. When did the character who has aroused our particular interest appear for the first time, and how was he portrayed? When were we given a deeper insight into his thoughts and feelings? What means did Shakespeare use in order to characterize him? Was it a matter of words, of gestures, of bearing, or was it his reaction to other characters, or the opinions he expressed? And to what degree has our notion of this character been influenced by what others have said about him? Where does the turning-point in his development occur, and how are the language and expression of this character modified as the play proceeds? Do our sympathies with this character change in the course of the play? After having read the whole play do we look at him and at the central issue of the drama from a different view-point? Are deeds and character consistent, do we know what motives lie behind his actions? These and similar questions may particularly arise at a second reading of the play.

The reader who sets out to re-tread the paths followed by individual characters will find a point beyond which he cannot go. Even if we see in our mind's eye a living figure, it is often difficult to define the qualities which are truly distinctive. For whereas Corneille, Racine and Schiller make it easy for us to recognize the motivation that lies behind the action of their heroes we find it difficult to detect these motives behind characters such as Macbeth, Hamlet or Brutus. Some questions remain open, there are sometimes even contradictions, and sometimes we feel that Shakespeare deliberately leaves us in the dark, so that we continue to ponder over the answer to the puzzle after the play is over.

Finally two warnings may seem appropriate. Firstly, it is not profitable for us to enquire too closely into Shakespeare's own convictions, his 'philosophy of life', or his opinions of his characters. He shows us a clearly structured world in which certain values prevail, but we can only guess at his own personal beliefs.

Only by looking at the fate of the characters, at the final turn of the action, at the manner of presentation as a whole, and by comparing contrasting situations can we draw conclusions about certain fundamental ideals and values. In this sense Shakespeare's plays have a 'moral', but it is implied indirectly and cannot be defined in an absolute way.

The second warning concerns the attempt to interpret a play on the basis of individual lines or passages. This is a temptation because in almost every play there are 'key passages' or phrases which seem to express the essence of the play. But here caution and restraint are called for. For these words are spoken by certain characters in certain circumstances; their application is often restricted to the context and limited by the mood and attitude of the speaker. Here, as in all studies of particulars, one must remember that a Shakespeare play is like a living organism in which every detail, each speech, each word, each moment, is linked to the whole structure, and also to the immediate surroundings, in such a way that details can be justly assessed only if we look at the play in its entirety.

Index

Index of Authors

Index of Plays

Main entries are in italics